Crossing Borders

Books and Pamphlets by Bernard Crick

The American Science of Politics

In Defence of Politics

The Reform of Parliament

Basic Forms of Government: A Sketch and a Model

Political Theory and Practice

Crime, Rape and Gin: Reflections on Contemporary Attitudes to Violence, Pornography and Addiction

Essays on Political Education (with Derek Heater)

George Orwell: A Life

Socialist Values and Time

What Is Politics? (with Tom Crick)

Socialism

The Labour Party's Aims and Values (with David Blunkett)

Labour and Scotland's Claim of Right

Essays on Politics and Literature

Political Thoughts and Polemics

To Make the Parliament of Scotland a Model for Democracy (with David Millar)

Essays on Citizenship

Crossing Borders
Political Essays

Bernard Crick

continuum
LONDON • NEW YORK

Continuum

The Tower Building, 11 York Road, London SE1 7NX
370 Lexington Avenue, New York, NY 10017–6503

First published 2001

British Library Cataloguing-in-Publication Data
A catalogue record for this book is available from the British Library.

ISBN 0–8264–5474–7 (hardback)

Library of Congress Cataloging-in-Publication Data
Crick, Bernard R.
    Crossing borders: political essays/Bernard Crick.
        p. cm.
    Includes index.
    ISBN 0–8264–5474–7
    1. Great Britain—Politics and government. 2. Great Britain—Social
conditions. 3. Political science. I. Title.

JN118.C75 2001
320′.01—dc21

                                                                        2001028259

Typeset by YHT Ltd
Printed and bound in Great Britain by Biddles Ltd, Guildford and
King's Lynn

Contents

CONTENTS

Preface

Crossing Borders – there has to be some title for a group of essays on different topics and on different levels. To have just said 'Essays', which I would ideally prefer, would pose too many indexing and cataloguing problems. I have explained in my previous gatherings why I enjoy the essays as a genre, and I have tried to characterize the essay as a genre in my introduction to *The Penguin Essays of George Orwell* (1984).

To name these earlier gatherings may help explain this title: *Political Theory and Practice* (Allen Lane, Penguin Press, 1973), *Essays on Politics and Literature* (Edinburgh University Press, 1989) and *Political Thoughts and Polemics* (Edinburgh University Press, 1990). For me, 'Crossing Borders' has three connotations: as an Englishman, to cross the border almost twenty years ago to make my home in Scotland, to have two sons who are half-Welsh, and at one time to visit Northern Ireland regularly and purposefully; as a scholar, to cross the borders of academic disciplines – a sense of the political is not limited to students of political science; and, as a writer, deliberately to write at different levels, sometimes for academic publications, certainly, but also for what used to be conceptualized as Fleet Street, now 'the media', in effect to write for the general educated reader, the active citizen, not simply the often all-too-internalized subject specialists writing for each other. If I am a disciple of Orwell in one clear respect, as well as biographer and critic, it is for his aspiration 'to make political writing into an art'.

It is sad when those who know a subject well do not enjoy writing, or what is now called communication; and equally sad when too many of their studies do not have relevance to the concerns of ordinary educated people. The British Political Studies Association have so honoured me of late that this sounds an ungracious biting of hands that have fed me. But I suspect that they have honoured me for being a lifelong gadfly rather than either an eagle or a tortoise. Thinking politically is too important to be left to either politicians or political scientists. By 'a sense of the political' I mean how to live with, conciliate amd make progress among the different values and interests found in any complex and civilized society – as I explain in my long-running book *In Defence of Politics* (5th edition, Continuum, 2000).

I thank Caroline Wintersgill of Continuum for giving me scope for this indulgence of essays, and for casting a critical and quietly dismissive eye on short humorous and satiric writings ranging from *Punch* to the *Guardian* which were funny at the time, I still maintain, but possibly only at the time. Being essays written at different times, corrected but not updated or rewritten, some repetition is inevitable for which I apologize to any who might notice. The opening essays here will give some clue as to the future big book I have promised and have been working on for many years, *The Four Nations.*

> *Bernard Crick*
> *Edinburgh*

CHAPTER 1

The Sense of Identity of the Indigenous British

May I take a step backwards, intellectually but not politically, and consider how complex was the British sense of identity even before the issues and problems raised by post-war immigration? I will argue that 'we' were always a pluralistic society pretending, for historically quite specific purposes, now largely forgotten or taken for granted, to be an homogeneous society and a unitary state. But the mask has grown into our skin when the reasons for wearing it have mostly abated and have had unhappy consequences in the new situation. The majority of the 'we' are very confused about whether our identity is British or English. We feel that our identity is under threat not, I believe, because of objective circumstances but because of the mental confusion between Britishness – common property to three nations, to a large element of a fourth and to immigrant ethnic communities – and Englishness, which is more specific and an identity as authentic and honourable as any of the others, so long as the English realize its specificity and do not claim generality. To anticipate: it is a minimal demand for any civil order that immigrant cultures should, in part at least, be British, but a quite unnecessary and mutually burdensome demand for them to be English. But may I begin personally – as is the custom with so many fine writers of immigrant stock?

This began as a paper given in 1993 at a seminar on national identities in the United Kingdom organized by the Commission for Racial Equality, and was revised for publication in *New Community*, April 1995.

CROSSING BORDERS

My name is almost certainly of Danish origin, and is not a
common name. Most Cricks seem to cluster in East Anglia, the old
area of the Danelaw, so I am not strictly 'Anglo-Saxon' as a Black
British friend calls me. And I am unusually aware of being a citizen
of a state with no agreed colloquial name. Is it 'England', 'Britain'
(properly only the name of a province of the Roman Empire),
'Great Britain' or the 'United Kingdom'? Our passports call us
citizens of 'the United Kingdom of Great Britain and Northern
Ireland', and before 1920 there would have been no 'Northern'. But
what do we 'old British' (or honorary Anglo-Saxons) reply when
faced by that common existential question in a foreign hotel
register, 'Nationality?'[1]

If that question is meant to establish legal citizenship, then
'British' is correct and is, I suspect, instinctively used by all 'new
British' (say post-1953 immigrants). But among the 'old British' it
is the least used name for a people as distinct from goods bought in
shops or in oratory demanding national unity. However, it is more
widely used by Aussies and by *both* Prods and Taigs in Northern
Ireland in the expletive form of 'Brits', often with an appropriate
strengthening adjective. Rather than 'British' many write in the
register 'Scottish' or 'Welsh'. The question does, after all, ask for
nationality and not citizenship (most hotel registers make a
nationalistic assumption). When those with an address in Northern
Ireland write 'British' one knows that they are almost certainly
Protestant and Unionist; or if they write 'Irish', then they are
Catholic and vote for either the SDLP or Sinn Fein. Occasionally
someone pompously and pedantically writes 'citizen of the United
Kingdom', presumably to evade the issue of identity; but they are
almost certainly members of the Northern Ireland Alliance Party or
more likely Scottish Tories.

The majority of my fellow English, of course, write 'English'. The
majority of UK passport holders are English; but I have a strong
suspicion that many write 'English' not as an assertion of nationality
and identity, as would the other nations, but out of a common and
mistaken belief, shared by most of the outside world, that 'English'
is the adjective corresponding to 'citizen of the United Kingdom'.
This angers me personally because my children are half-Welsh, I live
in Edinburgh and frequently visit Ireland, often for pleasure. And
this angers me intellectually because I believe that the United
Kingdom is a multinational state or a union of different nations

2

with different cultures and different histories.[2] It is more like Belgium, Canada or Czechoslovakia (as was) than Italy or France. And I like it that way. There is a saying, 'variety is the spice of life'. I have become a federalist, both in a European and in a United Kingdom context (and if it was at all realistic, in a British Isles context too). But while my honorary stepchildren studied Scottish history in school, I sadly note that south of the border the histories are almost entirely Anglocentric, few if any look at the British Isles as a whole; perhaps because it is so complex, even to the British. It is easier to pretend that English and British are the same.

Every nation, of course, is unique. Every nation has its own characteristics, but always some in common with others. And any one nation behaves more like any other nation than like any other human collectivity: say family, tribe, church, party or class. So far so good, but there is something particularly puzzling about the British, both to ourselves and to others. And now, for the first time anyone can remember in a people who have taken themselves so much for granted, have been widely envied for their psychological security, an anxious debate has broken out about national identity.

The first and most obvious reason is the new immigration or unhappily named 'race relations' (because there is no such thing as race). But I can see three reasons for anxiety quite apart from racial prejudice. Others will deal with this question more expertly than I. Its relative importance is sadly obvious, but it is relative and so I think it worth exploring whether, rightly or wrongly, it is seen by the 'old British', however prejudiced some of them may be, as more important than the first of the three factors I have in mind. Just as the old British are rightly urged to understand the new British, so the new must consider the nature of the old in terms more helpful than blanket reproof or noble disappointment.

(i) There is the old 'Britain and Europe' question brought to a head by 1992, Maastricht, talk of European Union and the split in the Conservative Party. The English (British?) doctrine of parliamentary sovereignty that arose in quite specific historical circumstances is now widely confused with real power and essential national identity (as I have argued elsewhere).[3] And do the islanders really think of themselves as Europeans at all? Well, yes, obviously 'Europeans', but are we truly of Europe rather than just alongside, and not culturally just as closely tied, or more so, to those emigrant Europeans (mainly so), the North Americans?

(ii) There was an unexpected side-product of Mrs Thatcher's zeal for centralization and her attack on the powers of local government: the creation for the first time of a national curriculum for schools and the specific need to produce a national history curriculum. But this politically contentious curriculum is for England and Wales only; Scotland and Northern Ireland have their own systems. Should it be British or English history? It is the latter pretending to be the former.[4]

(iii) Nationalist sentiment has grown in what geographers call the three peripheral nations. In Scotland in the spring of 1993 typically about 52 per cent of the people favoured a federal parliament and 28 per cent 'independence in Europe'. If a majority of the Welsh people do not favour even a strong subsidiary parliament let alone separation, yet a substantial minority already enjoy considerable cultural autonomy through political concessions made to the Welsh language. In Northern Ireland a minority of somewhat similar proportion actually wish to leave the UK and the attitude of the majority to the mainland if clinging, yet is sour not sweet – loyal to the Crown but not to Parliament, truculently British but certainly not English. Some think all this portends a breakup of the United Kingdom (personally I see that as either alarmist or optimistic rhetoric, but certainly the growth of nationalisms makes most accounts of Great Britain as a centralized, unitary state untenable, and may necessitate constitutional change – indeed necessitate a constitution).

English and British

But am I really talking about the British or the English? The Scots, the two sorts of Welsh and the two sorts of Irish certainly have problems and grievances, but do they really have a crisis of identity (as distinct from grievances) in the sense that, as I will argue, the English do – partly because they confuse Englishness with Britishness? Let me show this by turning to a Lord who is a history professor as a source of authority – a man who specializes in being a source of authority in an irritatingly Oxford way. In 1982

4

Lord Blake edited an up-market coffee-table book, full of lovely pictures and distilled prose, called *The English World: History, Character and People*. In his Introduction he tells us that:

> England's coastline has helped to shape both the history of the English nation and the psychology of the English character. . . . The long centuries during which the land was free from invaders meant that there could be a continuity of tradition impossible on the war-torn continent. . . . Some characteristics on which both natives and visitors have tended to agree have to do with national psychology: egoism, self-confidence, intolerance of outsiders, ostentatious wealth, social mobility, love of comfort, and a strong belief in private property. . . . We come to the cliché that Britain is an island, a fact that has been subtly decisive in so many aspects of her history.[5]

Notice that as he orates and pontificates he suddenly becomes aware that 'England's' coastline has the slight hiatus of the Welsh and Scottish borders, so while his flow of rhetoric cries out for Shakespeare's John of Gaunt declaiming 'England, bound in with the triumphant sea', yet even though he is such a very English historian and not a geographer, on this sad point of fact he has to concede, as a scholar, that '*Britain* is an island'. And having gone so far he might have noted that Scottish historians would not so easily accept or recognize the contrast between 'a continuity of tradition' of the mythic peaceful isle of Albion and the 'war-torn continent'.

He does, however, address the question of English identity with that fairly conventional yet interesting set of stereotypes. 'Fair play' is oddly missing, with its double meaning both of playing fair and of treating some heavy matters, such as politics and religious conviction, as a kind of play. Linda Colley has plausibly argued, amid much else, that this famous propensity may have emerged from the passion for field sports of the eighteenth century squirearchy.[6] Neither does he mention 'individualism' (perhaps to him that is synonymous with 'independence'), although Alan Macfarlane's *The Origins of English Individualism* (1978) is a serious thesis, positing the roots of the capitalist market in England far earlier than Max Weber, R. H. Tawney or C. P. Macpherson have argued. Nor does Lord Blake invoke 'tolerance'. His 'intolerance of outsiders' seems to me subtly wrong: John Bull isn't quite Alf Garnett or the nineteenth-century cartoon xenophobe, Ally Sloper;

ı Lord Blake is thinking for once of the poorest sections of the inner cities. Say rather a traditional coldness towards outsiders, a lack of positive welcome (but where was that ever not so except in the earliest stages of colonial societies?), a tolerant distance but not a postive hostility. It is far harder, indeed, even for a White visitor to get to know 'the real English' than the more hospitable Americans; almost as difficult as to get into the homes of the French. But 'tolerance' was and still is real, even if to a diminishing extent and even if it is always only a limited acceptance; perhaps this very 'keeping people at a distance' allowed the once famous tolerance of what they believe and how they behave. The French have long had two dominant views of the English: Voltaire's *'Angleterre tolerant'* and Guizot's *'Albion perfide'*. Does this contradiction reflect on the French – that they do not understand the rules of the English game? – or on the English, that they are remarkably tolerant, up to the point where national interests are threatened, but then they are ruthless? I'll return to this.

Certainly the *British* sense of identity is difficult to grasp. There is a far larger foreign literature about British culture and national character, once written by travellers, now by popular historians, sociologists and journalists, than that written by the majority English themselves. Already I have had to shift from 'British' to 'English', which is part of the problem. Foreigners often treat the two terms as synonymous for all practical purposes (except that all tours must include Scotland and Ireland and occasionally North Wales). Worse still, the modern English, forgetting their own history, have often treated the two as identical, angering the three other nations.

Let me apply a boring bibliographical test to a cultural matter. Look under 'nationalism' in the subject catalogue of any great library: under sub-headings you will find, obviously, Italian, French, German, Polish nationalism and so on, certainly Irish and Scottish, possibly Welsh; but under 'English' either very few books, or none. You will possibly find a handful of very bad, ultra-patriotic books about the defeat of the Spanish Armada in 1588 or the Empire from 1870 to 1914 apparently written for school prizes for not very bright kids in the private public schools.[7] Under 'British' you may find books on political history or sociology, but on national culture, virtually nothing, certainly nothing serious. George Orwell was thought eccentric, as a man of the Left, to write in 1946, *The English People*, a celebration of the national character – a rather different character, incidentally, from Lord Blake's. In the original version of 1941, *The Lion and the Unicorn*, the Englishman had appeared as radical and revolutionary. This is also the belief or ideology of the Society for Labour History, the publications of the 'History Workshop' conferences, Edward Thompson and of Raymond Williams. Admittedly one can find dramatic discussions of Englishness in some Scottish and Welsh nationalist writings, but they are often purely polemical English-bashing (in which my friends Tom Nairn and Christopher Harviey learned a lot from their masochistic English colleagues of the old New Left) and too often an easy answer to the complex questions of Welsh and Scottish identities.[8]

Why have so *few* writers in Britain addressed themselves to this question of English identity? I think the answer must be that in reality Britain is a multinational state, and that part of the art of governing it and holding it together for nearly three centuries has been an almost deliberate suppression by the English majority of English nationalism and self-consciousness. There are two sides to this coin. There is the famous self-confidence (arrogance?) of the English, not condescending merely to foreigners but also to the other nations of the British Isles, often forgetful of their presence, pride and peculiarities. But there is also a tradition of the old English governing class of statecraft by conciliation and compromise. This would have made the development of an explicit state-cult *English* nationalism in the nineteenth century counterproductive, at the very time when nationalism swept through everywhere else in Europe and when Mazzini's writings were on the shelves of all liberals in Britain and Garibaldi's bust alongside Kossuth's on so many mantelpieces. An English nationalism would have frustrated reconciliation with Scotland in the early nineteenth century (after the civil wars of the seventeenth and eighteenth centuries) and made impossible the attempted conciliation of Ireland (a story not of unrelieved oppression, but of oscillations between coercion and conciliation – as Irish historians now relate).[9]

The old Tories understood well that since 1688 the main business of government was holding the United Kingdom together. For that purpose the English ideology of parliamentary sovereignty arose. But an English nationalism would have been counter-productive. The English dominated the state, but the political elite was not a closed elite: it was open to the rich, the well-connected, and loyal adventurers and social climbers (the upwardly mobile, like Edmund Burke) from the other three nations. By the nineteenth century a positive cultural politics was practised: George IV visited Scotland that famous once and, to the delight of satirical cartoonists, on the advice of Sir Walter Scott, wore the kilt in Edinburgh Castle (albeit over warm, pink tights).[10] Victoria's children wore the tartan plaid, the old lady actually liked living in Scotland and where the young woman had been 'requested' by the Prime Minister, Lord Melbourne, 'to spend an appreciable part of the year'; in Ireland the children of Viceroys wore the green, just as in India the old Tories had fought off the ambitions of the Benthamite radicals employed by John Company to attempt a uniform, rational and secular administration of the whole sub-continent. The old Tories, to give the devils their due, had some empathy with native cultures. Indirect rule through existing divisions had been practised in the North American colonies even before India. 'Divide and rule' was always a half-truth at best: the general political tactic (which Tocqueville saw as such a startling contrast between the French and the British colonies) was to govern through existing divisions. The old Tory, unlike the Liberals and his modern successors, had something of a taste for cultural diversity.

What did become a state-cult in the nineteenth century was, of course, imperialism. But imperialism was open to each of the nations of the British Isles. Indeed Scots and Irish younger sons of impoverished aristocratic families were disproportionately active as empire builders, and exploiters. Was it some great prescience on Shakespeare's part that he carefully placed representatives of the four nations in Henry's camp on the eve of Agincourt, or was it commonly accepted that James VI of Scotland would succeed (for the pragmatic sake of peace) the old Great Queen? Nearly all of Kipling's tales of India had four stereotypical national types in them too, and – in an excess of imperial idealism – a Gunga Din could sometimes be the 'better man'.

There were some attempts to create a sense of British national identity, and certainly that sense exists but only in a narrow and specific context, seldom understood at home or abroad. It does not describe a general culture in the way in which 'France' and 'French' go together. Even Linda Colley confuses this point in her otherwise brilliant and widely praised *Britons: Forging the Nation, 1707–1837*.[11] Her thesis is that after the Act of Union of 1707 (still called the Treaty of Union in Scotland) a sense of British nationalism was invented and propagated precisely to bind English and Scots together (she excludes Ireland from her thesis, since it does not fit). Scots became North Britons. Further, she argues, this deliberate propagation caught on: the new British nationalism was popular: Left-wing historians, piously searching for ancestors and martyrs, have got the balance wrong. The long wars against France and the popular fear of Catholicism, both identified with tyranny and autocracy, created among all classes a popular and British nationalism. That is true, up to a point. But I am not convinced that the sense in which any one of us was or is British covers as many aspects of life as does 'English', 'Scottish', 'Welsh' or even 'Irish' (unionist). The Scots in the eighteenth century did not come to think of themselves as 'Britons' except when singing patriotic theatre songs. Most Scots were unionists (still are, if the word had not been appropriated by the Conservative Party), were loyal to the state, but had no doubt whatever that they were Scottish and proud of and strongly protective towards uniquely Scottish institutions (institutions, moreover, entrenched in the Act or Treaty of Union). Patriotic loyalty was and is given to the British *state* not to a national culture or national identity, unless that culture or identity is seen in much narrower terms than is usually meant by nation or nationalism. 'British' implies the union itself, the laws, the Crown and Parliament. (The Crown is very important as a symbol of the unity of the United Kingdom, if only because, unlike say in the United States, there is no constitution to respect or worship and Parliament by itself is too partisan and too prone to the kind of disrespect that even a royal family can accidentally earn.) Scottish loyalty to the union state was real, but it was highly and sensibly utilitarian not emotionally nationalistic. The union and the sovereignty of parliament guaranteed peace, order and free trade. The head was British but the heart remained Scottish.

Colley's claim that the invention of Britishness was in the first years of the eighteenth century implies that it was an early form of true nationalism. But does she not as a Welsh woman remember that it was once believed that the whole island was ruled by one king, Arthur, son of Uther Pendragon, patron of Merlin? This myth was propagated by both Tudors and Stuarts to bolster their dubious linear legitimacy. But Arthur, Sir Thomas Malory makes clear, was a king of all the *peoples* of Britain; so 'Britain' was a geographical expression and the name of a kingdom, but a kingdom with many peoples. States are coterminous with a single nation only in the strict doctrine of modern nationalism, seldom in practice. In medieval and early modern Europe, just as in Mogul India, kings could rule over many peoples. Great Britain was a dual monarchy from 1603 to 1707. Most Scots today live reasonably happily with a sense of dual nationality, as do most Welsh; but they express it as being Scottish and British, only most rarely as Scottish and English. With the same common sense as recent immigrants they assume that 'British' is a political and legal term, defining a culture of civil rights and duties, of protection and obligation, but not a culture in the full nationalistic sense of traditions, religions, rituals and customs – everything that Hegel called *Sittlichkeit* or Montesquieu called *moeurs*.

Do I labour an obvious point? But I suspect that the significance is often missed of fellow citizens calling themselves and being called 'Black Britons', 'Black British', 'British Asian' or 'British West-Indian' or 'British Afro-Caribbean', etc., but rarely if ever 'Black English', 'Black Welsh' or 'Black Scottish'. The new Britons have a truer sense than many of the English that being a British citizen does not and need not imply a common culture, only a common allegiance and a pragmatic, utilitarian sense of obligation. This is more like what it was to have been a Roman citizen in the Roman Empire outside the city of Rome itself than what it is to be an American. We can either say that there is no British way of life, only a common political culture, or that the way of life is the political culture. The old wartime army education book *British Way and Purpose* seemed to imply the latter. A true understanding of the United Kingdom as historically a relationship of four nations should make, other things being equal (which they are not – say poverty, say race prejudice), a pluralistic society easier to attain than we often fear, and the idea of assimilation, or anglicization, neither a possible threat nor a possible promise. To my ear 'assimilation' in American English refers to individuals whereas in English English it more often refers to the integration of groups which maintain recognizable and different cultural identities.

Notice that one does not usually say 'a British novel' or 'a British song'. The older indigenous cultures are distinctively English, Irish, Scottish and Welsh (and each with important regional variations). 'British' describes the legal institutional framework and the specifically political allegiances that bind together, or did bind together until the Irish rebellion of 1918–20, the British state or, to give it the legal title, the United Kingdom of Great Britain, Scotland and Northern Ireland (Wales was held, not wholly realistically, to have been fully assimilated in the early sixteenth century). We talk of British parliamentary institutions but of English literature. The phrase 'British culture' is seldom used in Britain, only – and somewhat mistakenly – abroad. The Irish, Scots and Welsh complain that their cultures are being anglicized. There are such tendencies but they are relative, far from absolute; and against them it must be seen that the English language has long ceased to be the exclusive property of the English and, indeed, within England regional variations are now far more acceptable. The other nations, let alone the United States and the new immigrants, have had a massive influence on English English, even. And language carries mutual cultural interpenetration. The educationalists drafting a new national curriculum for English in schools said that English must be taught 'in a multicultural context'. The Conservative Government intervened to strike out that phrase! Political will is substituted for social reality – as vainly as the Dane Canute's commands to the tides.

The English themselves

The stability and the internal peacefulness of the mainland United Kingdom in the last 250 years is not to be explained, as is so often said, by social or ethnic homogeneity. Great Britain is, I say once again, a multinational state and the largest component of it, England, is a notoriously class-conscious nation. Historically, Britain has been almost as much a 'melting-pot' as was the United States. Britain has experienced a great mingling of Celtic, Saxon, Danish and Norman-French, then in the late nineteenth century Jews from Eastern Europe, in the 1940s refugees from Germany and Poland and more recently larger numbers of Asians and West Indians. And yet historically it was the feudal kingdom of England that became militarily and politically dominant. So Englishness predominates in Britishness, but that Englishness, the national spirit and culture of the growing state, was influenced by, as well as influencing, the other nations. It has been well said that

'Englishness' is a relationship quite as much as a clear thing in itself. And it should always be remembered that 'nation' is a modern not a perennial concept, and that the intermingling of cultures in these islands had already taken place before four reasonably distinct geographical areas began to regard themselves as nations. It is very questionable whether before the end of the eighteenth century people saw nations as distinct cultures, or thought that every nation must be a state.

To say that will provoke some although appear obvious to others: when Machiavelli ends *Il Principe* with a call to Italians to throw out the foreign invaders from Italy, he no more imagined (as ninteenth-century nationalists read him) that Italy could then be one state than the ancient Greeks had thought of one state when they united, more or less, for the specific purpose of resisting the Persian invasion. Of course, 'had Machiavelli been living in the nineteenth century . . .', but he hadn't. And even the creation of unified states like Great Britain and Italy did not remove continuing, indeed changing, regional sub-cultures, in Britain national cultures as well.

So the British Isles is complicated precisely because an intermingling of cultures took place long before modern ideas of nationalism, and the cultures still travel easily across administrative borders. The Irish Channel, the narrow strait between Ulster and Galloway, was for centuries not a barrier but a swift sea-bridge in both directions for trade and migration, long before the notorious 'plantation of Ulster'. Galloway and Ulster are topographically and culturally very similar to this day, and industrial Belfast has been closer to Glasgow than ever to Dublin. The people of industrial Wales (the south-east) have far more in common politically, sociologically and linguistically with the neighbouring English West Midlands than with the Welsh-speaking but sparsely inhabited mountain country of the north and the west; yet they think of themselves as Welsh while resisting separatism.[12] And the populous Lowlands of Scotland, mainly of Saxon and Danish stock with a Norman-French immigrant aristocracy, have more in common sociologically with the inhabitants of the north of England than with the largely Catholic and once Gaelic-speaking Highlands. But, of course, nationalism has become an autonomous ideology, so inhabitants of northern England identify themselves, of course, as 'English' with the wealthier and more bourgeois south-east, even though sociologically, even in dialect, they are far closer to the

Lowland Scots. And the Lowland Scots have now romanticized, civilized and totally neutralized the once barbaric and threatening Highlands.

In 1989 a brilliant short history was published that broke from the anachronistic perspectives of modern nationalism and the English-bias of so-called British history – Hugh Kearney's *The British Isles*.[13] The author is a British citizen of Irish stock, born in Liverpool (an English city, a third of whose population is Irish) and who has divided a long teaching life almost equally between Scotland, Ireland, England and the United States. 'The viewpoint adopted in this book,' he says, 'is that the histories of what are normally regarded as four nations appear more intelligible if they are first seen within a British Isles context and secondly if they are seen in terms of cultures and subcultures.' He was disappointed, however, that the publishers insisted on calling it a 'history of four nations', he had wanted the title as 'The British Isles: A Multicultural Approach' – not a title, however, that would sell a book. But the past can only be misread if read in terms of modern nationalism.

Most histories of the British Isles are still heavily Anglocentric, dominated by English assumptions and English history; or if written from the standpoint of Irish or Scottish nationalism, then simply anti-English. All the good that's ever come to Ireland has come from the Irish and all the ills have come from England! But the interactions are equally important. The free and independent Ireland after 1920 did not become, as its revolutionary generation and most famous leader, Eamon de Valera, had hoped, a Catholic, peasant, anti-modern, anti-urban, pastoral, uniquely moral and Irish-speaking society. Only the constitutional status of the Catholic Church has remained, otherwise the Republic of Ireland is a fairly normal, pleasant West European state. The English language rebuilt bridges that nationalist politics had sought to destroy. And bridges are crossed from both directions. The East–West border was less important than most others in Europe, even before both countries joined the EC. And the dominant English have been greatly influenced, especially in working-class life, by the lifestyle of millions of Irish immigrants who commonly think of themselves as both British (not English) and Irish. And the English drama, novel and poetry have been vastly enriched by Irish writers. The great names of Irish literature: Yeats, Synge, O'Casey, Shaw, published from London, as do modern Irish novelists like Edna O'Brien and William Trevor. James Joyce would have published *Ulysses* in London rather than Paris if at that time the laws on obscenity had allowed.[14] David Hume and Adam Smith both worked hard, to the anger of modern nationalists, to take 'Scoticisms' out of their prose; but for the very good reason that they wished to be understood abroad, in France and Holland as well as in England. In their homes and among their familiars they spoke guid braid Scots.[15]

The cult of the gentleman

The English did not develop their own literature of nationalism because it would have hindered what was seen as the main task of English politics from the end of the seventeenth century until the secession of southern Ireland in 1920: holding the United Kingdom together. When nationalism was sweeping Europe as an ideology, the English appeared very unideological. Is this part of English national character? Conservatism hitherto always claimed to be an anti-theoretical theory, Burkean not Hayekian. One does not need big ideas, only sensible conventions, manners, a sense of tradition, above all actual experience. Things are best done by people who know how to do them already. Sentiments put into words are vulgarized and destroyed. A sense of tradition is better than the rationalism of Descartes, Bentham or Beccaria. But two other myths or ideologies were propagated in the eighteenth century before imperialism, both of lasting influence, each functioning to help hold the four nations together: one was political and the other cultural. The political was that the British had a unique and enviable talent for parliamentary government. This was not, quite obviously, democratic government, and not republican or civic in any French, Dutch or American sense; but specifically parliamentary government, with its once highly practical doctrine of parliamentary sovereignty – in the right hands. The social and the political hierarchy were intertwined. 'To make your mark in the world,' Lord Chesterfield told his godson, 'you must to Parliament.' And Dr Johnson provocatively observed, 'politics is but a rising in the world'. Government was in the hands of the rural gentry and their clients and tutors who gradually gentrified the new businessmen and industrialists. I take this for granted (the myth, I mean, not the reality); and literature on it is legion. But the cultural myth, while just as familiar, has been more rarely studied or taken seriously in political and social theory: the cult of the gentleman itself. Historically this was a great and specifically English cultural export; not merely to the three other nations in the United Kingdom, but throughout the world. Many immigrants had this idealized concept in mind before ever they set sail or flew in. Tariq Modood begins a wise essay, 'Biography and Identity', by recalling that his father was not alone in believing that 'the ideal of an English gentleman comes very close to what the Qur'an requires from the individual.'[16]

The gentleman is not an enthusiast. Protestantism had brought individualism but also the fanatic fervour of individual consciences following God's commands directly. In most of Ireland this was stubbornly rejected; in Scotland it was embraced enthusiastically, especially by the Covenanters: the Church (the Presbyterian Church) was a ministry by the people (at least those who were recognized as among God's elect, a not inconsiderable number). But in England there was, in reaction to the Civil War of the 1640s, a middle way: the Church of England claimed to be both Catholic and Protestant. The member of the Church of England ('believer' sounds too strong) had his or her Bible and conscience, but within a broad and temperate framework of episcopal discipline. The matter was political as well as theological. In the eighteenth century the offices of state, law and the army were restricted to members of the Church of England, but the tests of membership were loose: 'occasional conformity' was all the law required, four communions a year; hard for the scrupulous conscience of Catholic or Nonconformist, easy for those of a *politique*, tolerant, latitudinarian or simply cynical disposition. From the sporting field came a popular concept for political moderation: 'fair play', or you should never play for stakes that you can't afford to lose or in a manner that threatens your status as a gentleman.

A gentleman could not be an utter Philistine, but should show a well-informed and apparently effortless knowledge of 'letters' and 'literature' – a superficial knowledge, of course, for while one needed to know about everything that was 'going on', to specialize in any depth was ungentlemanly, the behaviour of a bore or a scholar, just as to be too intense was to be an intellectual. He had a library as well as a stable, though whether he read the books he bought as hard as he rode the horses is doubtful. A gentleman had country pursuits but also, if not his own town house, like the aristocracy, at least good lodgings for the season in London, Bath, Edinburgh or Dublin. The suburban semi-detached house with a bit of garden is the mass form of this ideal, in sharp contrast to the urban terrace of a citizen culture. The gentleman was not a citizen in the republican sense; however, as well as being a rural sportsman, an animal-lover and a fox-hunter, he also ostentatiously patronized the theatre and opera (such as it was, mostly Italian) – thus an eternal round of town and country. But reliance on a code of custom made even the well-educated gentleman cautious and conservative in cultural tastes. Right-wing modernists were few and far between even in the first part of the twentieth century. Apart from theatre, old England was a patron of the performing arts rather than a provider.

A gentleman should have feelings, but should normally conceal them. In misfortune, he is to be stoical, and in triumph, casual and self-deprecatory, not triumphalist. He still winces when cricketers embrace each other. He attributes success to luck, and is often right. 'Magnanimity is not seldom the greatest virtue,' orated Burke; and 'great Empire and little minds go ill together'. The gentleman should be able 'to speak his mind', but not eloquently; the favoured form of rhetoric is understatement – as Sir Geoffrey Howe knew when he destroyed Mrs Thatcher with one speech. He should not be ambitious, or if so only as a collector or pursuer of some harmless, even eccentric hobby or pastime. The highest social ambition was to sit in Parliament, but not to take office. An MP was no more or less respected for being in the Cabinet; there was perhaps a suspicion that he cared too much and tried too hard, not quite a gentleman ('like so many fellows nowadays, even in the Party'). A gentleman owned land, however small an estate (best to have inherited it, of course); and he was affably familiar with his tenants who were all small farmers and free-labourers. There had not been peasants or serfs in England since the Black Death of the mid-fourteenth century. A gent might drive hard bargains but not too hard, and he valued, as a gentleman, a reputation for benevolence – up to a point. He looked down on trade, but was not above marrying a spare son or daughter into acquired wealth. A successful merchant or citizen, 'a cit', could buy a small estate and, if he behaved like one, could become accepted as a gentleman. It was a difficult code of conduct but one that could be learnt and acquired, from either manuals or novels, though mostly by observation. Style became more important than content, manners than convictions.

The great (Polish-born) historian of the British eighteenth century, Sir Lewis Namier, wrote that England was the most snobbish of countries because there was 'an infinite gradation of social rank', no sharp cut-off points as in the ranks and orders of continental Europe where people knew where they were without pretence (or hope). That is what Lord Blake meant by mobility. In most of continental Europe people were clearly aristocrat, bourgeois or peasant. Somehow in England the lines between classes became blurred not by an attempted democratization of society, as to some extent in the French and American revolutions, but by their elongation. Famously the English upper classes were able to recruit talent from below. An English Figaro might rise into the nobility, not just outsmart them. So powerful was the ethic or ethos that there were extreme cases of noblemen, even of the blood royal, who were not always accepted as gentlemen. 'Who's yer fat friend, Alvanley?' asked 'Beau' Brummel famously to the face of the Prince Regent. And Lord Cockburn recalled in his *Memoirs* an old lady in Edinburgh saying, 'Kiss and tell, would he? The Prince is no gentleman.'

In the nineteenth century the route to gentility became simplified and commercialized with the expansion of old and the founding of new 'public schools'. They were public in the simple meaning that anyone could go who could pay. It was an expensive investment, on different scales for slightly differing qualities of product, but any product was guaranteed to be some sort of gentleman. Being mainly residential, they had ample opportunities for what was held to be the main object of education, not truth, not learning, and not especially religious or political orthodoxy either, but 'character' and leadership. And one should add that the product was supposed to be an all-rounder, a talented amateur, distrustful of the enthusiasms of professionals and specialists (a gentleman hired such people). Until the last twenty years the culture of most of these schools was not merely unscientific, but antiscientific. (This had disastrous effects on the British higher civil service.)

This new human ideal, half aristocratic, half bourgeois, of the English gentleman was, of course, emulated throughout Europe. It even affected the richer native inhabitants of the British Empire. And it was on offer to Scots, Welsh and Irish too: the sons of their landowning, merchant and soon professional classes came to the

English schools. But they were not fully anglicized, that would have rendered them politically useless. They were anglicized enough. Scottish and Irish accents, like folk song, were rather fashionable. Bad luck on the Welsh; their accent for a long time seemed irredeemably working class or lower-middle class.

Compared with France or Italy, the cult of the gentleman had a benign effect on landlord–tenant relationships in the countryside, but either removed a potential leadership class from urban workers and the petit bourgeois, or else rendered those leaders perpetually open to 'the aristocratic embrace', to being tempted by advancement, since it was so readily possible, up the social scale. And perhaps I should needlessly add, the gentleman was a man. The cult always raised certain difficulties for equality between the sexes, even in the gentry class. Small wonder that D. H. Lawrence became obsessed in his novels with the belief that sexual satisfaction with members of the same class was impossible for the English gentry. One reason for the decline of the cult, though its influence still is everywhere, is the rise in the last two generations of at least a relatively greater equality between the sexes.

The other nations of the British Isles have been, however, more radical, republican even, than the English and at times (as shown by playwrights, poets and novelists) openly contemptuous or, at best, ironical of the cult of the English gentleman. In Scotland, Wales and Ireland local community and 'roots' count for more than in England, especially the south of England: ordinary people tend to move less, and the occupationally mobile more often return at the end of their career to where they grew up. And despite English dominance, there has been more resistance throughout society to the complacent, anti-egalitarian and anti-intellectual aspects of the cult of the gentleman. The decline of that cult (as now vividly seen in the decline of standards of probity in the higher civil service as well as among Ministers, the heart of the old establishment) has exacerbated the English uncertainty about identity. The old implicit certainties are now almost gone, something explicit needs to take their place.

Signs of change?

Historically it should have been easier for the United Kingdom to provide a context for the integration of different ethnic groups. Not for one moment do I underestimate racial prejudice and poverty as exacerbating factors, yet they are all but universal. The peculiarity of the British situation as regards integration was that it was already a multinational state, but one in which the largest nation, the politically dominant nation, appeared to be losing its secure sense of identity. And most immigrants have settled, of course, in England, far more than in Scotland, Wales or Northern Ireland.

Perhaps Thatcherism, with its contradictory combination of an intense free market ideology and an intense chauvinism, was an attempt to find a new sense of English identity. And unhappily the new Conservatives, while somewhat scornful of the old cult of the gentleman, have far less historical sense or memory than the old Tories. The Thatcherites seemed to have lost all sense that they were governing a United Kingdom rather than an extended England. But it is worth noting that even England, certainly not Scotland and Wales, did not turn Thatcherite in its opinions. Public opinion polls clearly showed that most people's values still allowed for compassion, community care, environmental issues, the provision of such public goods as the Health Service, local authority education, free public libraries, etc. Thatcherites were in command because of the structure of the electoral system and the contingent disarray of the Labour Party.

A great change of opinion is taking place. There will soon have been half a century in which there has been peace in Western Europe, or at least no war. The Bosnian crisis is distanced with an almost neurotic realism because it appears to drag us back into the past. Otherwise the island psychology now seems less relevant, and in many ways inhibits new possibilities. The historic events of last year in Eastern Europe now suddenly make the whole European dimension of Britishness more relevant, important and attractive. The parties have changed sides on the issue. The Labour MPs are now the good Europeans and the Conservatives more divided. The Europe issue was the occasion of Mrs Thatcher's overthrow. But in relation to the demand for Scottish and Welsh subsidiary parliaments, her successor still confuses Englishness with Britishness and thinks that devolution (except in Northern Ireland) threatens the unity of the United Kingdom.

The crisis of identity that faces Great Britain and the fears that the long settled peoples have of the newer arrivals, all this is, I suspect, an especially English problem. The answer is not less

English nationalism, but rather that for the first time the English should develop, as the Scots, Welsh and Irish, a self-confident and explicit national feeling. Such a sense of nationality is no more a threat to the peace and stability of the United Kingdom than is Scottish and Welsh national feeling, nor the sense of ethnic identity of any of the new peoples – so long as Englishness is not confused with Britishness but, like the others, is seen as one culture within those laws originally framed for four nations.

I make no apology for having concentrated on the old British peoples. If they were understood better, and understood *themselves* better as *already* and historically a multinational state and multiethnic state, all the communties in the United Kingdom, old and new, might find it easier to deal equitably and justly with each other. And I have sought to describe and explain, neither to excuse nor to condemn. A balance sheet would be difficult to draw. The English cult of the gentleman has, until the last decade, created a certain moderation in British politics. It civilized an aristocracy and, compared with the former Habsburg and Romanov lands, prevented the class war that was as much politically reckless exploitation from above as rebellion from below. But gentrification had deadening effects on the old nineteenth-century entrepreneurial spirit (here Thatcher was right) and it had little empathy and sympathy with urban Britain (here the Labour Party and the old 'Two Nation' Tories were right). A new Englishness must recall that there was a radical tradition of positve citizenship as well as an establishment tradition of the loyal subject and law and order; but it will not lose entirely the distinctive gentry belief that the good life includes both town and country (phenomenologically, artefacts and nature), it will, as it were, green both the red and the blue, and it will grasp that toleration means, as the best English and Scottish political thinkers have long seen, the understanding, acceptance and at times even pleasure and pride in differences between national and ethnic communities, not a mistaken zeal for their diminishment.

Notes

1. See 'An Englishman Considers His Passport', in my *Political Thoughts and Polemics*, Edinburgh, Edinburgh University Press, 1990, pp. 94–103. First published in *The Irish Review*, autumn 1988.

2. The intellectually devastating argument of Pocock against Anglocentric history has been slow to sink in; see J. G. A. Pocock, 'British History: a Plea for a New Subject', *Journal of Modern History* 47(4), 1975.

3. See 'The Sovereignty of Parliament and the Irish Question', in my *Political Thoughts and Polemics*, Edinburgh, Edinburgh University Press, 1990.

4. See my critique of *The National Curriculum History Working Group: Final Report*, London, HMSO, 1990, in a review article of books on British nationalism and patriotism in *Political Quarterly*, October–December 1990, pp. 486–92.

5. Robert Blake (ed.), *The English World: History, Character and People*, London, Thames and Hudson, 1982, pp. 28–30.

6. Linda Colley, *Britons: Forging the Nation, 1707–1837*, New Haven and London, Yale University Press, 1992.

7. Gentle reader, please supply your own footnote references to taste but include references to Sir Arthur Bryant and Dr A. L. Rowse.

8. Tom Nairn's rumbustious *The Enchanted Glass: Britain and Its Monarchy* (Radius, 1990) is broadly right about the manipulative importance of the Crown in the business of holding the United Kingdom together, but he is cavalier to ignore utilitarian, pragmatic considerations, and ungenerous (unlike his friend Neal Ascherson in the companion volume *Games with Shadows*) to imply that apart from monarchy-worship there is no authentic English identity. Ascherson thinks that the English would disentangle their identity from the mental detritus of imperialism, if they did not despair, wallow in guilt or blame 'Europe' for everything.

9. Roy Foster, *Paddy and Mr Punch: Connections in Irish and British History*, London, Allen & Unwin, 1993.

10. John Prebble, *The King's Jaunt: George IV in Scotland, 1822,* London, Fontana, 1989.

11. I reviewed this at length, with respectful disagreement, in 'An Essay on Britishness', *Scottish Affairs*, winter 1993, pp. 71–83

12. See Kenneth Morgan, *Rebirth of a Nation*, Oxford and Cardiff, Clarendon Press and University of Wales Press, 1981.

13. Hugh Kearney, *The British Isles: A History of Four Nations*, Cambridge, Cambridge University Press, 1989. Perhaps because it is brief and nicely illustrated, its intellectual originality and interpretative importance (equal to Pocock's 'British History', *op. cit.*) seems to have been ignored. It should be basic to the so-called national curriculum for history, still so (though knowing better) stubbornly or nervously, under strong political pressure, Anglocentric. Keith Robbins's Oxford Ford Lectures (*Nineteenth-Century Britain: Integration and Diversity*, Oxford, Clarendon Press, 1988) appeared to be history to the Kearney and Pocock specification, until one saw that he dealt with the great difficulties of describing interrelations with Ireland simply by ignoring them!

14. The different traditions of Irishness are set out classically in F. S. L. Lyons, *Culture and Anarchy in Ireland* (Oxford, Oxford University Press, 1979) and British and Irish mutual images and confusions are discussed historically over a longer period by Oliver MacDonagh, *States of Mind* (London, Allen & Unwin, 1983). See also Roy Foster, *Paddy and Mr Punch*.

15. See J. C. Bryce, 'Lectures on Rhetoric and Belles Lettres', in P. Jones and A. S. Skinner (eds), *Adam Smith Reviewed*, Edinburgh, Edinburgh University Press, 1992. This is a good example of the *interrelations* between national traditions in the British Isles. Nationalists tend to exaggerate even significant differences, and always see threats more than obvious advantages in sharing mutually comprehensible branches of the English language. Brian Friel's play *Translations* is a balanced if sad meditation on this theme, not a simple lament for the decline of Gaelic. Both Irish and Scottish nationalists speak, properly and sensibly, of *preserving* the Gaelic, not of somehow making it the main national language. The Welsh national movement is fiercely divided between the cultural vision of a Welsh-speaking 'real Wales' (enclaves of geographical Wales) and a political, Home Rule vision of a whole-of-Wales with an English-speaking majority. (See the cool voice of Dafydd Elis Thomas in 'The Constitution of Wales', in my *National Identities and the Constitution*, Oxford, Blackwell, 1991.) Robert Crawford illuminates this whole issue in a highly original study, *Devolving English Literature* (Oxford, Clarendon Press, 1992).

16. Tariq Modood, *The Difficulties of Being English*, Stoke-on-Trent, Trentham Books, 1992. Since writing this essay an excellent research report has appeared on how ordinary fellow citizens among the three million with origins outside Europe conceive 'Britishness' and their own element of Britishness. See T. Modood, S. Beison and S. Virdee, *Changing Ethnic Identities* (London, Policy Studies Institute, 1994). But nowhere do the authors mention the fifteen million indigenous inhabitants who also have a dual identity. It cheers me that this essay is needed.

CHAPTER 2

For My Fellow English

For myself, I am a deliberate immigrant to Scotland because I came to love the country. I gave up a job to live in Scotland not to take a job. But so different is the culture, and so strong my Englishness, that however Scottish my political and constitutional views have become (for good reasons, as I'll seek to convince you), I am now, to be honest, too old to believe that I'll ever think of myself or be thought of as Scottish, as my young college friends in the late 1940s, whose Jewish parents had sent them from Germany as young children, were already English. (If, of course, it ever came to that, I'd take up citizenship at once in an independent Scotland, though I'd probably have voted against it.) At the heart of the matter there is, what Mrs Thatcher cannot grasp, or only grasp in an English context, national feeling, indeed nationalism. But nationalism does not necessarily imply separation. Most Scots, like most Welsh, have an intense sense of dual identity, and for most purposes live with it

---

From *A Claim of Right for Scotland* (Edinburgh, Polygon Press, 1989), edited by Owen Dudley Edwards, which were commentaries on the report of that same name by the Constitutional Steering Committee presented in July 1988 to the Campaign for a Scottish Assembly. This led to the setting up of the Constitutional Convention, which led in turn to Labour's and the Liberal Democrats' commitment to a parliament with real powers. Some of the arguments now seem dated; but this pre-history of the Scotland Act was an important influence.

comfortably, indeed find an enhanced quality of life in being able to live in two worlds, enjoy two cultures and their hybrids. But they perceive this, of course, as being Scottish and British, not Scottish and English. The real difficulty is that this sense of dual identities is not shared by most of the English.

The English immigrant in Scotland should be very sensitive to the 'English-for-British' linguistic and cultural trap. My tongue often betrays me. But there is such a thing as being so sensitive that reality is obscured. The heart warms to the honest clarity of mind of the third paragraph of A *Claim of Right for Scotland* (an exemplary piece of political thinking, even if almost totally ignored by the London media, who don't yet take the issue seriously and who don't read much):

> In this report we frequently use the word 'English' where the word 'British' is conventionally used. We believe this clarifies many issues which the customary language of British government obscures. Although the Government of the United Kingdom rests nominally with a 'British' Parliament, it is impossible to trace in the history or procedures of that Parliament any constitutional influence other than an English one. Scots are apt to bridle when 'Britain' is referred to as 'England'. But there is a fundamental truth in this nomenclature which Scots ought to recognise and from which they ought to draw appropriate conclusions.

I now want to draw the appropriate conclusions for my fellow English, or more formally to consider the consequences of A *Claim of Right* for the constitution of the United Kingdom as a whole. It does, indeed, call into question the whole character of the constitutional settlement that followed 1688 and 1707. And this is precisely why many English Conservatives so vehemently oppose any devolution or home rule, as well as why most Scots and a growing minority of English (I mean a probable majority of those who think about constitutional issues at all) now favour it. The traditional response of English politicians was to make conciliatory gestures and to search for compromise or compensatory positions, either Burke's great virtue of 'prudence' or Macmillan's or Wilson's soft fudge. But Margaret Thatcher practises a melodramatic either– or confrontationalism, the Union (God bless it) or separation (shudder, shudder!). She dismissed any middle ground whatever in her Glasgow speech of 4 February 1989: 'This Government believes in devolution to the individual citizen, a devolution now being practised in the United Kingdom. This Government remains committed to the Union, as committed as ever.'

Let us go back to the beginning, to the Act or Treaty of Union of 1707: part of the living memory of Scotland and just one part of the dead past in England. The very name and nature of it is still in dispute. The canny Scottish Lords of Appeal have never been drawn into judgment on any case meant to test whether alleged breaches of the Treaty of Union by Act of Parliament could be illegal. The response of English judges would be more robust and less equivocal: that Parliament has absolute power to legislate on anything it chooses, therefore no Parliament can be bound by the Acts of its predecessors, however solemn; so the Act or Treaty of Union is simply an ordinary enactment, and even if it was a treaty, treaty obligations can be overridden by future enactments (presumably even the Treaty of Rome).

The 16th edition (1964) of Sir Erskine May's *Treatise on the Law . . . of Parliament* intones:

> The constitution has assigned no limits to the authority of Parliament over all matters and persons within its jurisdiction. A law may be unjust and contrary to the sound principles of government; but Parliament is not controlled in its discretion, and when it errs, its errors can only be corrected by itself.

Practical men of both kingdoms in 1688 and 1707 saw the new abstract doctrine of parliamentary sovereignty as a gigantic bluff (a leviathan indeed) to maintain order, or in specific terms to ensure the Protestant succession and the end of religious and dynastic civil war, to ensure the predominancy of Parliament over the Crown, and to maintain the unity of the United Kingdom. Power was to be checked and balanced within Parliament, for to divide it between the kingdoms, even under one crown, was to risk anarchy. And men felt that they had come close to 'anarchy' or perpetual civil war in all three kingdoms. Yet every man of affairs in Scotland and England knew that the claim to absolute power was a legal fiction tempered by political reality and mediated by skilled statecraft, sometimes by good or ill fortune.

Did prudence or corruption predominate in the last debates of the old Scottish Parliament? The *Claim of Right* is still coloured by an old romantic nationalist view of history, in a specific nineteenth century form: that a Parliament must embody the life of a nation. 'The nation was not conquered,' they say, 'but it did not freely agree to the Union of Parliaments in 1707' (Para 2.5). Certainly there was bribery and corruption in Edinburgh, just as there was in Westminster to get the bill through the English House of Lords with the bishops in uproar. Yet modern historians suggest that most Scots believed that a hard bargain had been driven. 'The matters on which the Treaty guaranteed the Scots their own institutions and policies represented the bulk of civil life and government at the time; the Church, the Law and Education' (Para 2.6), indeed. And add to that commercial union and military security against the Highlands, vastly important and urgent matters. And Parliament itself was not as respected at the time as it became in legend. True, 'the nation' was not consulted, but nations never were until modern democratic times, and only then most rarely. Much public opinion of the day saw Parliament not as the national institution and the nation's pride but as a corrupt entity mainly serving the interests of the landowning class. But there was a national institution in which the middle classes and the people took pride, the Church of Scotland itself, the Kirk. And by the standards of the time it was a remarkably representative institution, at least the elect proceeded by elections. The elected Church Assembly had at least as strong a claim to be seen as the national institution as the parliament. That is why its establishment was so bitterly fought by the bishops in the English upper house.

It was not the case that Scotland suddenly became directly governed by England, but that what government there was (leaving aside trade and foreign affairs) became secured in the hands of the Kirk, local government and the legal profession. And with the growth of the modern Scottish Office, Scotland still exhibits an astonishing spectacle of almost complete administrative devolution, and one, moreover, mainly in Scottish hands. And that is, of course, *the minimum case for a representative institution in Scotland: that all this existing machinery should be subject to democratic control.* What happened was less that Scotland has suffered from having, in an aberrant epochal and regrettable moment, 'lost' its Parliament, but that the established Church it gained gradually lost its dominance over the nation's life and its role as the national institution.

Scotland is full of what the eighteenth century called 'peculiar institutions' but it now lacks an elected national institution. Therefore the common-sense argument is for some form of subsidiary parliament. But it is not a wholly rational or a common-sense matter. On the one hand, there is nationalism: Scotland is a unique culture and has its own history, it is not a meccano set of institutional arrangements that can be adjusted into the 'greatest happiness' equilibrium position; and on the other hand, there is what I call the 'English ideology' of parliamentary sovereignty. It may have outlived its usefulness, but it has left behind deep fears that the creation of any national representative institution in Scotland will lead to the breakup of the United Kingdom.

The English ideology of parliamentary sovereignty arose because from the end of the seventeenth century right up until the Government of Ireland Act, 1920, the major business of British politics was holding the United Kingdom together. Churchill's generation, even after the formation of the Irish Free State, had the history and mythology of this at their finger tips. They did not always succeed, as the Irish rebellion showed, but they knew they had to try, and it was part of 'the Great Game'. Irish historians once painted a lurid canvas of continuous coercion, but their modern successors paint a more complex picture in somewhat softer colours: first, they see the culture, commerce and politics of Britain and Ireland as inextricably intermingled, quite apart from claims of right and justice; and, second, they see British policy in the nineteenth century as reactive more than settled, as alternating spasms of coercion and conciliation. And these spasms did not always follow change of office between Whig or Tory, Liberal or Conservative.

Scotland was once almost as worrying to the English as Ireland. Memories of 'the 45' lived long. A barbarian army had got as far south as Derby. The depth of the scare, among Scottish unionists not least, is reflected in the savagery of the reprisals. When in 1780, in desperate need of recruits in the unpopular American War, the Government lifted some proscriptions on Catholics partly to increase the recruitment of Highlanders (the Gurkhas of the First British Empire), it provoked the Gordon Riots in London, anti-Catholic and xenophobic. And the fear of these, as shown in two novels of Dickens, echoed into the next century. The harsh treatment of Scottish radicals in the Napoleonic Wars was not just an aberration of Lord Braxfield. The maintenance of law and order and the preservation of the Union were inseparable concepts to both the English and Scottish political classes of that time. After the wars, the old memories and fears were still strong enough for the Government to feel the need to play cards from the other hand: conciliation. There was the ludicrous state charade of George IV's visit to Edinburgh produced by Sir Walter Scott and commissioned by the Cabinet. Only for political necessity did the dropsical Prinny wear the kilt that immortal once. And in the next reign but one, the young Queen was persuaded by Melbourne, at first reluctantly, of the desirability of spending 'an appreciable part of the year in Scotland'. Luckily she and Albert liked it. And at that time there was virtually a state cult of Celtic song, poetry and dance. Victoria's children wore tartan plaid and the children of a Viceroy of Ireland wore the green. It was later called 'cultural politics' in other contexts, but it was not then an insensitive and centralizing imposition of southern English culture and values.

By the last quarter of the nineteenth century any residual English fears that Scotland might become Ireland had all but gone. Yet this period saw the creation of the office of Secretary for Scotland in 1885 and the beginning of the gradual process which led to the modern Scottish Office in Edinburgh. This was part of, once again, an instinctive, almost routine, English conciliatory politics, triggered more by dubious analogies with Ireland than by actual threats or immediate pressures in Scotland. There was a Scottish Home Rule Association from the 1880s. Its ideas were prescient but its influence was minimal. And, to complete this stumbling gallop, when Liberal leaders in 1910 and 1911 began to talk of 'Home Rule All Round', and Asquith discussed in cabinet whether to bring in one bill, or to take the difficult or the easy one first, again the impetus was analogy with Ireland, a pre-emptive or reflex action rather than something dictated by the political power of the Scottish Home Rule movement. Also many ministers of the day, not just thinkers, were coming round to the federalist position of Gladstone's *The Irish Question* pamphlet of 1886. They were beginning to see the drawbacks in 'sovereignty of Parliament' and the constitutionless constitution it entailed. They were influenced by Canadian and Australian experience, American of course, and more immediately by the federal settlement in South Africa after the Boer War. Even a few Tories played with ideas of an Imperial federation. The Great

War brought an end to such speculations, as to much else. But the old English political class could exercise sovereign power with more flexibility, restraint and conciliation than they are usually given credit for. The inner paradox of the theory of sovereign power is the need for good judgement in when not to use it. Holding the United Kingdom together called for all kinds of restraints.

When the going is hard they can change their rigid ways. Since 1974 I've seen some very unlikely Northern Ireland Office ministers (seemingly sent there for punishment or to destroy themselves) mug the subject up, talk to the right people, get quite a feel for the ground, and do, for such circumstances, reasonably well. And things 'inherently inimical and contrary to the British Constitution' suddenly become possible, indeed necessary: statutory referenda, power-sharing, proportional representation and 'conditional sovereignty', even.

The Anglo-Irish Agreement of 1985 stated: 'The two Governments . . . declare that if in the future a majority of the people of Northern Ireland clearly wish for and formally consent to the establishment of a United Ireland, they will introduce and support in their respective Parliaments legislation to give effect to that wish.' And provision for such a poll or referendum was already in the Northern Ireland Constitution Act of 1973. It should give heart to the SNP. Why cannot this flexible attitude to the Union be extended to Scotland and Wales, though a majority of Scots might wish to vote for something different? Must political imagination only arise from the unhappy stimulant of violence?

The concept of sovereignty itself is the great obstacle to empathy and imagination in the English political mind. 'Our direct concern is with Scotland only', began *A Claim of Right*, 'but the failure to provide good government for Scotland is a product not merely of faulty British policy in relation to Scotland, but of fundamental flaws in the British constitution' (Para 1.2).

As I have said, the wide acceptance of the sovereignty of Parliament only took place in the eighteenth century. Blackstone set down the classic statement of the doctrine in his *Commentaries on the Laws of England* (1765–69): 'Parliament has sovereign and uncontrollable authority in the making, confirming, enlarging, restraining, abrogating, repealing, reviving and expounding of laws concerning matters of all possible denominations, this being the place where that absolute despotic power, which must in all governments reside somewhere, is entrusted by the constitution of these kingdoms.'

His sweeping assertion that all government needed 'absolute despotic power' did not go unchallenged. The parliamentary debates over the repeal of the Stamp Act in 1766 show that some still took the old-fashioned view that there were limits, other than practical limits, on parliamentary sovereignty. Taxation, then and now, roused deep passions. Could the Americans be taxed if they were not represented in Parliament, except by their own provincial Assemblies? The great director of the Seven Years War, William Pitt, had no doubts, and dragged himself in his last illness to protest in Parliament:

> that this kingdom has no right to lay a tax upon the colonies, to be sovereign and supreme in every circumstance of government whatsoever. They are the subjects of this kingdom, equally entitled with yourselves to all the natural rights of mankind and the peculiar privileges of Englishmen. . . the Americans are the sons not the bastards of England. Taxation is no part of the governing or legislative power. The taxes are a voluntary gift and grant of the Commons alone . . . Here I would draw the line.

He was, however, in the minority.

Edmund Burke in his great speeches on 'Conciliation with America' and on 'American Taxation' was to rail at Lord North's claim that the American refusal to pay taxes threatened the sovereignty of Parliament. Do not ask, he said, 'whether you have a right to make them miserable, have you not rather an interest to make them happy?'

> Leave America, if she has taxable matter in her, to tax herself. I am not going into the distinctions of rights, nor attempting to mark their boundaries. I do not enter into these metaphysical distinctions; I hate the very sound of them. Leave the Americans as they anciently stood. . . They and we, and their and our ancestors, have been happy under that system. . . Be content to bind Americans by laws of trade; you have always done that. Do not burden them by taxes, you were not used to do that from the beginning. Let this be your reason for not taxing. These are the arguments of states and kingdoms. Leave the rest to schools; for there they may be discussed with safety. But if [not]. . . you will

30

teach them by these means to call that sovereignty itself into question.

And that is precisely what has happened, then and now. By opposing all concessions and slamming the door on any discussions of change (even within her own party in Scotland), Margaret Thatcher, very like Lord North, has raised the stakes dramatically and foolishly. Some will think that she has, indeed, strengthened the hands and hearts of separatist nationalists in Scotland. Perhaps. But I think it more likely that her intransigence has swept mere devolution off the agenda and is turning, almost overnight, devolutionists into federalists in the Scottish Labour Party (however slow our leaders are to catch up with their followers). The whole constitution of the United Kingdom is called into question, and there is no secure way forward for Scotland unless it is.

Unhappily while Mrs Thatcher has turned her back on Burke, Labour's leaders still echo him. They plead for *and rely upon* a prudence which is not there. They seek vigorously, like Mr Hattersley, to fudge the sovereignty issue. They can sound equally magnificent, perhaps, but the impact is equally futile. Like Burke, they are hedging the fundamental issue. For Burke clearly in the above passage was not attacking sovereignty as such, but its abuse in bad policies. Labour's present leaders also believe in 'unlimited and supreme . . . sovereignty' but want it in their hands, and would, indeed, if it ever fell into them, exercise it more prudently and benignly, truly chockful of radiant and sincere concern. But by the time Burke spoke it was too late. The Americans did not just want better treatment, they wanted constitutional guarantees for a defined area of self-government. They were not prepared to wait for a more friendly government, and to trust for restraint, like good English politicians, to friendship alone.

It used to be argued, in private by the main draughtsman of the Scotland Act of 1978 before he retired from the Scottish Office, and in public by John Mackintosh MP, who had he lived might have given the campaign that lift it needed, that the details of the devolution bill were of secondary importance. Not to worry, get an assembly of some kind off the ground and as its authority grew so its powers could be amended. Such a process would be politically irreversible. But Jim Ross has recently seen the catch in the Burkean argument from prudence. His 'A Fond Farewell to Devolution'

(*Radical Scotland*, Dec./Jan. 1989) is a remarkable and important document. He was, of course, the secretary of the committee who produced *A Claim of Right*.

Ross simply argues that in 1978 'we were innocent enough to suppose that future Ministers would not dare withdraw powers once granted. We now know better. We used to think that governments under the British constitution were fussy and interfering but not fundamentally undemocratic. We now know that the British constitution is inherently authoritarian and is quite capable of spawning a Government to match.' So he concludes that the objective must be, however politically difficult, a constitutionally protected Scottish Parliament, such that only by some special and difficult procedure, involving that body too, could Parliament wind it up, change its powers or cut its funding (as has been done to local government).

In 1981, with the events of 1979 very much in mind, I remember trying to set this question for an English school examination board: 'Devolution was a concept invented by Harold Wilson to obscure the hitherto clear distinction between local government and federalism. *Explain and discuss.*' The teacher assessors understandably threw it out as too difficult. There was plenty of choice in the paper. I just wanted to see if *any* English sixth-formers would go for it. But it would have been fully comprehensible, then and now, to any Scottish sixth-former. Assessment might have raised some difficulties. The *Claim of Right* sees the English constitution as a barrier to Scottish rights to a national representative institution. But it is now widely canvassed, as never before (except within the old Liberal Party for most of this century!) that the constitution is an obstacle to all our British civil liberties. The lack of restraint upon government has reached epic proportions.

The Political Quarterly, a journal not famous for sensationalism, had a recent issue on 'Is Britain Becoming Authoritarian?' (January 1989). Wyn Grant wrote comprehensively of 'The Erosion of Intermediary Institutions'. There is no need to labour the point that many political thinkers have seen intermediary institutions as essential conditions for liberty. But Wyn Grant sombrely pointed out that the erosion is not simply a product of Thatcher's deliberate policies but follows from another strong tradition, rooted in the classical economists, which sees any intermediaries between individuals and the state as threats to true competitive, atomistic individualism. And Mark Stallworthy wrote in the same place of 'Central Government and Local Government: the Uses and Abuses of Constitutional Hegemony'. It is an almost definitive listing of the extent to which powers and discretion of local government have been radically diminished (contrary to Tory tradition quite as much as to Labour's – in some respects more so). He sees it as a new, imposed constitutional settlement, and concludes: 'A constitutional settlement which is resistant to dialogue and which confers an unconditional legitimacy on imposed central solutions is antithetical to reasonable expectations within a purported liberal democracy.'

There has been a centralist tradition in the Labour Party (as Wyn Roberts reminds). Old Fabianism had one thing in common with Leninism: that the party should act for the good through control of the central state, and a belief that most intermediary institutions were irrational, reactionary or obstructive. But there was also a pluralist tradition, more concerned to do good through people, in ordinary social groups and communities, than to do good to them from however heavenly a height. This centralist tradition was unhappily apparent in the half-hearted support, if not open opposition, given both by government ministers and by many Scottish Labour MPs to the devolution bills of 1978. Things done by a government simply for political survival carry little conviction among ordinary people. Yet the fear was real among Labour activists, in Scotland as well as in England and Wales, that the welfare state would suffer if central power declined. But that was before Thatcher's massive demonstration of how much of welfare, not merely in the personal social services and housing, depended on the strength of local government. So in the last ten years there has been an extraordinary conversion among Labour intellectuals and thinkers to constitutional reform. It is hard to think of any prominent figure on the Left who now makes the old Footite defence of parliamentary sovereignty. Some of the motives for this change are obvious, a process for constitutional traditionalists of both Left and Right not unlike aversion therapy. But there has also been a movement away from mere pragmatism in the Labour centre and right, a recovery of thought by the thoughtless, a reanimation of values. Among those values is a positive sense of community. And at the same time, for quite different reasons, former hard or obscure Marxists, in searching for a basis for an humanistic and liberal approach, have been rediscovering pluralism. Philosophically, they now say with Harold Laski that 'all power is federal': and empirically they say that while class divisions are still important, other social groupings are too; therefore the old 'class analysis' is too simple to describe modern or post-industrial society.

These two groups have, together with Liberals and Social Democrats, swelled the adherents of Charter 88's call for constitutional and electoral reform. Charter 88 arose in London, with no direct reference to Scottish conditions, but a remarkable cross-section of people have come together convinced that, because of a breakdown of traditional restraints on which civil liberties depended, a formal constitution is now needed. The actual Charter 88 statement only says of Scotland that 'Scotland is governed like a province from Whitehall' (well meant but not wholly accurate). Among Charter's eleven demands there is 'Guarantee an equitable distribution of power between local, regional and national government.' So do even they see Scotland as just a 'regional government'? This is far less than the *Claim of Right*. But some of the original sponsors read that demand more radically than the bare words suggest. Anthony Barnett called his inaugural article on Charter 88 in *New Statesman and Society* (2 December 1988), 'A Claim of Right for Britain'. He said that 'along with the sustained and detailed *A Claim of Right for Scotland* Charter 88 points towards a new kind of politics in Britain'. And he quoted from Neal Ascherson's Mackintosh Memorial Lecture: 'It is not possible to build democratic socialism by using the institutions of the Ancient British State. Under that include the present doctrine of sovereignty, Parliament, the electoral system, the civil service – the whole gaudy heritage. It is not possible, in the way that it is not possible to induce a vulture to give milk.'

This is not merely true for democratic socialists, though the admission is long overdue from many of us; even to build a more liberal, decent regime needs formal constitutional law. The kind of reasoning behind the Charter is found in *1688–1988 Time for a New Constitution* (1998, edited by Richard Holme and Michael Elliott), in which I was not the only Labour contributor to a kind of Liberal Democratic popular front. So the climate of reformist opinion in England for *Claim of Right* ideas could be favourable, if they are argued. The English dimension must not be forgotten or neglected by Scottish publicists, or simply made a target of abuse.

Potential allies need to be convinced in terms relevant to themselves.

National movements can spend, like political parties, too much time arguing among themselves. English Charter supporters, let alone Mr Hattersley, need to be convinced that Scotland's rights go beyond being graciously given the powers of a hypothetical English region. The case for English and Welsh regional government may be good. It rests on democratic and on administrative theory (there are few signs of any popular support). But in Scotland there is massive popular support for Home Rule, substantial support for independence (though some of that may be tactical), because Scotland's case also rests on nationalism and a long national history. How can any of my fellow English be so obtuse as not to recognize that Scotland, for all the interconnections and friendliness, is a nation? Or so condescending as to think that what Texans, Bavarians, Quebecois, Gujaratis and white Tasmanians do, cannot be done by Scots – that is operate a federal system? And why should a federal solution be deemed impossible because of the numbers of English? It depends what constitutional guarantees are given and how and by whom they are guaranteed. The Scottish Constitutional Convention will have some proposals to make.

As all of us write, the Convention faces great difficulties. Will the SNP return to it? Both parties have their internal difficulties, not unknown to the other. But may I just say this to fellow Labour Party members, always remembering what Pericles said in Athens so long ago, that 'the secret of liberty is courage'? We must have the courage of our democratic convictions, let alone of our electoral numbers, to make things as easy as possible for those separatist nationalists who would want to come into a devolved assembly or a federal parliament and leave to the future the 'final decision'.

Can we not say, as even Mrs Thatcher has said over Northern Ireland, that if at some future date the people of Scotland should vote in a referendum for separation, 'independence in Europe' or whatever, then so be it. As I've said, I'd take up citizenship happily, not trek south to Yorkshire or Surrey again. And a referendum should offer the Scottish people the three realistic alternatives which everyone knows there are: the status quo, a federal parliament or independence. The Campaign for a Scottish Assembly might have been wiser to picture the convention as producing, initially, three such packages (for just one needs little work) and to put these to the

Scottish electorate. Let them decide. Then would come the time for an elected convention, officially or unofficially, to provide a fully drafted constitution. And can anyone seriously doubt the practical sense and justice of conducting those elections on any other but some form of proportional representation? Again consider Northern Ireland which has set, in that respect, no necessary precedent for the mainland, even by having PR for its European seats. Should we be less flexible and inventive than Thatcher's ministers?

What if the Government refuses (as is overwhelmingly likely) to hold such a referendum, or to facilitate an official election for a constitutional convention, or to respond to the proposals of a convention however constituted? And what if, as is at least possible under the present electoral system, the Conservatives are still in office after the next election (the heart will not let the head say, 'if Labour loses again overall')? What will happen then? There is no knowing. Opinions might grow stronger but still not translate into appropriate, understandable, historically precedented behaviour. Or could there be real trouble? But my vision of civil disobedience is neither of riots, nor of Jim Sillars and Donald Dewar politely disputing who shall cast the first symbolic stone at the windows of the Secretary of State for Scotland, but of respectable, worried, conventional local government officers all over Scotland beginning to ignore legal injunctions and to organize an election for a Scottish Parliament.

The heroic version of Irish independence centres on the fighting, bloodshed, atrocities and 'the lads of the column'; and the realistic version on the resulting stalemate and war-weariness on both sides. But there is a civilian version also: that at some stage law-abiding and home-abiding family men in three-piece suits and watch chains began to post their official returns on this and that to Dublin's Mansion House and not to the Castle. Pray God Scotland's right can be obtained peaceably and without 'troubles'. Much will depend on the character of the response when propositions are made. It will be a test for the English political mind at a bad time. It is dangerous to affront the rights and pride of a nation for whom the present English Government has lost politically all right to speak.

CHAPTER 3

On Scottish Nationalism

The British general election of April 1992 frustrates for the while the hopes of three-quarters of the people of Scotland for some kind of parliament. Currently there is heady talk of Labour, Democrat and SNP (Scottish National Party) supporters, perhaps even the parties themselves, together with various civic bodies and pressure groups, organizing an unofficial referendum, if they can agree on its terms. But they will certainly have second thoughts. It would be hard to organize and the cause would be greatly damaged if an unofficial poll had the low level of turnout associated with local elections. Moreover even a large vote might draw no Government response, and what then? That three-quarters of the people in Scotland want a national parliament is undoubted and, to my mind, the broad justice of its argument is strong in terms of civic political theory; but the very reasonableness and moderation of it make talk of 'forcing the Government to listen' extremely unlikely. Scotland is not Ireland and rhetorical analogies to Eastern Europe in 1989

A review article for *Government and Opposition*, Summer 1992, of Roger Levy, *Scottish Nationalism at the Crossroads*, Scottish Academic Press, 1990; Tom Gallagher, *Nationalism in the Nineties*, Polygon, 1991; Paul H. Scott, *Towards Independence*, Polygon, 1992; Christopher Harvie, *Cultural Weapons*, Polygon, 1992; Ian Donnachie and Christopher Whatley (eds), *The Manufacture of Scottish History*, Polygon, 1992; James G. Kellas, *The Politics of Nationalism and Ethnicity*, Macmillan, 1991.

forget that physical oppression, not merely the unfairnesses and injustices of an antiquated constitution, is needed to bring masses of people onto the streets threateningly; and even then it needed a sudden realization that the old order was collapsing, triggered by an external failure of power and will, and was now fragile, brittle at the best, not complacently stable. References to Catalonia may be nearer the mark but cut no ice with the electorate.

There is a place for political speculation, but my imagination fails to come up with a scenario which would simultaneously move during this parliament both Westminster-Whitehall and Scotland towards a referendum. Referenda can now occur in Great Britain but only when governments find themselves in deep political crisis and divided in their own ranks – as happened to Labour over Europe and then Scotland in the 1970s, and to the Conservatives when they allowed a referendum in Northern Ireland on 'the constitutional question' (not forgetting the small but politically awkward Welsh Sunday opening or closing question which led to county by county referenda). The vote for a Scottish subsidiary parliament was carried in 1979 by a thin and unconvincing majority but did not become law because of the famous wrecking amendment carried in the Commons against the Government, eventually leading to its fall, requiring a 40 per cent vote of the electorate. Yet if Labour had gained a working majority of seats at the general election of April 1992, it was pledged to legislate for a Scottish parliament during its first year in office; and this time with neither promise nor threat of a referendum – so great is its dependence on Scottish seats and so great the apparent change of opinion since 1979 both in Scotland as a whole and in the Labour Party in Scotland.

Small wonder that the last two years have seen an outburst of books on the Scottish question in general and on Scottish nationalism in particular; almost all were published in Scotland, however, and got little attention from English bards or reviewers. But before helping to fill that gap one must attempt to clarify both the context and what we are all talking about when we say 'Scottish nationalism'. English commentators have got very confused about both, and so obviously must foreign observers. The Confucian Mandarins, it is said, thought that good government depended upon 'rectification of terms' (the nominalist theory of language that seems common sense to the ignorant and self-evidently true to the pedantic): that every concept must have a unique and original uncorrupted meaning. They were plainly wrong on both empirical and logical grounds. Ernest Gellner once argued against Peter Winch's *The Idea of a Social Science* that we cannot understand a society simply by knowing its concepts, we must understand the working of them in social relationships. Some usages are more confusing than others.

The day after the recent local government elections in Britain (7 May, 1992) a front-page story in the *Guardian*, written by two very experienced London-based journalists, reported that: 'Scottish home rule supporters, fighting to turn the district elections into an unofficial referendum on the constitution, were dealt another blow when the nationalists failed to make a significant impact.' It is hard to pack more confusion into one sentence, heightened by the *Guardian*'s fanatical modernist prejudice against capitalization. If 'Home Rule' had appeared in upper case readers could have been alerted that they were dealing with a term of art, going back to Gladstone's Home Rule Bill of 1886 (how much bloodshed might have been spared had that Bill been passed!). But it was not a separatist Bill, though supported unanimously by Parnell's Irish Parliamentary Party who nevertheless clearly saw themselves as nationalists and were unmistakably Irishmen. The Westminster parliament was to retain control of defence and foreign policy and power to levy taxes for those purposes; and the status of the Crown was unchanged. The term has been revived in the last three years by Scots who want more than 1979-style 'devolution' but less than independence, even 'independence in Europe', the slogan or policy of the SNP. A Scottish home-ruler wants the powers of a Scottish parliament to be entrenched and wants it to have a limited power to vary UK rates of taxation or to levy additional taxes. If SNP politicians say that they 'favour Home Rule', more likely 'accept Home Rule', they mean as a bide-a-while or half-way house to independence. (This is to state the usage, not to enter into the intricate argument as to whether entrenchment is possible within the existing UK constitution – personally, I doubt if it is, but that is precisely what has drawn home-rulers into a general concern for reform of the UK constitution and towards federalism, or what both James Kellas and I are happy enough to call quasi-federalism.[1])

The *Guardian* adds to the confusion by printing 'nationalist' when they plainly mean 'Nationalist', that is supporters of the SNP. For there are many nationalists who are not separatists. The leaders of the SNP did, indeed, publicly declare that they were treating the local government elections as a referendum on the constitutional question; but no one else did, and with only 21.4 per cent of the Scottish vote (Labour 38.99 per cent and Conservative 25.65 per cent) they signally failed to make it so. One of the most remarkable features of Scottish politics in the last decade has been the gradual shift of opinion among both Scottish Labour MPs and constituency activists from deep and bitter divisions to almost unanimous support for constitutional change. In 1979 some, like Robin Cook and Tam Dalyell, broke the party line and campaigned openly against devolution, as did Neil Kinnock in Wales. Now Cook is outspoken in favour of a Scottish-led general constitutional reform, and Dalyell is unusually quiet. Part of the shift of opinion was, of course, a political reaction to Labour being out of power in the United Kingdom while having such dominance in Scotland, at a time of unparalleled government intervention into local government. But part was a growing feeling of national identity. The old, proud and secure cultural and historical identity came to be felt as incomplete and insecure, threatened even, without a democratic national institution.

It mattered less in the nineteenth century when the Church of Scotland could plausibly claim to be *the* representative national institution. Now the Church has become just one among the other four great carriers of Scottish tradition – the Law, local government, education and the language and its literature itself, the practitioners of each of which now feel insecure alone. The political and the cultural threads have been drawn together not just by the centralizing tendencies of British government but by a new generation of Conservative politicians who have lost the real historical sense of their predecessors (however much they go on about 'heritage' – a blue haze with little real content). Part of the content of that sense of history was that one of the main concerns of English politics, perhaps the main concern since 1688, was holding the United Kingdom together. They now take for granted what can never be taken for granted. The price of living together, for nations as for individuals, is eternal empathy and effort (that should be part of the pleasure).

The pressure on Labour's leadership grew irresistible to join in talks with other parties and civic bodies to establish a Scottish Constitutional Convention. It began work early in 1990, even though the SNP refused to join unless there was a prior pledge, even before deliberations, somehow to hold a 'three-way' referendum (between 'as is', 'devolution/home rule' and 'independence [in Europe]'). The Convention's Report[2] of 1991 was endorsed by the Labour Party in the sense that both Kinnock and Hattersley stated that the legislation to be introduced would be on the lines of the report. Two events had precipitated the establishing of the Convention. One was the publication of a pamphlet called *A Claim of Right for Scotland*,[3] written by a committee of Scottish notables commissioned by the Campaign for a Scottish Assembly (CSA) which had arisen in 1980 to continue agitation and argument for a Scottish assembly. It was an impressive document, well reasoned, historically grounded and written in the powerful rhetoric of the plain style (deserving comparison with some of the great pamphlets and state papers of the American Revolution; quite unlike what we are used to in recent British reports, whether official or unofficial). Basically it combined two arguments. First, there was an historical argument that the Act of Union was, in fact (as it is always known in Scotland), a Treaty of Union, and that the English had forgotten both the terms and the spirit and were eroding the equal national rights of Scots. Second, they advanced the familar argument of modern nationalism, that nations have a right to self-determination; but like their parent body the CSA, they made clear that they favoured using the right to remain in the United Kingdom, but on different, negotiated terms. The two Nationalists on the committee privately took the view that it was for a future elected Scottish parliament to initiate the final choice (a view now shared by many others, either tactically or in principle).

The other event that led the Scottish Labour Party into the Constitutional Convention as proposed by the *Claim of Right* (and indeed began to turn the Scottish region of the Labour Party into a *de facto* Scottish Labour Party) was the Govan by-election of November 1988. Jim Sillars took from Labour a seat that had had a 16,000 majority – one of the biggest electoral upsets on record. The shock was and is profound. The SNP claimed it as a vote for independence, especially as Sillars had produced the politically brilliant slogan, endorsed as a policy, 'independence in Europe' (it released many old fears, and seemed less of fantasy). But the opinion polls at the time were showing that about a third of those intending to vote SNP in Scotland favoured devolution or home rule, not any form of independence! A good deal of the SNP vote is a protest vote, but a specific protest, as the Govan result clearly demonstrated (for Labour won it back at the general election), at Labour when it is felt to be 'not doing enough for Scotland'. The unexpected result in fact correlated perfectly with a poll taken shortly before which had asked, *inter alia*, that simple question.[4] But at the same time about a quarter of Labour's potential voters said they favoured independence! Unlike in Northern Ireland, the constitutional issue in Scotland, real but protean, cuts across party lines and makes voting behaviour, especially in by-elections, unpredictably volatile. And one should add, as Scottish Office ministers must daily ponder, that about 40 per cent of their voters favour a devolved parliament![5] Notice in passing that discourse in Scotland has moved from 'assembly' to 'parliament' over the last decade – something more than devolution but less than independence is envisaged. But Scottish Labour leaders will ponder whether they won back Govan not just as part of the general package of a general election (in which by-election results are often reversed) or because last April most Scottish voters who wanted a Scottish parliament really did believe that Labour would win and could deliver it. That credit now spent, and not having been able to deliver, Labour can look forward to some unwantedly exciting by-elections. It will be very unwise for any Scottish Labour MPs to die in the next five years.

It should also be noted, in fairness to the executive of the Scottish Labour Party, that they had made a decision a month before the Govan result to circulate *A Claim of Right* to all constituency parties for comment, and supportive comments were already coming in (scores of constituency activists with whom I have talked claim that their opinions were changed, confirmed or quickened by reading it). And their leader, Donald Dewar, had made a rather low-key speech, poorly reported even in Scotland, but nonetheless a public speech, supporting the idea of a Convention. South of the border, virtually none of this was reported. Govan got huge publicity in the London press and broadcasting media, but the normal processes of Scottish politics are scarcely reported at all, only spectacular events, like Govan, poll tax, Lockerbie and child abuse in the Hebrides. London thinks it knows it all and liberal and independent newspapers, not just old Thatcherite editors, usually act as if the distinctive factors of Scottish politics (indeed Scottish life in general) are eccentric, residual and in terminal decline – Scottishness is no more than well advertised tartan tourist attractions.[6] Most Scottish correspondents of London newspapers are stringers or part-timers with neither the status nor clout, unlike their collegues in Northern Ireland, to file regularly (violence, of course, always helps to create news values).

The next big event after Govan to bring English political writers shuttling up (and down) to Glasgow and Edinburgh was, ironically, a non-event, a rogue poll in January 1992, in the excitable pre-election period, which showed 50 per cent of Scottish voters going for independence (a result never before or since repeated).[7] These two events reinforced the misconception of the London media that most Scottish nationalists are separatists and the confusion between nationalism and Nationalism. Moreover two rival political parties had a mutual interest in trumpeting this dodgy figure and presenting 'the real issue' as 'the Union or Independence', and in asserting categorically that all middle positions were 'impossible' or 'unstable': the Government and the SNP. Both seemed to believe that sovereignty is indivisible. Both were confident that they would benefit electorally if the Labour Party and the Liberal Democrat vote in Scotland could be squeezed by polarizing the constitutional issue. They tried but the results were not spectacular; the SNP share of the vote increased but by far less than anyone expected; and the Conservatives did marginally better, but still remained a minority who can only claim legitimacy in national terms by stating that there is unequivocably a British *nation*, that Great Britain is a single nation rather than a conditional Union of nations (which they concede in the case of Northern Ireland).[8] I pedantically said that 'the Government' rather than the 'Conservative Party' had a mutual interest with the SNP in perpetuating the fallacy of the excluded middle; for the Scottish Tories are more divided on the devolution issue than English politicians who do not regularly read *The Scotsman* or the [Glasgow] *Herald* can be aware of. Before the general election, several Tory candidates and constituency chairmen broke ranks to warn of the danger of this 'either/or' tactic (with 40–45 per cent of their voters favouring devolution and a stern 6 per cent independence!). And after the election it is by no means clear that the Prime Minister may not slip away from Thatcherist confrontationalism into the more traditional conciliatory approach of English Conservatism, as Macmillan and Heath had cleverly pre-empted Plaid Cymru's political revival by big concessions backed by real money on the language question.[9]

***

Roger Levy's *Scottish Nationalism at the Crossroads* is an excellent account of the internal politics and organization of the SNP, the best there is.[10] But no party exists in isolation and Levy makes the fundamental mistake of seeing authentic nationalism wholly in terms of the SNP. He is not obviously a sympathizer but he accepts their conceptualizations and account of themselves too readily. Thus he treats the growth of nationalism in the Scottish Labour Party in a chapter headed 'The New Separatist Coalition' and speaks of the 'tartanizing of the Labour Party'. This is questionable on three counts: Scottish nationalism is not necessarily separatist; 'tartanizing' suggests a set of traditional attitudes rejected by almost all modern Scottish nationalist writers who draw far more on economic history than on the pseudo-history of Stuart mythology and Walter Scott's opportunistic ambivalence (the Tory unionist celebrant of Jacobitism);[11] and it underestimates, in so far as there could be a common interest growing up between some SNP and some Labour activists, how much that comes from a thinly concealed and intellectually formidable federalist tradition within the SNP.[12] The basis for any coalition would be to agree to work together for a negotiated parliament within the United Kingdom, but to disagree within that parliament whether to go forward to independence or not. The crypto-federalist in the SNP presents Home Rule as only a stage towards independence, but some (call them the covert-federalists) would be realistically happy with half a cake so long as it had plums in it and they took part in the baking. (As we may see in South Africa, transitional coalitions can prove long-lasting.) Roger Levy's 'tartan coalition' would not be tartan, more democratic socialist inclined; and the risk of a split is as great or greater in the SNP as in the Labour Party.

Tom Gallagher's *Nationalism in the Nineties*[13] argues the case for the SNP to adopt a more flexible strategy and to realize that terms like 'sovereignty' and 'independence' are now highly relative, especially in the light of their slogan 'independence in Europe', or aspiration perhaps, policy scarcely. The book is by implication also a case for 'common ground', since the editor is a member of the Labour Party, unlike the five other contributors who are all members of the SNP – though they each, to their honour, put one in mind of Orwell's remark that no writer can be a *loyal* member of a political party. And Tom Gallagher might have tried a little harder to find at least one other author in his own position. Bob Purdie uses the experience of all Ireland to warn that rigid intransigence can lead to violence, and from Northern Ireland he draws a sense of honourably divided loyalties. Isabel Lindsay, who resigned from the SNP executive to work in the Convention and has become Convenor of the CSA, lets the cat's head, at least, pop out of the bag:

> For short-term expediency the 'Scotland in Europe' concept was projected as an easy escape route from the problems of seeking a constitutional settlement with England, an escape into a utopia in which strong influence could be wielded and generous regional grants received, where great change could be achieved without changing much.

She is not in any way anti-European, on the contrary; but she has a rare sense that for small nations 'developments in the European Community involve an inherent dilemma. . . .Whatever the ultimate constitutional status that Scotland attains, Europe will be an arena of problems as well as opportunities but not the source of easy solutions.' Tom Gallagher himself might have pondered her words before allowing his generosity of spirit and empathy towards the problems of the Baltic republics to lead him into castigating the SNP for doing nothing to help their struggle for statehood. There is little shortage of gesture politics. A soft breeze of romanticism pervades some beguiling and intricate talk of 'a Europe of the regions'.

Three books of essays are in the same 'Determinations' series on culture and politics as Dr Gallagher's and are each, in different ways, expressive of nationalist thinking.[14] 'Determinations' is meant by its editor, Dr Cairns Craig, to express the determination of Scottish writers to achieve 'self-determination', both in culture and politics with, of course, 'dialogue . . . about those international issues which directly affect Scottish experience' (so long, I sadly add, as they are heartening to the cause; so there is nothing realistic, as yet, about how the determinations of the international capitalist market can be avoided by states of any size – consider Eastern Europe). The Scottish sense of identity and Scottish culture are both remarkably resilient. Each of these books rightly claims that Scotland is in the middle of a literary revival, and 'the vigorous imagination' of Scottish art has become world-famous. We may look back on this generation as having a merit akin to the Irish revival around the

turn of the century, and an influence on all writing in English akin
to that of the Anglo-Irish writers – even if the giants seem missing,
or perhaps a more democratic culture needs fewer giants. The
difficulty for the 'Determinations' school of writers is, however, that
the case they make for the strength of both Scottish identity and
culture denies the very connection they want to find with political
institutions. There is an almost paranoid tone, at times, of claiming
that the culture is threatened by an increasing anglicization unless
Scotland gets its parliament. This is most unlikely. It is like the
fears of the English anti-federalists that if the logic of Maastricht
unwinds the English will soon cease to be English. In truth, I think
Dafydd Elis Thomas, the scholarly former President of Plaid Cymru,
is right: culture, language and national identity do not necessarily
depend on having a sovereign nation state. The case for Scottish
Home Rule is a democratic case and Scotland is a more democratic
society, by and large, than England, but a frustrated democracy. The
culture and the language are, however, astonishingly resilient and
will survive political disappointments and loss. For myself, I
celebrate both, but do not confuse them.

Paul Scott and Christopher Harvie become tedious and raucous
when they are trying to find cultural offence. Scottish nationalism is
much more than anti-Englishness, and if some of that is
intellectually intolerant, it is very rarely socially intolerant (a
mutual national characteristic?). They are right that English and
Scottish Office ministers and politicians have been provocatively
offensive to Scottish claims for a representative institution; but the
educated English public have a great respect for Scottish, Welsh and
Irish literature, sometimes an exaggerated respect. The trick of the
nationalist polemic is not to compare like with like, but to show
that English politicians, businessmen and tourists have no respect
for or understanding of Scottish culture. Indeed, but nor do they of
English either. Scottish intellectuals, unlike English, pride
themselves on having the common touch and on speaking and
writing in the vernacular; but there is no evidence that the
commonality regard them any differently than, say, readers of the
Sun do those of the *Guardian*.

Paul Scott works too hard in his collected essays at trying to find
English threat and hostility, where others might find only
indifference and (to him) an annoying and condescending tolerance.
But some of his essays are profound and telling evocations and

analyses of the Scottish intellect and tradition. Anyone wanting to know what it is all about should read him. And his love for and understanding of the humanistic values of the Scottish enlightenment, when Edinburgh was indeed 'the Athens of the North' and Scottish natural and moral philosophy was admired throughout Europe and the American colonies, makes his nationalism far removed from the infernal metaphysical marriage of Herder's *Volksgeist* with Meinecke's *Staatsraison*, or the *Blut und Boden* nationalism which has killed so many and has now returned amid the ruins of Soviet power to mock and torment the civic tradition. Christopher Harvie has done solid work on British and Scottish history and holds the chair of British Studies at Tubingen. He has recently joined the SNP and is a prolific writer in the press and in anthologies. But he suffers from a kind of social historian's disease; everything is related to everything else and everything he now writes goes round and round in huge swirling circles, vortices or corkscrews. It is very hard to understand what he is saying, except that Scotland's future lies in modern Europe (so long as it is socialist). The 'is' and the 'ought' intermingle promiscuously. He raises every issue one wants to hear about, but then dashes on – or back – to another. He seems to think he is writing for the ordinary man, but he must have some doubts for he allows 'Punter' to ask him at the end, in an imaginary dialogue (which unhappily I have not imagined), *just what* is he proposing? To imagine 'what sort of country we wanted Scotland to be', he replies: 'Scottish nationalism is about how people understand and run a smallish community, without exploiting anyone.'

Neither Scott nor Harvie seems willing to give due weight to the inter-relations of the nations of the British Isles, that what we call 'Scottish', 'English' and 'Irish' are and always were inextricably intermingled. At some imaginary point of time was there a Scotland that was fully Scottish and an England unaffected by the others? The most frequently imagined time was, of course, when Arthur was King of all Britain. One does not expect nationalist rhetoricians to be interested in what is in common as well as genuine differences, many of which can be properly described as national characteristics; but one hopes for something more subtle from the scholarly. Paul Scott is aware of the point at times. He can quote T. S. Eliot on the value of the cultural diversity of the four nations of these islands. He says that the English usually forget this; but so can he. He recalls an exchange once famous in Scotland between a nationalist intellectual, Stephen Maxwell, and the late John Mackintosh, in which John said he could not go all the way with the SNP because he had a sense of dual nationality, British and Scottish.

Now, of course, there are two answers to this. In the first place, 'British' implies reciprocity and this has been denied by the English who have never understood the distinction between British and English. Secondly, autonomy or independence does not preclude a secondary or wider loyalty.[15] Yet a sense of dual national identity does not imply that one or the other must predominate. If either is threatened and needs institutional protection, then federalism is a more obvious response than tearing out part of the heart. And to say that the English have *never* understood the distinction is either 'forgetful' or rhetorical blather: one of the main state policies in the eighteenth and nineteenth centuries was to build up a (at first somewhat artificial) *British* patriotism. And this meant not developing a state-cult of English nationalism, rather imperialism and the Crown, in whose service the four nations combined. But the distinction, well known to the old Tories, has been forgotten by the new suburban breed.[16] It is reasonably clear that 'English' and 'Scottish', etc. refer to cultures and 'British' refers more narrowly to mutually agreeable political and legal arrangements, so long as they are mutually agreeable (and in Scotland they are not, certainly in the present form). Loyalty must, in any case, always be conditional.

The 'Determinations' anthology *The Manufacture of Scottish History* promises more than it fulfils. It is a lively set of essays, not all by historians, decidedly amateur or hastily compiled compared with the six detailed monographs in, whose title and intention it echoes, Hobsbawm and Ranger's *The Invention of Tradition* (which includes Hugh Trevor-Roper's account of the myth of the tartan kilt). A modern Irish book of such a title would now celebrate the emancipation of historical research from nationalist agitation; the great Irish historians of today are secure enough in their national identity not to need bad history and to be able to see the Irish rebellion not in teleological terms but as a contingent coincidence of events in British (sic) politics – it was only afterwards that an Ireland apart (somewhat apart) from the United Kingdom came into being, never before. These essays are, in fact, less concerned with trying to give a true judgement of the relative weights of interrelationships than with either claiming that past Scottish history has not been nationalistic enough or has shown the wrong kind of nationalism – the tartan traditionalist kind, not Harvie's postmodern, technological, small nation Europe kind. One looks in vain in their long bibliography for Hugh Kearney's magisterial 'attempt to examine, within short compass, the interaction of the major cultures of the British Isles from the Roman period onwards'. Modern nationalists can survive reading it but can claim little respect if they won't respond to it:

> To concentrate upon a single 'national' history, which is based upon the political arrangements of the present, is to run the risk of being imprisoned within a cage of partial assumptions, which leads to the perpetuation of ethnocentric myths and ideologies.[17]

But this is precisely what the nationalist as against the national historian wants to do. The national historian should keep the conscience of a nation and put the truth before it, not preach some disputable orthodoxy.

James Kellas's standard textbook *The Scottish Political System* is now in its third edition, and its unopinionated good sense and sound political judgement make it underrated or unknown to the 'Determinations' populist light cavalry. Now he has written an extremely thoughtful analysis of types of nationalism in the modern world. He looks back too, and has no doubt, against both Gellner and Kedourie's different datings of it as a modern phenomenon, that the Declaration of Arbroath of 1320 is a kind of nationalism, but a very different one from that of democratic societies and nothing whatever to do, in fact the contrary, with any notions of 'sovereignty of the people'. This Rousseauistic or Jacobin concept is invoked freely by such writers as Harvie and Scott, by SNP spokesmen (even with a majority of the people against them) and even by some members of the Convention. They do not seem to notice its contradiction to their 'Europe of the nations', nor to their belief in a bill of rights restraining even the powers of an elected parliament.

Nationalism can live without belief in sovereignty. That is one of the concepts that can now blind eyes to the real nature of the modern world, just as nationalists are too often tactically inept by feeding internally on their own 'determinations' and understanding their opponents only in stereotypical terms. Was it Orwell or Koestler who said, 'know thy enemy as thyself'? The greatest dilemma for Scottish nationalism, home rule or separatist, would be if the English Tories returned to historical form and attempted conciliation; offered some kind of representative assembly with few powers and minimal facilities.[18]

Notes

1. The implication is there and now grows fast. Mr Alistair Darling, MP for Edinburgh Central, was an opposition spokesman on constitutional affairs in the last parliament and strongly defended Roy Hattersley's view that 'the sovereignty of parliament' was the good key to the whole British system, and would be threatened by proposals for entrenchment and judicial review. But he is now reported to be considering seriously proposals for a United Kingdom federalism. See also James Kellas, 'The Scottish Constitutional Convention', *Scottish Government Yearbook, 1992*, ed. Lindsay Patterson and David McCrone, Edinburgh, Edinburgh University Press. My essay 'The Sovereignty of Parliament and the Irish Question', in *Political Thoughts and Polemics*, Edinburgh, Edinburgh University Press, 1990, suggests that recognition of the difficulty of governing the other nations led the English in the past to a prudential way of exercising sovereignty as if in a federal state.

2. *Towards Scotland's Parliament: A Report to the Scottish People by the Scottish Constitutional Convention*, 30 November 1990, Rosebery House, Edinburgh, EH12. See also James Kellas, *Scottish Government Yearbook 1992*. (These Yearbooks are an invaluable source on recent Scottish politics; they are about to become a quarterly journal of analysis and record, *Scottish Affairs*.) James Naughtie's 'Labour 1979–88' is a good overall account of Labour's changes, in Ian Donnachie, Christopher Harvie and Ian S. Wood (eds), *Forward! Labour Politics in Scotland 1888–1980*, Edinburgh, Polygon, 1989.

3. Edinburgh, July 1988, Campaign for a Scottish Assembly. *A Claim of Right for Scotland* is reprinted in a useful volume of essays of the same title, edited by Owen Dudley Edwards, Edinburgh, Edinburgh University Press, 1988.

4. See William Miller, 'Can We Believe in Opinion Polls?' in David McCrone (ed.), *What Scotland Wants*, Edinburgh University, Unit for the Study of Government in Scotland, 1990.

5. So did I. Why else throw so much good time away on writing, with David Millar, *Standing Orders for the Parliament of Scotland*, Edinburgh, John Wheatley Centre, 1991?

6. This distinctiveness is demonstrated beyond doubt in William Miller, *The End of British Politics: Scots and English Political Behaviour in the '70s*,

Oxford, Clarendon, 1981. But few English textbooks bother to include substantial sections on Scotland; they systematically confuse 'English' and 'British'. See my 'An Englishman Considers His Passport', *Irish Review*, Autumn 1988.

7. See Peter Kellner, 'Why the Tories Won' in *The BBC-Vacher's Guide to the New House of Commons*, Berkhamsted, Vachers, 1992, pp. 9–13. He quotes figures on the constitutional question from an NOP election day poll, thus likely to get more realistic answers than in polls on that question alone. Nonetheless, Scottish voters went 9% for outright independence; 19.5% for independence inside the EC; 44% for devolution; 24% for no change; with only 3% don't knows. And 17% of voters in England and Wales would support some form of independence for Scotland; 36% devolution, 24% no change and 17% don't knows. Thus there is no real sign of English hostility despite some backbench Tory MPs beating Drake's drum loudly.

8. The Northern Ireland Constitution Act 1973 and the Inter-Government Agreement of 1985 commit Her Majesty's Government to bring in legislation if a majority of the people in Northern Ireland 'clearly wish for and formally consent to the establishment of a United Ireland'.

9. See Dafydd Elis Thomas, 'The Constitution of Wales', in Bernard Crick (ed.), *National Identities and the Constitution of the United Kingdom*, Oxford, Blackwell and *Political Quarterly*, 1991. Dafydd clearly puts preservation of the language a long way in front of gaining a Welsh parliament, indeed he sees clearly that a Welsh parliament would be a numerical threat to any hope for a genuine bi-linguality in the whole of Wales.

10. Edinburgh, Scottish Academic Press, 1990.

11. See Murray G. H. Pittock, *The Invention of Scotland: The Stuart Myth and the Scottish Identity, 1638 to the Present*, London, Routledge, 1991. And consider also two books whose authors, while strong nationalists and anti-Unionists, both attack the tartan myth and denounce the SNP for claiming a monopoly of patriotic virtue and for having no sensible idea of how their aspirations could become realizable policies: Neal Ascherson's *Games with Shadows* and Tom Nairn's *The Enchanted Glass*, both London, Century Hutchinson, 1988.

12. See especially Neil MacCormick, 'Unrepentant Gradualism', in Owen Dudley Edwards (ed.), *op. cit.*, and 'Nations and Nationalism' in his *Legal Right and Social Democracy: Essays in Legal and Political Philosophy*, Oxford, Clarendon Press, 1982.

13. Tom Gallagher (ed.), *Nationalism in the Nineties*, Edinburgh, Polygon, 1991.

14. Paul H. Scott, *Towards Independence*, Edinburgh, Polygon, 1992; Christopher Harvie, *Cultural Weapons*, Edinburgh, Polygon, 1992; and Ian Donnachie and Christopher Whatley (eds) *The Manufacture of Scottish*

History, Edinburgh, Polygon, 1992.

15. Dafydd Elis Thomas, 'The Constitution of Wales'.
16. See my 'The Sovereignty of Parliament and the Scottish Question', in Norman Lewis (ed.), *Happy and Glorious: The Constitution in Transition*, Milton Keynes, Open University Press, 1990.
17. Hugh Kearney, *The British Isles: A History of Four Nations*, Cambridge, Cambridge University Press, 1989, p. 1.
18. James Mitchell, *Conservatives and the Union*, Edinburgh, Edinburgh University Press, 1990 reveals more differences within the Conservative Party towards Scotland than are often remembered or taken seriously.

CHAPTER 4

The Politics of British History

You have no idea how historians usually behave if you are not astonished at what happened in 1994 at the famous annual Anglo-American Conference of Historians at the Institute of Historical Research (IHR). For the first time ever they stayed together in plenary session, listening attentively and seriously to unfamiliar, or at best semi-familiar matter, rather than splitting into their time-honoured, semi-private special period or special subject closets. What kept them together then was the very matter of Britain, 'The Making of the United Kingdom'. The revised papers are the first of the books listed in the note below. That it was done at all is more commendable than whether it was done well or badly; in fact it was done rather well. And it has triggered off a kind of pioneer's race to stake out choice claims in print in the new historiographical

---

A review article in *Political Quarterly*, July 1996, of Alexander Grant and Keith J. Stringer (eds), *Uniting the United Kingdom? The Making of British History* (Routledge, 1995); Steven G. Ellis and Sarah Barber (eds), *Conquest and Union: Fashioning a British State 1485–1725* (Longman, 1995); John Robertson (ed.), *A Union for Empire: Political Thought and the Union of 1707* (Cambridge University Press, 1995); Brendan Bradshaw and John Morrill (eds), *The British Problem, 1534–1707* (Macmillan, 1996); Robert G. Asch (ed.), *Three Nations – A Common History? England, Scotland, Ireland and British History* c.1600–1920 (Bochum, Brockmeyer, 1993); Roger A. Mason, *Scots and Britons: Scottish Political Thought and the Union of 1603* (Cambridge University Press, 1994).

territory. 'Kansas or bust', as it were; and on none of these well-packed wagons need be written, as in Lincoln's anecdote, 'busted'. Truly, much is contentious but all is good. Each of these books is slow going but intellectually exciting, to be read by all who follow politics seriously. They show a lively British history, both empirical and thoughtful, fully recovered from the methodological narrowness and parochiality of Namierism. Pioneers all; but here my metaphor may bust a wheel, for several of the pioneers ride in more than one wagon.

The prophet John Pocock was in the lead wagon above and on the manifest of three more, and his wagon-train master John Morrill also rides in four. I distance this with humour because in times of debased public rhetoric it is hard to write, without sounding portentous, that all this is an event of historical significance, and of potentially direct political importance if it leads to a new way of looking at who we are and what we might be doing. The old jingle 'Politics without history has no fruit; history without politics has no fruit' has its truth. But the history that fruits in the popular consciousness is too often bad history: a selective memory that serves only the perpetual short-term politics of the next election. The diminishment of Anglocentric history may not as yet have penetrated the ignorant and prejudiced skulls of those Tory education ministers and their servile or supine advisers who first presumed, contrary to English political tradition, to legislate for a state national curriculum, and then to attempt to fine-tune the history and English curricula to old patriotic airs, melodies of aggressive nostaligia, a kind of unsatiric *Beggar's Opera*. But they now have something to be worried about when educational (I use that word as a near-synonym to commercial) publishers like Macmillan and Longman force the pace. Textbooks will not be slow to follow. Attempts were made over fifteen years ago to get something about Scotland and Northen Ireland, at least, into GCE Politics syllabuses, but they foundered through the unwillingness of the teachers (and most examiners) to break new ground, to abandon the safe lowlands of 'British politics' as English politics with an occasional awkward exception (which can always be avoided if an examination papers allows, as liberal dogma too often allows, wide choice).

The director of the IHR in his foreword eschews the delights of deep epistemological thought about the relation of historiography to political ideas and public opinion; he just says on behalf of his committee that 'It was our view, given the uncertain nature of present-day "Britain" and "Britishness", that such a conference had a pronounced topical relevance' – good English understatement. He adds, 'Historians are too wise to claim that there are easy lessons to be learned from their discipline, but they know that history matters, and the scholarship and insights embodied in these essays can undoubtedly play a vital role in informing current debates about the future of the United Kingdom.' Not yet, but they will in time – in time one hopes for the next generation of Conservatives to recall what the precursors of this sorry lot took for granted as the very stuff of British politics: that we are a multinational state and the main business of politics has been, since the Act and Treaty of Union of 1707, holding it together – with broad success as regards England, Scotland and Wales, but with signal failure in Ireland (a failure not necessarily in the parting, but in the violence of it and the bad political legacy it left – even though literary, cultural and social interpenetration and mutual concern remain remarkably close).

Rethinking of how to present history is now proceeding rapidly. Notice that the still somewhat Whiggish title of the conference, 'The Making of the United Kingdom', gains a change of verb and a question mark in the book's new title. The question mark presumably implies a reasonable slight doubt about the future of the Union (or the form of its future), but far more it reflects the scepticism of modern historians that there was an inevitable dynamic for the feudal kingdom of England to create a state embracing, for a time, all of the British Isles. As a rising star of Irish history, Hiram Morgan, argues in the Bradshaw and Morrill collection, this was not even a settled policy of Tudor or Stewart rulers and councillors: they cared more for ensuring that Ireland and Scotland did not come under the domination of Catholic France or Spain, which could then threaten England directly, than for the great cost (in every sense) of conquering and governing the geographic periphery. Indirect rule became the custom of the expanding English state long before the American colonies, long before India. English colonies in Ireland certainly, but the colonization of all Ireland? A nightmare until it became thought of as a dubious necessity. In Scotland neither colonization nor permanent occupation nor anglicization was ever consciously attempted.

John Morrill, Reader in Early Modern History at Cambridge University, puts the claim of the new history and its own history concisely in *Conquest and Union*:

> Our starting point must be the work of John Pocock, whose plea for 'British History: a new subject' has been the delayed action inspiration behind most recent development in the field. In 1975 he called us to a holistic approach to what he has termed 'the Atlantic archipelago', insisting that we must adopt a pluralistic approach which recognises but does not exaggerate the extent to which such a history must contain 'the increasing dominance of England as a political and cultural entity'. He went on to show how the component parts of these islands 'interact so as to modify the conditions of one another's existence', and that 'British history' denotes the historiography of no single nation but of a problematic and incomplete experiment in the creation and interaction of several nations.

Each of these books, in different ways and for different periods, follows this Pocockian agenda (and even some reaction against it). The history of these islands is shown as continuous interaction. From the time of the Norman invasion of England, followed by the occupation of part of Ireland and a cultural permeation of Lowland Scotland, to the present, almost nothing of major political importance in one country did not affect the others. That the timetables and contingencies of British and Irish general elections complicate and delay any new settlement in Ulster today is simple to grasp compared with the three-way diplomacies and divisions of the seventeenth century. Our English Civil War will never be the same again. The concepts of 'wars in the three kingdoms' gains currency because Charles I would not have run out of money and had to summon the Long Parliament had he not been defeated by the covenanting Scots in the Bishops' War, towards which Parliament, broadly sympathizing with the Scots on the church issue, would not vote supply. He would not then have challenged Parliament in the field had it not, when faced by the rebellion in Ireland two years later, against all precedent taken command of the army itself. And the rebellion in Ireland was triggered in part by Catholic fear, on the part of both the Old English and the Gaelic lords, that his attempt to impose ecclesiastical conformity in Scotland would be extended to Ireland where, a crucial fact of the history of these islands, the Reformation had failed and the Counter-Reformation had begun to solidify a hitherto largely unfocused Irish consciousness. Thinking of such complications at almost every time and on every level should induce a more problematic, pluralistic way of looking at English-becoming-British state-craft.

It also strengthens more subtle ways of considering national identity. Yes, people do feel threatened; but perhaps as much by the mental muddle arising out of old bad history as by external (or internal) malevolent forces threatening British (or is it only English?) identity. The picture that emerges in the new 'British' or interactive perspectives of the Act and Treaty of Union (the one in one country, the other in the other) cuts away two rival false perpectives. On the English side, there was nothing inevitable about it and a lot of contingency – certainly not Macaulay's historical destiny of the English state, the teleological acount of the UK current in the old textbooks – empire, power, unique role as mother of parliments, fair play and all that. On the Scottish side, the nationalist account of sell-out and betrayal looks very thin. Some bribery, certainly – there always was; but to lose a parliament then did not mean what it would now mean to lose (or gain) one. The Scottish commissioners drove a hard bargain: the establishment of the Kirk, the entrenchment of the legal system, full participation in the English economy and imperial trade, and by implication the continuance and growth of a different system of local administration and education. The Kirk was as much, possibly more, the national institution, certainly closer to the common people, than the parliament. Overall, of course, the great desire in Scotland was to ensure at least peace after 'the killing times', and to avoid civil war over the succession; these were as much national concerns and equally important parts of the national consciousness in the Lowlands as later ideas that every nation must constitute a state, both as of right and to survive at all, let alone that every state must hurry to turn its diverse peoples into one nation.

Such a way of looking at things at least can modify passionate bad arguments in difficult enough complex situations like Northern Ireland. The Scottish example suggests that neither Protestant British consciousness nor Catholic Irish consciousness is necessarily threatened by the formal institutions and identity of the state, whatever tolerable settlement can be reached, however fudged the great principles. It is not only modern English Conservatives who find dual identities hard to operate: some on the left still want to simplify complex histories by romantically or lazily accepting nationalist assumptions, so that if all Ireland and Scotland went their own way, things would be simpler (for theorists). An example of this is an interesting editorial by Raphael Samuel in *History Workshop Journal* (autumn 1995) precisely on 'Four Nations History'. On the whole he finds it pleasing, albeit mainly in the negative sense of rejecting the old Anglocentric approach; but the alternative seems to him to be Scottish separation (he still talks about Tom Nairn's rashly titled *The Breakup of Britain* as 'prophetic' and, rather appallingly and not with his usual appealing political innocence, Samuel says: 'The civil war [*sic*] in Ulster was opening a new phase in the history of Irish separatism.' That is a memorable example of the kind of nationalist teleology against which the 'four nations' school now argues, and Irish scholars have long argued. He is upset that the revisionists see English revolutionary ideas in the mid-seventeenth century as a consequence of the collapse of royal authority, not at all as a main cause. He makes a very perceptive distinction between the disaggregative use of 'four nations' history, as in Hugh Kearney's *The British Isles: A History of Four Nations* (1988), and Linda Colley's aggregative half-use of it (she ignores Ireland) in her *Britons: Forging the Nation, 1707–1827* (1992). But then, when he asks rhetorically whether the English can 'go on calling themselves "Brits" if the Act of Union . . . is repealed', he totally misrepresents Christopher Smout's demonstration in the same issue of *History Workshop* that Scots have long felt closer to Europe than the English, as showing them to be more interested in that than in 'reconceptualising cross-border relationships'. There is no hint of separatism in Smout's subtle, pluralistic view of Scottish identity (indeed, on identity questions in general). Contrary to Samuel, Smout concludes that if the Scots are less frightened of Europe than are the English, that may be because 'nearly three hundred years of political union have taught them how readily one can be a member of such a union without sacrificing national identity or cultural integrity: but that is another story'.

The Scots can acknowledge a Britishness precisely because they have remained securely Scottish – whatever SNP intellectuals or their fellow-travellers say in spite of the majority opinion of their compatriots, and whatever their friends among the remnants of the English old New Left think, respecting every other nationalism but their own (well, nearly every other – the Balkans have taught a few lessons). The Hanoverian project that Colley described with such beguiling vigour failed, or rather only half-succeeded. The half is very important, but if 'Britishness' defines a civic nation, it does not define a comprehensive national consciousness or culture. If Britishness is a national culture at all, it is narrowly and precisely a civic one to be distinguished from civil society as a whole; it is those institutions which gave the historic four (or now three-and-a-half) nations a common citizenship: the Crown, Parliament and the laws. Asian Britons see this more clearly than most English do. That is why they call themselves Asian Britons, etc., and not Asian English, Asian Scots, etc. They are as law-abiding as the rest of us, are loyal to those institutions and seek their protection; but beyond that see no reason to seek to assimilate English culture fully, rather maintaining their own religion, culture and customs within British laws (not at all unlike, in this respect, the Welsh and the Scots). It is the English, several writers note, who are muddled on this distinction. My hypothesis is that whereas Scots could be both good unionists and good Scots, as Sirs Walter Scott showed the world, the older generations of English statesmen suppressed a conscious and explicit exaltation of Englishness in the interest of holding the UK together by Britishness. That would be the political equivalent of the new historiography's rejection of the misleading Anglocentric approach. But there is now a price to be paid for this suppression in the xenophobia over Europe, even if John Major's 'Union in danger' cry over the proposed Scottish parliament appears to find no resonance in English public opinion.

However, the new history has its critics and its limits. In the *Three Nations* volume (no time or space for the Welsh, apparently), Keith Brown, a Scottish historian, announces himself 'unconvinced of the notion of a British people', and he invokes Irish allies to resist being swallowed by a 'Pocockian monster', however nice it is, he says, of the 'Anglo-American historical establishment' at last to take Irish, Scottish and Welsh history seriously. His historiographical point is simply that some topics lend themselves to the interrelations of the nations approach, but others are peculiar and particular to national history. Broadly speaking, the national histories lead us better into social history and the interactive approach leads better into political history. But Brown also hints that Pocock's prescription, possibly like Linda Colley's, could lead to an all-embracing British super-state mentality, not just to better and less nationalistic historical explanation.

In Pocock's own case, it plainly has – to the embarrassed surprise of some of his many admirers and debtors (among whom is myself). But, as ever, middle positions are possible. The fallacy of the excluded middle is only good for fights. One can applaud Pocock's historiography as warmly as John Morrill while sharply differentiating it from his political philosophy. In recent lectures and writings, notably a lecture at the Woodrow Wilson Center on 'Some Europes in their History', he has doubted that the very concept of Europe was meaningful, or constant enough 'to be lived with honourably'. In a notable article three years ago, 'History and Sovereignty', he said that his native New Zealand's identity lay in a reciprocal relationship with Britain, and that Britain by its decision to withdraw from it unilaterally to become a Europe state, 'left it clear that those who took it did not repect us and at least doubtful what room they had left for respecting themselves'. Strong words. I ventured to reply, more in shock than anger, that I feel no loss of self-respect by feeling somewhat European, as well as British, English, and Scottish by residence and political conviction, and being father to half-Welsh children. For we can compound, as Smout has demonstrated so precisely for Scotland, many identities. While I do not give much respect to my country for pretending to be an imperial power for too long after most of the former empire wanted it despite the speedy postwar withdrawal from India, I would have more respect for our ruling rulers had we been in Europe from the beginning.

Pocock really does believe that in Britain sovereignty and national identity are inseparable. This must be the basis of a theory of British exceptionalism that he owes us. Because of that, to him no compromise was possible in 1775 and 1776, so better that the Americans went their own way than that we British compromised on sovereignty and risked Westminster being swamped by colonials. (If New Zealand were as big as Australia, would he still take that view?) And he sees 1707 as a *fully* 'incorporating union' because it left the Westminster Parliament the legally unchallenged sovereign (depite most opinion in the Mason and the Robertson volumes, and a brilliant essay on the Union debate by Mark Goldie in Bradshaw and Morrill). He lives in a world of definitions, not noticing that sovereignty had to be restrained in political reality – quite apart from the formal terms of the treaty – to preserve the hard bargain the Scots drove and the English felt the need to accept. The 'incorporation' of 1707 fell far short of that which James I and VI had dreamed of in 1603 and for a wasted while had schemed. Pocock told the assembled Anglo-American historians that 'the language of confederation was profoundly alien to British discourse and has remained so' – a most curious and cursory view of Commonwealth history. Actually, he may be broadly or verbally right. Federal constitutions were always thought good for colonials but not for us at home. But that only shows that *discourse* is not always a good guide to practice, either political practice or the historian's practice of explaining what actually happened. Ideas and circumstances need linking in different ways and to different measure on different occasions. The history of ideas and the history of events must be married, but to be fruitful each partner has to be equally important. The English theory of parliamentary sovereignty was a grand guarantor of peace in times when the big fear was civil war; but in all other times the trick of sovereignty was when not to exercise it – as Charles I, Lord North and Lady Thatcher in their different ways could never quite grasp, above all confusing of sovereignty with power. Parliamentary sovereignty is a concept with a contingent history which includes declining British power; and, as circumstances change, it may have had its day, or simply be less important than it was. The new times, looking outward and inward, are more likely to be with the 'F' word.

If there is one criticism of the editing of these admirable and important volumes it is that these mighty concepts like 'sovereignty' (nationalism itself, citizenship, toleration, freedom, ideas of political obligation, etc.), which do shape what practical politicians think of as practice, are not treated systematically other than by John Pocock, but are scattered throughout discussions of events. Few historians as yet dare to produce revisionist accounts of enduring and changing national characteristics to set against dubious nationalist stereotypes of national character. Better accounts are needed, not silence.

CHAPTER 5

Why the Northern Ireland Peace Process Must Take So Long

Few people here will, I am sure, agree with everything I am going to say nor particularly want to hear some of it. But, before I come to the current situation, I want to stand back and look at some of the basic factors in the Northern Ireland question, and the way we conceptualize them, matters that get lost in the day-to-day accusations and counter-accusations reported in the press, sometimes stirred by the press, for Northern Ireland often furnishes a marvellous working holiday for committed journalists. But it may at least be a change from what you will hear when you have the legendary Great Elks of Ulster in front of you, with their familiar mixture either of self-justifying rhetoric or, in the other case, grim and angry suspicious reticence, both knowing that any half-way honest hints about realistic possibilities may be reported and used against them back home. Let me try some common sense and common morality about this highly complex matter from a political philosopher who has been visiting Ireland continuously since 1969 and mixing, from time to time, in highly unacademic quarters, mainly motivated by what killed the cat – curiosity about what is

---

This was a lecture jointly sponsored by Ireland House, New York University, and the National Committee on American Foreign Policy. A shortened version was published in the National Committee's newsletter, *American Foreign Policy Interest* (June 1996). A long time ago? But I still think the basic analysis and conclusions hold.

on one's doorstep and won't, as most of my fellow countrymen wish, go away.

I want to address five broad points: first, about basic preconceptions; second, about what it is like on the ground; third, about bad history and the significant past; fourth, about the state of opinion at the moment; and fifth, about what is likely to happen.

Basic preconceptions

There is now an almost inevitable process toward an acceptable settlement in Northern Ireland, but I want to explain why the so-called peace process will, in the nature of the problem, inevitably take a long time, quite apart from any short-term foot-dragging there might have been. The so-called peace process will be a matter of negotiated stages, with pauses to test popular acceptance, not a sudden breakthrough by big men around a table ready for television, with a final treaty to be signed by the two prime ministers in the presence of the American President of the day. Notice that I said an 'acceptable settlement' rather than a 'just solution' or 'final peace'. There are three difficulties with thinking in terms of a 'just solution'. First, there are solutions only to logical puzzles or invented games. In such real and extreme conflict situations when anyone cries 'I've got a solution', one knows that one is dealing with a fanatic, an innocent, or a crank. In the real world only reasonably acceptable resolutions are possible to extreme conflict situations, and those imply both big political compromises and a willingness to use coercive power against would-be wreckers of popularly acceptable compromises. Second, to argue about the historical justice of claims to sovereignty is a fruitless way of reaching agreement. That familiar mode of pseudo-historical argument would give back Manhattan to the Iroquois Confederacy and Israel to the Philistines.

I often think of what Albert Camus had to say to his fellow intellectuals and to journalists in France during the far more bitter and bloody Algerian conflict:

> The role of intellectuals cannot be . . . to excuse from a distance one of the violences and condone the other. This has the double result of enraging the violent group that is condemned and encouraging to greater violence the violent group that is

exonerated. If they do not join the combatants themselves, their role (less spectacular, to be sure!) must be merely to strive for pacification so that reason can have a chance.[1]

What it is like on the ground

In Northern Ireland, however, one does have to come to terms, as part of a settlement, with the injustices of the immediate past – the abuses of the old Stormont regime and some occasional excesses of police and army in fighting terrorists. While they hammer away with the irrefutable awkward fact that a clear majority in the North do not want a united Ireland, Unionist leaders would do well to admit some of the past abuses of majoritarian democracy and show some contrition. It would help mightily. But though ordinary Nationalists see the constant recall of these abuses as useful advocacy and propaganda, their leaders are well aware of the danger to their professed fundamental cause, Irish unity, if these charges were well answered by arrangements for power-sharing, equal rights, and constitutional reform in a Northern Ireland still part of the United Kingdom.

Notice also that though I believe that an acceptable settlement will come, I spoke of the 'so-called' peace process. The process is aimed at peace. Peace is, indeed, a goal, a principle, and a standard more applicable to the situation than 'justice'. As the philosopher Thomas Hobbes reminded us, we cannot avoid death but we can create societies in which the chances of violent death are minimized from whatever cause: civil strife, guns, gross poverty and starvation, or automobiles even. Yet a possible danger in using the rhetoric of 'peace process' is that it disarms our expectations that fanatics on either side, scorning compromise, which is the stuff of politics, will attempt to wreck it; they may even redouble their efforts as it gets closer to realization. We see that happening in the Middle East at the moment. It may recur in Bosnia. So to make 'the ending of violence' the test of the peace process is impractical. We have to steel ourselves against such a situation in which things may get worse before they get better. I have been saying that for twenty years in mordant letters to the British press, for sometimes human fear of provoking violence has inhibited possible political initiatives or necessary actions. The early ray of hope, the power-sharing government of 1974, was destroyed in a spontaneous general strike of Protestant, Loyalist workers; and Harold Wilson, then prime minister, nervously refused to permit the general officer commanding (GOC) to tear down the barricades, which he said could be done with minimal casualties because the rebels would not stand up to the army. Wilson had his press officer in unattributable briefings say that the GOC had advised the contrary.

In such situations it is always likely that things will get worse before better, that this year there would be a breach of the cease-fire by the IRA, whether spontaneous (I mean elements out of control of the leadership) or conniving and tactical, to force their way to the table and get it set up quickly. A recent scholarly study by a Scottish sociologist reminded us bluntly that there is 'a core of people whose hatred of the other side is so great that any hurt invited on them, no matter how awful, is cause for rejoicing'.[2] These emotions are, of course, reciprocal. Also, he showed that the Loyalist community has animating myths of history every bit as elaborate, passionately believed, and dubious as the Nationalist community, if less well known outside Ulster. Short of violent passions there are two communities defining each other by religion, each deeply suspicious of the other, fearful of each other, and often hating each other, polarizing or stereotyping every issue, great or small. One is fearful that to give an inch is to lose all, religion and identity. Witness the gradual diminishment of the Protestant population in the South – therefore, the loyalist cry of 'not an inch', 'no surrender'; while the Catholic community in the North has traditionally believed that its faith was threatened by godless secular laws maladministered by bigoted Presbyterians and that the proud consciousness of being Irish could be secured only as citizens of an Irish state.

So the problem has often been called that of the double minority or the double majority. The Catholics have a majority in the island of Ireland but a minority in the North. The Protestants have a majority in the North but a minority on the island. And it is all so very small: about a million and a half in the North, with a ratio of about three to two Protestant to Catholic and about four million people in the Republic – a bit like Jews and the state of Israel. More people who feel themselves to be Irish in some significant sense, in part at least, live outside Ireland as citizens of other countries. Not simply the United States, but Australia, Canada and Britain have large numbers conscious of being Irish. I mention this for a purpose, to remind you that many people carry double identities regarding national consciousness and that national consciousness often does not demand, still less historically depend on, a separate state. As an Englishman living in Scotland and identified with Scottish causes, I am very familiar with these double identities. My Scottish friends think of themselves as Scottish and British, but they never say, it is worth noting, 'and English' – just as Unionists in Northern Ireland say 'British' and not English. British is their allegiance but not their culture.

Sinn Fein Nationalists believe, of course, that multinational states are inherently unstable and are corrosive of 'true nationalism'. It is an exclusive nationalism that pays only lip service to there being 'two nations' in the island of Ireland. Opinion surveys, however, now suggest that this is no longer the view of a clear majority of Catholics in the North, whatever their leaders say. Nevertheless, the distrust between the two communities is so great that talk of their gradual integration, as even a middle-term policy, certainly with respect to primary and secondary education, seems to me fatuous. Searching for 'what we have in common' in a Quaker, Hindu, Unitarian style is a pleasant activity undertaken by churchmen at ecumenical conferences, but it can identify only a very basic level of human rights or minor levels of social or sporting co-operation, necessary conditions indeed for a settlement but far, far away from sufficient conditions. The best that can be hoped for is tolerance between two different communities, and tolerance implies informed understanding of real differences so that no one causes offence by accident even when he or she is resolved not to do so deliberately. Fortunately it is the common policy of the British and Irish governments to move toward creating more institutions in the North that reflect the equal existence of two communities rather than piously or hypocritically making gestures toward a common culture.

Bad history and the significant past

Before coming to the present and pointers to the future, let me just try to lay to rest or exorcize two powerful historical ghosts that still haunt and shape people's imaginations, especially sympathizers of

Sinn Fein in this country, in Australia, and indeed among some of the old left in my country: the ghost of nationalism itself and that of partition. There is now a surprisingly wide measure of agreement among professional historians in Ireland, Britain, and this country (so much so that nationalist intellectuals use 'revisionism' as a term of deadly abuse), and though the new history has been in the schools in both parts of Ireland for a decade or two, there are few signs that it has reached the consciousness of political activists. Its conclusions suit the case of neither extremity, and so the historians are comprehensively abused as 'revisionist' (which is indeed what professional history is all about, continual revision).[3]

To the Nationalist it is a matter of faith that there was an Irish polity before the English or Angevin invasions and that the nation was coterminous with the island of Ireland. Neither proposition is true. There were tribal societies of rich Celtic cultures but no concept of a nation or common political institutions. As so often in the history of the expansion of Europe, unity came from foreign conquest or attempted conquest. A consciousness of being a nation began to form in the mid- to late sixteenth century partly as a general response to alien rule, whether direct, as in the Pale, or indirect through the clan chiefs, as notably in Ulster, but more so through a failed attempt to spread the Protestant reformation to Ireland. That it succeeded in England and Scotland and finally in Ireland is the key to modern history. But not until the mid-nineteenth century did consciousness of being a nation create the demand, even then a minority demand, to be a state. Even Tyrone's rebellion in the 1590s was far from nationalist in our modern sense. He rebelled, first, for the traditional rights of the chiefs or the earls and then broadened the cause to the religious rights of the common people; but in a typical feudal manner, he appealed to the Queen against her ministers. Only when Elizabeth would have none of that and reinforced her hard-grudged garrisons did Hugh O'Neill offer Ireland to Philip of Spain; he did not attempt (as would happen centuries later in Poland and the Balkans) to invent an Irish lineage from the legendary high kings. He was no more a nationalist in the modern sense than were the English of his time who in 1603 gave the throne, without fight or murmur, to a Scottish monarch. Peace, stability, avoidance of civil war, and respect for rights of inheritance (kingdoms were properties of dynasties, not of their peoples) were more important than national consciousness.

National feeling was very strong in the Cromwellian and Williamite wars, but it was fatally attached to the House of Stuart, not to an Irish sovereign or state. James II had no more interest in being king of Ireland than Bonnie Prince Charlie had in being king of Scotland; both used those unfortunate countries as bases to regain the great prize and pickings of England. Even when a belief grew in the nineteenth century that every nation should constitute a state, the Irish Parliamentary party, both of Parnell and Redmond, stood, right to its end in 1918, not for separation but for what Gladstone had tried and failed to deliver in 1886, 'home rule' – powers of self-government within the Crown similar to those of Canada, Australia and New Zealand. Separatist nationalists there were, famous in song and story, but they were a small minority until that fatal day when a politically stupid British general rose to Padriac Pearse's calculated bait and shot out of hand by military court martial all the leaders of the hopeless rising but one. As is well known, as they were dragged under arrest from the post office and the South Dublin Union, they were abused and spat upon by the crowds. But a week later they were heroes and martyrs, the power of Redmond's party was broken, and Sinn Fein rose to a sudden ascendancy.

Then came the second great ghost of Nationalist mythology: that partition was a great betrayal by Collins, Griffith, and the Free Staters, a failure of will when the British will to continue fighting was indeed crumbling. But the main reason for accepting partition was not reluctance to carry on fighting the British or the wily tongue of David Lloyd George but a grim recognition, clear enough ever since 1886, that the Protestant people in the north would not accept rule from Dublin even if it were still nominally under the Crown. Ulster had been an armed camp since the immediate prewar gun-running at Larne. The Protestants said 'Ulster is right, and Ulster will fight', and they obviously meant it. Neither the provisional Irish government nor the British government had the will or the power to take them on. The loyalty of the army could not be taken for granted. It was then a noticeably sectarian force. Many of the squaddies came from Protestant orphanages or from marching brigades attached to Sunday schools, and many of the commanding officers were of or connected to the Anglo-Irish landowning ascendancy. I hasten to add that the modern army is thoroughly professionalized and the modern squaddie can't tell one sort of Paddy from another and would shoot either if given orders. But in

1920 a great and deliberate political compromise was made, realistic, painful, and, I think, courageous. Though de Valera attacked partition continually in Irish politics, his behaviour suggested that he recognized the reality. John Bowman, the Irish scholar-journalist, showed conclusively in his *De Valera and the Irish Question* (1982) that when, in Britain's hour of desperate need before the United States had come into the war, an emissary from Churchill dangled under Dev's nose unity after the war in return for Ireland's joining the war against Nazi Germany, he showed no interest. It is not surprising that as a shrewd politician he preferred the independence, neutrality, and church–state constitution of the Republic to such a speculative gift-horse, let alone the daunting problems of how an Irish government could enforce law and order in a resisting Ulster. Then and now the British army would be needed to do it.

The state of opinion today

Things have moved a long way since then, even since the beginning of the troubles in 1968. Article 1 of the Anglo-Irish Agreement of 1985 states that

> The two Governments (a) affirm that any change in the status of Northern Ireland would only come about with the consent of the majority of people in Northern Ireland; (b) recognize that the present wish of the majority of the people of Northern Ireland is for no change in the status of Northern Ireland; (c) declare that if in the future a majority of the people of Northern Ireland clearly wish for and formally consent to the establishment of a united Ireland, they will introduce and support in their respective Parliaments legislation to give effect to that wish.

Now if that is one of the definitive versions of the famous 'guarantee' that is supposed to put Protestant fears to rest, it must be recognized that even though it is politically and diplomatically sensible, it is hurtful to Unionist pride,[4] for it clearly implies that sovereignty is not absolute and that Northern Ireland is not a normal or integral part of the United Kingdom but a conditional part. Leave aside that the condition for departure is most unlikely to be met. The conditionality still hurts. I have heard that from members of the UDA or its sympathizers.

The name of the UDA, 'Ulster Defence Association', should be taken seriously. The predominant ideology of the UDA is defensive, a fear that Britain might pull out. It is a militia in waiting, unfortunately with time on its hands, and some of its members engage in racketeering, gangsterism, and sectarian killings that they attempt to justify, of course, as reprisals. The UDA in effect is waiting to take over public buildings and offices in the North on the day when the drums of the British army play 'The World Turned Upside Down' again and sail off from Belfast Loch, as once from the quays of Dublin and Cork. The UDA has the numbers to do this.

The IRA is a terrorist organization designed to break the will of what its members see purely as an occupying power. Therefore, unlike the UDA, it is small in numbers and hard to penetrate. The IRA recruits mainly through family connections and its nationalist ideology is extreme, a strange and specific compound of the cult of 'blood sacrifice', class socialism and a belief in purification through violent deeds.[5] Its leaders are less the leaders of a mass movement in the community (nor is Sinn Fein if one compares its voting strength with the SDLP's) than a self-justifying sect that depends for its operational effectiveness not on the support but on the tolerance of the community, a community once oppressed and still suffering some discrimination. But it is a tolerance that has limits that include indiscriminate bombing.

The UDA is more numerous but less disciplined than the IRA, so it is easier to penetrate. As defenders of Ulster, its members are firmly rooted in much of the ideology of the Protestant working class but hardly if at all mirror the voting habits or intentions of the working class. So without formal party structure and tradition, small wonder that the leaders of their legal offshoots, the small pretend political parties of the UDP and the PUP, can be more flexible and open in their responses than the leader of the DUP or the predominant UDP. In fact, the UDA has been earnestly and acrimoniously discussing a 'political alternative' in one form or another for more than twenty years. But I have formed the impression that there are not so much political and violent wings but that alternatives are always being weighed in each heart and mind according to circumstances and opportunities. I suspect that the process is somewhat like that in the IRA, as Gerry Adams once put it pithily: 'the Armalite in one hand and the ballot box in the other'. So the militant Loyalist leaders are freer to speak out politically, and they are now a serious factor in the equation (hence one part of the complicated election arrangements to ensure their presence at the table) because of the proposals they make for social justice in the North (even though they are opposed to unity) and because they could be provoked to return to violence, not because they are likely to get many votes.

Both Paisley and Trimble are much more constrained than the Loyalists. Paisley is constrained by his total belief in his mad theology (he *does* believe that the Pope is the Anti-Christ of the book of Revelation) as well as by his party and by his church elders who believe that struggle is sacred and compromise in principle is dealing with the devil. David Trimble has imposed upon him the constraints of an organized party machine containing party activists whose minds are not only as stuck in the past, as are those of many Nationalists, but who are at least as likely to use public issues as counters in competition for party office as are activists in other established political parties. Any public sign of willingness to compromise would not make things easy for him. Perhaps he is as stubborn and rigid as he looks or must look. But I suspect that he had a lot to live down when running for the party leadership. As a young man he was a leading member of William Craig's Vanguard Unionist party when that hard man, in the abortive Northern Ireland Constitutional Convention of 1974–75, reached agreement with John Hume and the SDLP on 'power sharing for the emergency' government, and it failed in the Unionist caucus by only three votes, having stirred Paisley's jealousy.[6]

What are, however, the fundamental constraints? Figures in an MRC Ireland poll in January of this year (one of the biggest ever conducted)[7] show that the UUP, with 27 per cent, has pushed the DUP down to a very small 8 per cent and that the SDLP, at 21 per cent, has kept Sinn Fein down to 7 per cent despite the fact that the poll was taken before the ending of the cease-fire and despite the prominence that Hume risked giving to Adams before and after the cease-fire. From other figures in the same opinion poll and figures on constitutional options obtained late in February in a joint *Irish Times* and *Guardian* poll,[8] the results strongly suggest that the ordinary people of Northern Ireland, although showing no signs of a majority in favour of unity, are far more flexible about internal reform than are their leaders. Gerry Adams continues to state that 'an internal settlement is not a solution' and that 'the Irish people as a whole have an absolute right to national self-determination' while also saying that 'peace, to be sustained, must be based on a just and lasting negotiated settlement'. But neither side is talking about 'negotiated surrender'. Forty-two per cent of Catholics in Northern Ireland in the *Irish Times* and *Guardian* poll favoured links to 'both the UK and Irish Republic', only 27 per cent wanting to 'become part of a united Ireland'. On both sides of the line the door seems open to halfway houses. Neither the unity of Ireland as a unitary state nor 'remaining a normal part of the United Kingdom' are serious options despite what the leaders believe or have to say in the context of their parties. The negotiations will be about internal institutions and the extent of an institutionalized 'Irish dimension' or 'cross-border co-operation' or both.

Although official Unionists appear to be as rigid as Sinn Fein, 51 per cent of the Protestant community expressed the opinion that President Clinton and the US government have been even-handed, as against 41 per cent who disagreed (I would have guessed far more). And 67 per cent of Protestants thought that Clinton's efforts had been helpful in moving forward the peace process, as against 26 per cent who thought them unhelpful. I don't read this finding as so much the acceptance of actual policy but as a reflection of declining paranoia. On second thoughts, that is too strong. I mean a declining sense of embattled isolation in the Protestant community. Other figures show that 68 per cent of Protestants view in a positive way the Irish government's efforts for peace. The British in Northern Ireland don't get much support in mainland British opinion. Consider the cross-national figures on possible solutions. The large minority favouring independence for Northern Ireland in both the United Kingdom and the Republic of Ireland is an option not officially offered, and so a case of people thinking for themselves or snatching at straws suggests to me a strong negative wish to be rid of Northern Ireland – something that cannot possibly be offered. The *Guardian/Times* poll identified the most popular Catholic option in the North as links to both countries (42 per cent), and the *Belfast Telegraph*-sponsored poll found only 39 per cent of Catholics favouring unity, whether federal or unitary. Now I don't read that, as David Trimble has, as a Catholic majority for the union. I read that only as a cautious and sensible desire to see what will be offered down South before giving up many of the utilitarian advantages of the British connection. Most of us are nationalists of one kind or another, up to a point; only fanatic Nationalists say 'national freedom' or 'unity at any price, any sacrifice'. But I do read the figures as showing openness to the possibilities of radical reform in Northern Ireland.

What is likely to happen

There is plenty to bargain about, and most of it would be acceptable to the people in both communities in Northern Ireland if and when their leaders can escape from the dogmas propounded by old party regulars. That is why the peace process is going to take a long time. Reform in the North will come first, and new kinds of North–South relations, possibly of East–West relations, will evolve gradually. The results that revealed the highest level of polarization in the January survey were recorded in response to the question 'Are changes in the police necessary?' Despite the reforms of recent years, 74 per cent of Catholics answered 'yes' and 71 per cent of Protestants said 'no', indicating that the leaders of both communities are not going to be able to take risks precipitously. Just as it takes time for the Royal Ulster Constabulary to attract more Catholic recruits and for local policing to be made more communal, so it takes time for the message to sink in that the risks of going back are greater than those associated with going forward. The real risk to the Unionists of infinite procrastination is not losing votes but seeing the most able of their sons and daughters desert the province. If Adams really does lose all influence over the IRA, things will lapse, and there could be chaos worse than before. No one will be left to negotiate with, openly or covertly. It may be a new thought to them both, but both Adams and Trimble have a mutual interest in seeing the other keep power in order to maintain movement in their parties.

If David Trimble does see the need for compromises, he can't address them too quickly. The inevitability of real give-and-take negotiations has to sink in the minds of his party stalwarts. If he goes or if his party splits, only Paisley will benefit. John Hume has his troubles too. He used to favour power sharing and reform in the North as valuable in themselves, without closing the door to gradual integration of the two parts of Ireland. If the two communities can work together, it may dissipate Protestant fears. But some of his colleagues believe that reform in the North is meant to put off indefinitely the unity of Ireland. Others see a Northern settlement soon as essential, whatever happens in the next generation. John Hume once spoke cautiously and widely across this fault line of 'some form of unity in an Ireland of the future'.

Certainly elementary history and social science suggest that attitudinal change that would be sufficient for enemies of yesterday to work together tomorrow is a generational matter, not something to be settled around a table in one session dictated by the timetables of Irish, British and American elections, although each of these will have its effect on the long process – some hastening, some necessarily delaying the process. A realistic sense of time scales for different objectives is needed. But bought time must be used productively.

Let me end with a parallel case. Long before Mandela and De Klerk sat down together, Mandela had been exchanging viewpoints with South African government ministers; in the end, he was virtually negotiating the terms on which he would agree to be released. But then it took two and a half years before the understanding that had been reached could safely be put to the two parties, for what emerged was a great compromise, very obvious to the Afrikaner Nationalist side, but as great on the ANC side in terms of its past aspirations and rhetoric: the ANC dropped both the simple one-person, one-vote ideas of a majoritarian democracy unrestrained by courts and a written constitution, and they set out to convince the business community that they wished to support, not nationalize or in effect smash, the one flourishing economy in Africa. During that long period there were many alarms and excursions. The leaders attacked each other, sometimes genuinely and sometimes not to alarm their followers; but once the ANC saw that it could not win and once the Nationalists saw they could not continue to govern without producing catastrophe, they settled down to negotiate, knowing that they depended on the other not to lose control of his followers.

That the principals have not been meeting each other matters less in Northern Ireland than it did in South Africa. Every day they meet journalists and others who do meet the other community's leaders. No matter that some of the messages are disinformation. Leaders would be stupid not to know the other's bottom line despite the good old rhetoric and genuine distrust, even hatred. When negotiations begin, much that is unexpected will emerge from argument and compromise. Much is unpredictable. Serious negotiations are like that. When I once asked underground activists in South Africa what they really stood for, they invariably said 'To force them to the table.' 'What then?' 'Why, Professor, one negotiates, of course.'

Yet the broad outlines of the unfolding future agreement are already sadly clear to dispassionate observers and to the two governments most concerned. There will be periodic referenda on Irish unity, results that the Republic, if it wishes, may be able to influence to some degree by constitutional reform. There will be a power-sharing parliament at Stormont or possibly some new site; there will be a Bill of Rights and a constitutional court containing Irish members. Legislation governing equal opportunities will be strengthened. There will be an official provision for joint citizenship. There will be a network of cross-border and trilateral public utilities and non-governmental organizations, some of which exist in cooperative fact if not in joint name already. (Buses and trains do not stop at the border.) I say this pattern is sadly clear because it is basically what was offered at Sunningdale in 1973, first delayed for one generation by the Protestant workers' strike and the inflexibility of Unionist leadership and then for another by the belief of the IRA that they could destroy the will of the British government to protect the legitimate interests of the majority in the North and somehow to reverse, but they never knew how, the rapidly declining enthusiasm of the Republic to take on or over the North.

We need to consider why the IRA called its cease-fire at all and why the UDA, after a bloody year in which it showed its ability to kill more than even the IRA, did so too. All the opinion polls showed overwhelming support for both cease-fires and for negotiations. My friends in or in touch with both communities in Northern Ireland reported that the women had been saying to the militants in the streets, 'Where the fuck's this getting us?' 'What the fuck's the use?' But real negotiations will take time because there are some on both sides, alas, who are irreconcilables and to whom danger, violence, and 'the struggle' have become a way of life. So we must not flinch from a settlement or endanger it, like the Israelis, by believing that 'peace' will end all violence.

Notes

1. For a longer discussion of this general issue of principle, see 'A Final Footnote to Rally Those Who Grudge the Price [of Peace]', in my *In Defense of Politics*, 4th edn, Chicago, University of Chicago Press, 1993, pp. 242–72.

2. Steve Bruce, *The Edge of the Union: The Ulster Loyalist Political Vision*, Oxford, Oxford University Press, 1994, and my long review of this work, 'Talking to the Loyalist Paras', in *Bullan*, vol. 2, no. 1, summer 1995.

3. Hugh Kearney's *The British Isles: A History of Four Nations*, Cambridge, Cambridge University Press, 1989, is a comprehensive and brief example of the new history.

4. See paragraph 1 of *The Northern Ireland Constitution Act 1973*: 'It is hereby declared that Northern Ireland remains part of Her Majesty's dominions and of the United Kingdom, and it is hereby reaffirmed that in no event will Northern Ireland or any part of it cease to be part of . . . the United Kingdom without the consent of a majority of the people of Northern Ireland voting in a poll held for the purpose of this section and in accordance with Schedule 1 of this Act.' See also the commentary in my 'The Sovereignty of Parliament and the Irish Question' and in 'Northern Ireland and Theory of Consent', both reprinted in my *Political Thoughts and Polemics,* Edinburgh, Edinburgh University Press, 1990.

5. W. B. Yeats imaginatively caught this in his great final rant, *Under Ben Bulben*: 'When the rifle knocks man dead,/Something drops from eyes long blind,/Man becomes himself again/. . .'

6. I was nominally the constitutional adviser to Vanguard but in fact was used as a minor go-between by William Craig to report its discussions to John Hume and, at that time, Paddy Devlin as a gesture of trust. Though Craig disliked the Republic and, I assume, the Pope, he loved a real parliament in the North more, even if it meant power-sharing. After the negotiation collapsed, I was fairly free with my tongue in private, saying that any royal governor of an American colony in the eighteenth century would have known how to turn three votes, but the Labour Northern Ireland Secretary was then Meryln Rees who, in other circumstances, was a man who possessed a wholly admirable probity. His highest civil servant at the time, who had served in Aden, seemed to share my views about priorities when peace was at stake.

7. Commissioned by the *Belfast Telegraph* and printed on January 16, 17 and 18.

8. As presented in the *Guardian*, 29 February 1996.

CHAPTER 6

The Legacy of John Smith

By the time this appears the immediate mourning of the death of John Smith will be over and obituaries will have been many. But because his politics and image were, in almost all respects, so close to what we strive for in *Political Quarterly*, a reminder is due of the astonishing character of a group of those obituaries and a reflection upon them may make a useful tribute to the good man we have all lost. One of the tabloids had this to say in its editorial:

> The Labour Party has lost an outstanding political leader. But more than that, the nation has been robbed of a man who could have made a fine Prime Minister . . . we recognised that as a man he had few equals in public life . . . .
>
> **Three words speak volumes about John Smith's character: integrity, decency, honesty.** It would be rare to say that of a man, even rarer, sadly, to say it of a politician . . . .
>
> **Perhaps his greatest achievement was that he convinced much of the country that the economy could be safe in Labour's hands.** He was the bank manager you could trust, the safe pair of hands, the wise old friend whose advice you rely on . . . .
>
> Labour's new leader . . . will not find general election victory falling into his lap. Success at the ballot box will have to be

An editorial in *Political Quarterly*, July–September 1994.

earned, in the way Smith was earning it. **That, surely, will be his epitaph: John Smith had made Labour electable.**

This was not the temperate *Mirror*, it was the scorching *Sun*. 'Integrity, decency, honesty' are words not often associated with that newspaper. And almost exactly similar passages could be quoted from the *Mail* and the *Express*. 'Hypocrisy is the tribute that vice pays to virtue'? No. This remarkable outburst of honesty was something more than that. Well, perhaps something of that. But human beings do more often tell the truth, unless there is a strong reason not to – as too often in politics and in press wars. But then why did they not even hint at that before? The answer is obvious. And there was no gibing at the difficulties of the Labour Party (that came days later), no *Schadenfreude*. Perhaps there is a long German abstract compound noun needed for envy-of-the-wicked-for-the-virtue-of-the-just. Such a concept would be closer. But we are more inclined to read it as a release of hidden fear.

The *Sun* prides itself on sinking down to earth, having its ear ever closer to the ground. They do not always get it right, as when their Scottish edition endorsed the SNP in the last general election. But they knew from the public opinion polls and probably from private readership surveys that Smith stood high in public opinion. There were good paragraphs in most of the broadsheets too (notably by Andrew Marr in the *Independent*) about Smith embodying 'the virtues of the ordinary'. It was as if there was a sudden collective recognition of a vacuum in British public life that he had begun to fill.

'John Smith made Labour electable'. That the *Sun* came out in the open and said this so strongly (in page after page of an obituary issue that will be a collector's item) may do much to explain their previous violent animus against John Major, who far from rising above his party was, in their eyes, threatening to sink it.

To say that John Smith was above party would be unnecessarily provocative as well as untrue, but he was a man whom ordinary people had, indeed, come to see as someone they could trust, someone whom they would like to see representing this country, indeed someone whom they seemed to see as representative of this country, not just of his party. Indeed the country, the message of the opinion polls is also clear, is (we will not say 'alienated', no one is sure what it means) somewhere between being irritated, fed up to the teeth and frustrated with mere party politics and being ribaldly cynical at the ding-dong ' "You did it!" "No, you did it!" ' long-running spectacle. Of course, they have no choice, except by voting silly in protest or, more often, by not voting. This is gall to politicians but they have brought it on themselves by excessive combatitiveness and daily exhibitions of abuse rather than even the pretence of stating issues plainly, relating policies to principles and appearing to reason, and be open to reasoning, about their consequences.

Each morning on Radio Four and each evening on BBC or ITV one hears every issue analysed primarily in terms not of merit or national interest but crudely of how it will affect party fortunes at the next election or how it will affect the leadership struggles. This follows, of course, how senior politicians speak off the record to journalists. In this respect the media is but the mirror. But one does wonder if at times the BBC should not, as we all have to do when driving at night, put a hand on the mirror to block out all that strong, dazzling but unfocused light so that the way ahead can be seen more clearly. But then the parties watch the BBC and ITV so closely to see that statutory 'balance' is observed that independent analysts and commentators are used less and less; and every issue, however complex, is presented by confrontation between pairs of brain-damaged light-weights or obese heavy-weights.

Perhaps Smith was respected so much in the country for the very reasons that he was criticized for by the hotheads and the unreflective in his own party and by the have-to-be-clever-every-day metropolitan columnists. He did not seize all chances to appear on the box every day making melodrama out of any issue great or small (as a slave to that galloping diurnal myopia created by the media's hunger for news more than features – especially when every good feature writer ends up by accusing everyone else but their own paper of 'short-termism'). Smith saved himself for key occasions, and was the more effective for that. It was not indolence but common sense. His currencies of moral outrage and of forensic demolishment were not debased. He could appear to give a lead without pushing himself or without muzzling his frontbench team. He led by example not diktat. But he was determined that neither the party nor himself should get involved in intricacies of policies on everything prematurely, even if that meant removing from the most prominent of the party's activists the delusions and delights of the old Footite 'policy committees' (which Kinnock had already and wisely failed to resuscitate). Smith knew that one of the hardest things in opposition is restraint, knowing that nothing great can be done by tomorrow, not devaluing the moral coinage out of frustration by crying havoc on every parliamentary occasion and by rising to every baited provocation to produce policy on the hoof, thus plunging his own party into wild rearings and false-starts pell-mell.

John Major saw all this in the remarkable tribute he paid to John Smith two days after his death, speaking to the Scottish Conservatives on a revised script. He deplored that 'there is too much knocking, too much carping, too much sneering' – and well he might; but he went on to say with shrewd vigour 'If politicians fight, in party and across party, like ferrets in a sack on every issue, is it surprising that the public turns away?'[1] Notice that he put 'in party' first. He must have envied how John Smith had been able to escape from the sack (which does, of course, need the help of the party).

So the *strength* of the tributes of the right-wing popular press on John Smith's death shows how much they feared that he was becoming seen as a national figure as well as a party leader, and doing this moreover by seeming to embody ordinary virtues of intelligence and common sense, not the heroic, headstrong virtues of Mrs Thatcher. Part of press rage at Major has been his failure to do just this (or to make up his mind whether to play son of Thatcher or, his first and best instinct, stepson of Baldwin). And the *content* of the tabloid tributes revealed, for a moment, like a flash of lightning, or a secret blurted out under shock, why they feared John Smith and therefore tried, like the Prime Minister, to expropriate his attributes at the moment of death. The country trusted the man.

Writers in the *Guardian* and the *New Statesman* might regret that he had not produced a 'philosophy of opposition' or a 'restatement of Labour's values' (sometimes a polite way to say that he had 'abandoned socialism'). But the country trusted John Smith, and the right-wing press feared him, because somehow he radiated honesty, trustworthiness and concern for society, the public interest and sociability. He radiated an ethos, not an ideology, and one that was not vacuous but could be easily read. He could whole-heartedly and unequivocally accept the reality of the free market, but he implied all the time that there is more to individual and social life than ruthless competitive individualism. There is concern for others and social justice. He implied that we should all take for granted that rights and duties must both support and qualify each other and that all power must be exercised with social responsibility and be held to public account. No ranting against 'the capitalist system', but by accepting it he could be a stern, reforming critic of its shortcomings. He could radiate a wry scepticism that top businessmen always know best how to run public bodies as well as they can run firms, a scepticism that is not entirely unshared by their employees. All this appeared not in print but in how he behaved, what he did and the sub-text of all that he said. The public saw this. They could grow to recognize what the dandy princes of the ageing New Left could not, a kind of ethical socialist, but one very much with his feet on the ground. The parties still contain some MPs of strong and transparent moral sincerity. But he seemed to embody an admirable mixture of sincerity and a reasoning practicality. He was not the theorist of the 'new realism' of which Eric Hobsbawm wrote, Kinnock strove to follow and Scargill identified and ranted against, rather he was its self-confident exemplification. Public example counts for more in politics than cleverly drafted speeches or comprehensive manifestos.

In other words, the man and woman in the street expect that applicants for the post of 'national leader' should measure up to a common job description of 'must be of good character and trustworthy'. So many political leaders in radio and TV interviews appear to ordinary people to be lying, wriggling, blustering and avoiding the point most of the time. And yet they crazily wish for such prominence and they lie awake hoping for that phone call at dawn. They take their mobiles into the bathroom with them, or make sure that their wife or London companion is wide awake first. Plainly Westminster has become such a self-isolating island that MPs enter up on the score card marks for each other's appearances on a quite different and more indulgent scale than that used by the public. They clearly believe that a professional foul is almost as good as a goal scored, but to the naive public a professional foul is a foul.

To return to the light of the *Sun*. 'John Smith had made Labour electable'. Can this heritage be inherited? The leader must rise above the dog fight; but how?

Some simple homilies might be in order. To speak honestly about the mistakes of the past, and candidly about the difficulties of the future. To remember that what goes over well in the House usually goes over badly in the country. To speak the odd good word about the odd good deed or decision by a government minister (the public regards as a load of rubbish the claims of party leaders to be right on every issue while the other lot are always wrong; as David Blunkett sometimes shows, the occasional lofty bone thrown to Virginia Bottomley is often more effective than setting his bark on automatic pilot). To resist by all means premature commitment to details of policy and residual party tendencies to overload manifestos (outside advice on policy is more valuable for being more candid and more useful for being less committing, even dispensable). To remember that while good government is not just reactive – the belief of the old Tories – equally it does not do to stick to plans regardless of changing circumstances (which was the mark of inter-party integrity claimed by both Thatcherites and the old Labour Left, to the amazement and cost of the public). To act as the leader of a team and loftily to indulge differences of opinion more often than throwing a well-laundered sheet over the combatants. To complete the education of the party begun so well by Neil Kinnock that it is the uncommitted or volatile electorate that has to be persuaded of the rightness of the cause, not its own self-appointed holy men. To begin the education of the country about what Britain can and cannot do within our historically diminished powers. To get some sense of time into social reform and the project of a society more democratic, egalitarian and libertarian: 'Where there is no vision shall the people perish', but equally 'Rome was not built in a day'. One could continue making certain basic platitudes pregnant . . .

A new leader, however, will also have to consider the structure of the party system and the institutional system that have led to such excesses of uncontrolled power and self-righteousness among prime ministers (certainly to go back to Wilson and Callaghan who in some ways opened the door to the powers exercised very differently by Mrs Thatcher and Mr Major's ministers), especially since no one can now pretend that such 'strong government' has solved the problems it addressed, and for which it was allegedly needed. The Labour Party has begun somewhat nervously to put constitutional reform on the agenda. A new leader must make sure that it stays there.

The importance of the pledge to devolve many powers of central government cannot be overstated, but it must go with a clear argument that within statutory limits, not simply ministerial discretion (thus challengeable in the courts), how local governments exercise new and broader powers should be up to them. There should be no demands for equality of result nor limitation or proscription of Conservative or Democratic-Liberal local regimes. 'We will not act as Thatcher did to London and the metropolitan boroughs.' 'Let the local electorates and the courts decide.'

A leader must detach himself from still dominant opinion in the Labour Party at least enough to show that he appreciates the worries of the public at the prospect of *any* party gaining an absolute majority nationally and locally with the present lack of constitutional restraints. This must mean inheriting and giving greater prominence to John Smith's commitment that a new Labour government would set up a process of consultation followed by a referendum on electoral reform, and to making clear that the acceptability of the results would not be limited to the token gesture of the Plant Report's over-compromised conclusion, nor simply to electing a new second chamber and/or the Euro-elections.

A Labour leader who invited talks tomorrow with the Democratic-Liberals about election pacts and a common programme might well be going beyond what is deliverable at present in both their constituency parties, however much attitude surveys would seem to favour this. But doors must be opened both privately and publicly, as a minimal test of candour and honesty in a new leader. Something that, while short of shock therapy, could change the discourse of and open up new horizons in British politics, would be simply to speculate out loud what might happen if Labour did not gain an absolute majority. What is obvious to every political commentator could surely be seen to have been heard by a party leader?

For a Labour leader to ferment rather than damp down a debate on proportional representation (too late to put it out) could educate the plungers into a more prudent and public-spirited hedging of bets. Even if Labour wins the next general election (although the recent local election results − a surer guide than the Euro-elections − make this far from certain) against the Conservatives (themselves with a new leader), the margin might be such that the put-your-shirt-on-it, winner-take-all brigade may come to see, if the leader broke taboos and talked about these things publicly, speculated or mused aloud, that the chances next time would be greater in alliance, or with a reformed electoral system. For that is what the public want to hear. The short-odds of being the major party in a long-lasting coalition could seem far more sweet and sensible to MPs and party activists alike than the thrills and spills of first-past-the-post. The old system is no way to run a party, let alone a government meaning to provide good, democratic and representative government to a country of fellow citizens.

John Smith was very cautious in all these respects, perhaps too slow, appearing too obviously only willing to consider coalition and/or electoral reform if absolutely necessary, by which time it might be too late. But the Labour Party has moved a long way, especially in Scotland. The Scottish Constitutional Convention (while failing to agree a precise system) did, after all, come out in favour of PR in a Scottish parliament, indeed with gender equality for fair measure; that the powers of that parliament should be entrenched and with a litigable bill of rights – and other radical innovations too which together would imply some major changes in Westminster. When the final session of that sadly abortive Convention was held, John Smith (who had taken no active part in its proceedings) chose to speak for Labour. He did not do this to upstage Donald Dewar, then Labour Shadow on Scottish Affairs, but to give, as Shadow Chancellor, the full weight of the Shadow Cabinet's pledge to legislate the broad outline of the Convention's proposals in the first year of a new government. He must have known what he was doing.

Some of the Scottish Labour MPs still have private reservations about such a strong form of devolution but they all realize that politically they must endorse it, and that it must include PR, otherwise they lose ground immediately and spectacularly to the SNP ('remember Govan!') and the Scottish Liberals. Such is politics. But most are convinced on grounds of democratic principle. John Smith was somewhere between these two never entirely contradicting poles. If there had been a Labour government the method of election and operation of the new Scottish parliament would inevitably have widened horizons of expectation at Westminster. No one could have missed that. And the whole logic of the Convention's proposals to which Labour assented was to assure the present Liberals and the absent SNP that Labour would be extremely unlikely to be able to rule alone.

And, come to think of it, once you think that far, *what are the real differences between the two opposition parties?* There are sensible and well rehearsed answers to that. But what are the differences worth compared with the differences between them and Conservative policies and conduct? That is an exam question too difficult to attempt if there are any choices. A new Labour leader should assume that it is not compulsory.

Note

1. Can the PM [John Major] read Yeats as well as Trollope? 'We pieced our thoughts into philosophy /And planned to bring the world under a rule, / Who are but weasels fighting in a hole.'

CHAPTER 7

Still Missing: A Public Philosophy for New Labour

It was a famous victory. Let me be quite clear, unless my very title suggests squeezing, however gently, sour grapes: I stayed celebratorily drunk, without needing to drink very much (unlike on some previous occasions), for several days afterwards. Everyone I spoke to was full of joy at having 'got rid of that lot at last'. Normally civilized and somewhat noncommittal neighbours showed savage exaltation watching the box as familiar face after face at the declaration of poll tried to put a brave face on it, sometimes failing spectacularly, sometimes achieving more dignity in defeat than they appeared capable of in office.

No need, surely, to remind us of what everyone knew, from psephologists in demand to my homely neighbours, that the Conservatives had imploded, had earned themselves an almost unprecedented unpopularity (perhaps only paralleled by the popular hatred of Neville Chamberlain after the fall of France, from which not even Churchill could save them five years later), and had signally failed in what they had always given themselves and been given credit for: 'strong government'. They had, like their former colleague, Jonathan of Arabia, fallen on their own sword, and how. With hindsight we now realize that the election was over long before the official campaign began; there was little change of

From *Political Quarterly*, September 1997, in the post-election issue. First published as 'Still Missing: A Public Philosophy?'

opinion from within two months of the 1992 result, as if Conservative voters had suddenly realized what they had done, as if they had each trusted to others to mitigate the unwanted consequences of their habitual, but now somewhat excessive loyalty. Edmund Burke's dictum had again proved sound: general elections are 'decided on the conduct of the late ministry'. (And, as their leadership election has shown, they have not learned any lessons from the reasons for their defeat; but that is another story, and Labour cannot count on that for ever.)

Labour, New Labour I mean, fought a brilliant tactical campaign. Even if there was (thinking of the future, as we occasionally must) an ominously low turn-out for such a great event, it did show that many Conservatives who could not bring themselves to vote against their party could not this time bring themselves to vote for it either. Broadly speaking, the great tactic consisted in giving as little target as possible to the enemy, making manifesto promises small but perfectly formed and realizable, persuasive to the public that there had been a clear, if not always clean, *break from the past*; a break almost as spectacular as that one had encountered in the 1950s among – where the phrase originated – young Germans. And that break, of course, was really a continuous process of modernization begun by Neil Kinnock (whose defeat showed how great was the burden of the past to be overcome in the public mind), and continued by John Smith so positively that Tony Blair could be elected to the leadership with few illusions held by us all that he meant to accelerate the process, even amid some uncertainty about quite where he was going. Cromwell had remarked that 'an army never goeth so far as when it knows not where it is going'.

Ideas in politics

Animating ideas are important in politics. The Old Left believed that passionately, but many of their ideas were the wrong ideas. They confused means with values and ends. If equality was both a value (better say egalitarianism in conduct) and an end (always better to have said an egalitarian society), then nationalization was plainly a means and not an end, and the wrong means at that; and it became treated not merely as a value, but as a shibboleth. Even Marxists seemed to have missed the fact that Marx had said that socialism could only follow the economic expansiveness of capitalism. The Old Left were right to realize that the capitalist market when applied to wages does not yield a just and socially tolerable result, as is now seen all over the former Soviet bloc (without considerable public control or mitigation of the consequences by a state dedicated to welfare), but they saw the answer in terms of ownership more than control, and they paid little attention to theories of and realities of public finance and, above all, taxation. Well, they were, of course, in favour of taxing the rich to help the poor, but they were so vague that perhaps they actually helped discredit, rather than fortify, graduated income tax as a fundamental principle of social justice. The assumed link between politics and economics was simply not there. In the 1960s only a very few of the Old Left were bold enough to advocate and attempt to theorize incomes policy in face of political opposition by otherwise – and what an 'otherwise'! – left wing trade union leaders.

Thatcher, however, taught us all that pragmatism is not enough. She may not have actually read Hayek, but friends, creeps and courtiers had. Keith Joseph habitually referred to 'the noble philosophy of Professor Hayek'. Thatcher peddled an effective populist version of market liberalism, which also served to discredit the vague economic paternalism of the old grandees, the old Tories. Unhappily for the party, it knew no bounds and so served as a rationalization for an unmoralized, unrestrained, man-on-the-make individualism (not what that former professor of moral philosophy at the University of Glasgow, Adam Smith, was talking about at all); and this even penetrated beyond the backbenches of the parliamentary party.

Tony Blair clearly saw, as Carlyle famously told Margaret Fuller, that the universe had better be accepted, indeed not ungraciously. Capitalism had brought unique prosperity to much of the world. Perhaps like Kinnock he had read, or read about Hobsbawm Mark II; or more likely it was clear-minded common sense. But how was the *growing* gap between rich and poor to be bridged, especially without frightening the electorate by any criticism that the Conservatives had lowered income tax far too much, hence a large part of the cause of the growing public sector borrowing requirement (PSBR)? So leave that aside and turn to the excellent PR polemic that Conservatives had actually raised taxes, so many taxes, if one looked at indirect taxation. And indirect taxation, thundered the opposition frontbench, is regressive. But what is progressive? The answer to that simple riddle is widely known, but is taboo in the inner party as shown in the July 1997 budget, whatever its other considerable virtues. In the outer party (and among the proles) there is still a suspicion that the Labour Party, old or new, cannot in public plausibility long compete with the Conservatives as being the party of purported lower taxation and static income tax.

Tony Blair made speeches in opposition that seemed to be working towards a reasonably coherent public philosophy,[1] difficult to name emotively on the hustings, but which modern historians might well call radical liberalism, but a liberalism attempting to theorize the somewhat contingent provincial roots of British liberalism by taking on board, or sharing, the pluralist, decentralist tradition in British socialism. There was always a tension in the thinking of the British labour movement between the centralists, whether Fabian or quasi-Leninist advocates of a party-led state, and the decentralists, the pluralists, the municipal and local government tradition, or more idealistically speaking, the small group, co-operative, community tradition. When Blair talked of 'social-ism' he seemed to be, not rejecting the democratic socialist tradition, but coming down in favour of that latter side of it. Man is, indeed, a social animal, and to stress this is not entirely banal politically when we have been told, *ipse dixit*, that there is no such thing as 'society'. Blair had a brief encounter with *Spirit of Community* Amitai Etzioni, whose publishers claim on the dust-jacket of the sequel (*The New Golden Rule: Community and Morality in a Democratic Society*) that he has been 'very influential on New Labour'; indeed they generously reprint in their press release the new Clause Four. There were even references to Tawney in Blair's speeches, but more for his Christian socialism in general terms than for the fiercely egalitarian inferences for policy that Tawney drew from it in *Equality* and in *The Acquisitive Society* (which are not now books to be seen on your shelf when the leader's men come to tea, unless like me you are known to be interested in the history of ideas). But too often when he spoke about restoring a spirit of 'community', he linked community to 'society' and to 'nation', as in clause four as amended. They are rather big as communities go, or are not communities at all in the pluralist, decentralist and, indeed, sociological senses of that key concept. Etzioni himself is extraordinarily muddled on this point.

The sense of solidarity that a whole nation or society can feel is a different thing from the 'community feeling' of a group small enough to maintain an informal, traditional or voluntary moral order, as distinguished from 'society', which may or may not have a moral consensus, but needs central and general legal restraints and procedural consensus to maintain order.

It is too early to judge whether the actions, even if not the words, of the new government are based on presuppositions that may come to constitute a new and coherent public philosophy recognizable in the public mind. 'Modernization' was an effective slogan, but was never defined as a theory, except negatively as 'not Old Labour'. Its most concrete manifestation was not in ideas but in campaign tactics and organization. Blair had, of course, to be circumspect in the long election campaign and in the still longer run-up. He had to embody concern for obvious social problems, but also reassurance to Middle England that he wouldn't go dipping into their pockets for the sake of other people's consciences. In office we have not heard much of 'community' so far, and 'stake-holding', which had a little run, handicapped by the many different meanings, strong and weak, which were heaped on its back, is now quite out of sight way down the field.[2]

Far from 'community', it is 'individual enterprise' and the creation of the conditions for 'equality of opportunity' that are now stressed. But individualism and individual enterprise may destroy real communities and 'equality of opportunity' can work against both egalitarianism and any actual lessening of the gap between rich and poor, that is unless there are strong anti-poverty policies to sustain, even to create, communities *as a prior condition* for the results of equality of opportunity to prove reasonably just.

The public sector

To attack poverty in the way that not merely old Labour, but all Labour dreamt of,[3] is now either off the agenda or far into the future, thanks to pledges given during the election not to raise the PSBR, not to step outside the old government's expenditure targets both overall and in each department for two years, similarly not to raise income tax. I write before the budget. The campaign tactic on taxation has made the limits for manoeuvre extremely small, and therefore exaggerated importance is given to one-off and relatively small matters that cost little or nothing, and even to some prime red-herrings. Harold Wilson made the mistake, let it never be forgotten, of abandoning any clear public philosophy or general policies for simply ticking off triumphantly a list of manifesto pledges fulfilled, many or most of which rapidly proved irrelevant or unadaptable to changing circumstances, if not simply a product of electoral rhetoric more than the needs of government in the first place.

Take the case of the two sectors that are not merely part of old Labour's dream but of current public, middle-class concern; two factors that helped in the Conservative debacle. Who seriously doubts, except the two frontbenches apparently, that our common schools and the health service are grievously run-down, not primarily by maladministration or by their organization (though faults there are in both), but by being under-resourced (the polite word for underfunded). Since the expenditure required in both cases, to have gone beyond the immediate palliative of the budget, would have involved tax rises including income tax, whether they meant to or not ministers by concentrating on cheaper or no-cost problems have perpetuated the impression that the methods and ability of teachers and the greed of hospital administrators and high-tech doctors are to blame. There are problems, especially with the costs of the internal market in the NHS. Teacher training has been neglected by both the universities and successive governments, then run down deliberately by the last government in favour of learning on the job, as if teachers were garage apprentices. As Philip Turner's book *Second Class Ticket: The Neglect of State Education* (Sheffield Hallam University Press, 1995) persuasively argues, a succession of Conservative ministers, ignorant of conditions in our common schools, were determined to make a name for themselves by doing *something*, or *anything*. The somethings have been products not of consultation and research, but of prejudice fortified by willpower and a craving for publicity in the manner of the Lady of so many of our sorrows. Then the next minister has done something else, big, and equally disruptive to the good business, on the whole in such safe hands, of teaching our children and grandchildren. Labour will not make that mistake, but it will have to concentrate on matters that need relatively little money; and likewise in the health service.

The poverty question touches both these great services.

Intellectually Labour sees this. A new committee is being set up to go over the ground again of the suppressed Black Report on *Inequality and Health* of 1980 that demonstrated correlations between high levels of ill health and poverty. But with the taxation pledges tying our hands, and the political fears behind them, there will be depressingly little the government can do, except say 'told you so' with solemn gravity to the Tories. The budget was, indeed, very astute politics; because they were led to expect no increase at all, the media missed the inadequacy of the actual increases. If schools were to be properly resourced, teachers properly paid and thus respected, it is likely that crime could be reduced and economic potential enhanced.

Politically both these services serve most of the middle class as well as the poor, and survey evidence has been impressive that the Liberal Democrats were right, that people could and should have been asked to pay more through income tax for those two great good common causes, and would have done so willingly enough. It is a long argument and a matter of political judgement, but I find the belief of Labour's inner circle that the 1992 election was lost on the taxation issue at least unproven. It was at least as likely that, in a broad historical view, if any one factor can stand alone, Kinnock needed a year or two longer, after having brought the party back to a sense of reality, to convince the public, or rather to let it see for itself, that the Labour Party had put behind it the left/right years of disruption. Too late now, but with the lead the party had in the polls for almost the whole period of John Major's feeble second innings, surely the tax question could have been taken head-on rather than evaded? Political popularity is not just basking in sudden sunlight but is the opportunity to persuade and change opinion. A popular leader can and should use his position, however gradually and carefully, to bring the public as well as his party into a sense of reality. Lincoln, Lloyd George, Churchill and – sorry to mention it – Thatcher were bold to bring public opinion round, and so were many lesser people on lesser occasions. Does the modern technology of opinion research somehow inhibit rather than arm the capacity for political change? Certainly we don't like paying more income tax but we may like the decay of our schools and our health service still less. Leadership is striking some balance or creative compromise, not dropping one of the terms of the paradox. To have accepted Ken Clarke's allegedly tight and realistic, but in fact crudely optimistic figures, may now be cause for regret even in the inner party; and even when responsibility for higher interest rates has been shuffled off. Suppose the bull had been taken by the horns, and that the margin of victory had been less. A smaller majority without its hands so tied would be a stronger government more likely to maintain popularity.

Even with hands tied one might hope to hear more of a rhetoric, not, indeed, of socialism ('what's in a word?') but of *public service* and of restoring, yea enhancing, *public services*. 'Public interest' and 'public-spirited' are concepts worth restoring to old prominence in new contexts. This leads straight into another problem, theoretical and practical.

Pluralism and devolution

When the leader was new to his leadership he talked much and well about Britain and British government being over-centralized, about the need for devolution and subsidiarity as paths to better government and more public involvement. This was one key link between old and new in the Labour Party, and also a bridge to liberal-democratic opinion. I do not hear this now as one of the major themes of office. Yes, elected government will be restored to London and with an elected mayor; but no major speech or statement so far on restoring, indeed many had hoped enhancing, the powers of local government. Talk of English regions seems to have been quietly dropped. And yet the very roots of the Labour Party's ethos were in civic and municipal government. The new English MPs seem mainly professionals who see London as the sole centre of real power.

When in the 1970s and 1980s so many real or pretend Marxists of the New Left began to adopt a more realistic attitude to politics (I would even say, to think politically for the first time), they drifted into the Labour Party, reinventing the wheel as they went along. I mean they wrote about democratic theory, the need for constitutional law and often, quite literally, joined Charter 88. (I remember Neil Kinnock in animated conversation naming several of their leading spirits as 'Trotskyites', and my attempting to persuade him that they were now rabid ex-Trotskyites and born-again democrats.) They were also pluralists almost without exception. They had not given up the Leninist theory of the state to embrace easily either Mr Sidney Webb's Fabian centralization or the English obsession with the sovereignty of parliament. Many of these 'last of the Labour intellectuals' are now in what would have once seemed unlikely alliance with right-wing activists in the constituency parties to resist the implied centralism of the NEC's Party into Power proposals for allegedly 'reforming' inter-party democracy.[4]

Even five years ago I felt confident that this decentralist theory of administration and pluralist theory of power had penetrated to anyone at all thoughtful in the Labour Party leadership. It seems not. Even the whiff of victory, let alone the reality of office, threatens to bring back the old instinctive, unthinking centralist beliefs. They mean to do good for us all in the localities, so long as we do not want different kinds of good for ourselves. Scotland and Wales are now, of course, exceptions to the general rule of central sovereignty. They are not seen as the extreme cases of a general desire to devolve as much government as possible from Whitehall and Westminster, they are simply exceptions born of political necessity as far as most English Labour MPs are concerned. That many people in Scotland argue for devolution on democratic grounds, meaning 'republican' ideas of citizenship and participation, not primarily on nationalist grounds at all, is almost always missed in England, largely due to the London-based media. It is easier to treat the Scottish demand as purely nationalistic, for then it does not challenge what seems to be the easy acceptance in England of the continued derogation of local government.

Take one key example. Labour even in opposition accepted the principle of a national curriculum for schools. Little thought was given about why there should be one at all, or to the dangers of opening the door to political intervention in the curriculum (as has happened). Sensing that the Conservatives were trying to make it a popular political issue, bizarrely arguing and assuming that centralization would raise standards, Labour said, in effect, 'me too'; and now shows little sign of wishing to return education to local control. Local control should be reformed, made more democratic indeed; but the matter is not even raised. And if we are content or condemned to have a national curriculum, because presumably pluralism has lost out to centralism as the implied public philosophy, consider what a curriculum it is with no place in it, once again proudly unique in Europe, for civic education,

education for citizenship itself. That should be a priority for a Labour government, unless the modernization of New Labour is simply concerned with education for industry, neither for citizenship nor for leisure as part of the quality of life itself. Are these old values lost? But also consider how Conservative ministers made direct, highly prejudiced and fatuous interventions into the detail of the history and the English curricula. Again, it is better not to have a national curriculum at all, especially in education, especially if the public philosophy of New Labour has concern for subsidiarity, devolution, pluralism: as much as possible should be done by citizens in localities, not by ministers and civil servants in Whitehall – even if that leads or reverts to different standards and practices and (not unheard of in central government) to some gross mistakes. The price of liberty is astounding variety, even in an egalitarian society. But if a nationally controlled curriculum is maintained, then it should be reformed simply to become guidelines (somewhat on the German model for *Politischebildung*) in terms of which local authority advisers would have to publish curricula within the parameters of which teachers would create syllabuses, or syllabi if they care.

In conclusion

What many of us had hoped for in a public philosophy of New Labour were three broad elements. First, indeed, a full-hearted acceptance that the production, physical distribution and pricing of goods are best handled by free enterprise and the market, and that the immediate institutional form that the market takes (all markets need a framework of law) is the EU. So far, so good. But also that it would use the powers of the state and enable powers in local government to mitigate if not remove, through the taxation system, unjustifiable inequalities and poverty whether arising from low wages or unemployment. Yes, that will take time: 'patience and time', as Tolstoy's General Kutuzov said to his young officers, too eager for immediate battle: but the process has to be seen to be beginning,[5] and the agreeable and ingenious device or expedient (I will not say gimmick) of the one-off windfall tax is, indeed, one-off, a fitting punishment to the privatized utilities, but more likely a gift soon spent than a lasting pump-primer for the young unemployed. We hoped that New Labour would have had some formulated intention (I will not use the discredited word 'plan') to avoid the permanence of the underclass already with us, and would have begun to argue the ill consequences for society, as well as the moral shame, of such a permanence, unless public revenues are increased in a fair manner (cf. the philosopher John Rawls, if you want). Here even a symbolic increase in the top rate of taxation would have sent a message of more than symbolic importance, intention and hope. The public rage in the pre-election period even in the Conservative tabloids at the salaries and bonuses of the 'fat cats' could still be worked upon. The readers of those papers know sardonically and bitterly that their bosses are overpaid and that there are many in the firm quite able to step into their shoes if they emigrate to purer points of capitalism like Hong Kong or Moscow. The argument that a few pennies in the pound on top incomes would discourage leading entrepreneurs is fatuous, the kind of thing that is said in letters to *The Times* and the *Daily Telegraph* but which no sensible person believes. They are just being greedy, I mean individualistically acquisitive within the law. New Labour has surely well earned the trust of business without such unnecessary and potentially self-defeating concessions. The unconcern of the stock exchange to Labour's advance, victory and budget was proof and tribute to that.

The second element in the hoped for public philosophy of New Labour was the democratic impulse: *to open up and devolve the processes of government, and to try to create a positive culture of active citizenship.* There are some signs of this both in the promises of constitutional reform and in the greater informality and openness of Labour ministers, but so far these seem to be piecemeal responses to outmoded habits of office and particularly gross anomalies (like the peerage in an upper chamber), not guided by any as yet discernible and announced general principles. Scottish and Welsh devolution are, indeed, big steps forward but, as yet, are not being presented as part of a general policy of devolution (underpinned by a philosophy of pluralism rather than the growing irrelevance of sovereignty theory). The key to the link between comprehensive constitutional reform and a positive citizen culture is, of course, electoral reform – some form of genuine proportional representation (as is part of the Scottish proposals). There is the political paradox that most of the new Labour MPs say they favour PR, but older MPs point out that they are the winners in the great and disproportionate swings of the first-past-the-post race-track gamblers' excitement system. But it is swings and roundabouts. On the Glorious First of May the electorate took the electoral law into its own hands by tactical voting: better for Labour to institutionalize and stabilize this by PR, rather than trust the Conservatives to carry on rendering themselves so spectacularly unpopular.

The third element should be a clear enunciation of aims and values. We are already a highly libertarian society. *We need to be, should aim to be, a more egalitarian society and a more democratic society, in both manners and procedures, at every level*; and one in which the values that shape our behaviour should be, indeed, a respect for individual talent but also an encouragement, through education and example, of sociability (no longer do we say 'fraternity'), a realization that each one of us is ourself at our best when others recognize this by how we behave to them, when we show a concern for the well-being not merely of friends and neighbours but of strangers. The palpable decency, honesty, good intention and competence of the new government compared with the last has already created something of this atmosphere, but comparisons will fade in memory; and it must not appear to depend *too much* on the personality of one man but on the example from above of observable collective will and behaviour and a revitalized civic democracy in the constituencies and local government from below – revitalized by a clear public philosophy.

Notes

1. 'The basis of such socialism lies in its view that individuals are socially interdependent human beings – that individuals cannot be divorced from the society to which they belong. It is, if you will, social-ism. It contains an ethical and a subjective judgement that individuals owe a duty to one another and to a broader society – the Left view of citizenship' (Tony Blair in *Socialism*, Fabian Pamphlet 565, July 1994). There is no need to mock, as some have done, that hyphen: it is a worthy explication. But what worries me a little is that 'citizenship' to be meaningful, not just rhetorical, must imply devolution and strong local government, philosophically even pluralism, in practical terms there must be something for citizens to do; but there was no specific commitment to that elsewhere in the speech: it has to be inferred from the logic of what he

said, and inferences from unstated premises in leaders' speeches have their perils, even in a democracy.

2.   Nonetheless, one can tear the prescription 'stake-holding' right out of Will Hutton's books *The State We're In* and *The State to Come* and still leave the most brilliant and comprehensive diagnosis of our social and economic problems, even if they are out of favour, one gathers, with Little Brother and the inner party. Not that they look for second opinions. They have little use for intellectuals and do their own thinking entirely. (I sometimes think of them as, in the light of post-war university expansion, Count Frankenstein's children.)

3.   Things get very confusing; I for one am not Old Labour. I polemicized against the Bennites and the Footites hard and had no tolerance for either the infiltrating wreckers nor the Social Democrat deserters; but I am not sure that I am New Labour either. I rather think not. I rather think that the inner party have not heard of 'the fallacy of the excluded middle'. Much of the party, I suspect, is basically excluded middle.

4.   As seen in the rapidly growing Labour Reform Movement and their series of consultative papers, notably *Rebuilding the National Policy Forum* (PO Box 5219, Birmingham, B13 8DY or on http://www.zynet.co.uk/ecotrend/LabRef/).

5.   See my *Socialist Values and Time* (Fabian Tract 465, March 1984).

CHAPTER 8

The Decline of the Political Book

Walter Bagehot once said that the reason there were so few good political books was that too few people who can write well know anything. But nowadays, with the growth of the social sciences, many more people know a lot but cannot write in a way that is publicly accessible. And this election has revealed a new type of political writer who does know a lot, who can write (or else Penguin would not have selected William Wallace, David Willetts and Tony Wright to write those three widely abused *Why Vote for. . .* books), but who is under awful constraint to say almost nothing.

In the 1930s good political books were common, today they are few. If that judgement sounds a wee bit categorical, I can only confess that it comes from four years as reviews editor of *Political Quarterly* and from being a judge in the Orwell prize for political writing. But if the proof of the pudding has to be in the eating, then chew over the Penguin list of books in print. They used to lead non-academic political publishing. Now there are two and three-quarter columns of books under Politics and nineteen under New Age! Now Swampie is king, for a day.

'What I have most wanted to do,' Orwell famously wrote, '. . . is to make political writing into an art'. He wanted to bring intellectuals into politics not simply by nagging them that creative freedom depends on good politics, but by reassuring them that

The Guardian, Saturday essay, 29 March 1997.

artistic integrity need not be the price of commitment. The stress must have been on 'loyal' when he also wrote 'No writer can be a loyal member of a political party' – for at that time he was a member of a political party. In 1941 in *Horizon* he bit hard a big hand that had fed him. In an essay titled 'Wells, Hitler and the World State' he railed that H. G. Wells had underestimated Hitler, making him a figure of fun, not realizing his deadly seriousness; and spouting 'World Government now!' as a meaningless answer to immediate crises. Orwell saw Wells as reflecting, like too many intellectuals, indeed he threw the whole of 'the Left Book Club' into the charge sheet for fair measure, 'the sheltered conditions of English life'. But 'in Europe', he meant in continental Europe, something different stirred.

> One development of the last ten years has been the appearance of the 'political book', a sort of enlarged pamphlet combining history with political criticism, as an important literary form. But the best writers in this line – Trotsky, Rauschning, Rosenberg, Silone, Borkenau, Koestler and others – have none of them been Englishmen, and nearly all of them have been renegades from one or other extremist party, who have seen totalitarianism at close quarters and know the meaning of exile and persecution.

If the polemic at Wells seems fair enough, his side-swipes at his fellow English either implied unreal high standards for political writing or most unfairly ignored a whole clutch of writers who wrote for the very audience targeted and most valued by both Wells and himself. Think of R. H. Tawney, Harold Laski, G. D. H. Cole among academics and H. N. Brailsford, Fenner Brockway and Kingsley Martin among intellectual journalists. What was the audience? Wells and Orwell still called them 'the common man', those whom Virginia Woolf had called 'the common reader', an almost extinct species today. They were mainly those whose only university was the free public library.

My students, all part of post-war university expansion, found it hard to imagine that political books were once written in plain English not in social science, whether in the Marxiological or the American methodological dialect. Now we must raise the stakes a little, alas, and talk not of the common man (if he or she is politically literate it is now without the help of books) but of the general educated reader. Yet even for that narrower audience the case is the same. Consider that Penguin complete list. Indeed the age of reason seems over. The printed book now has a very much diminished role in preserving a citizen culture; no, I would say in beginning to try to create one. This country has never had a citizen culture, unlike France, the Netherlands and the historic imagery of the United States.

Not for one moment do I wish to deny that there are a few fine political writers who reach the general reader – such as Neal Ascherson, Ian Bell, Will Hutton, Simon Jenkins, Joyce Macmillan, Andrew Marr. But any list, if impressive, will be short. I am using political writing to mean writing about political issues: reasoned advocacy. There have been some reasonably honest biographies of living politicians, say Ben Pimlott on Wilson and Rob Shepherd on Powell, if far more truly awful ones: uncritical popular hagiography of Wilson, Thatcher, Heseltine even, Major and Blair. Such campaign biographies could be said to have marked the beginning of the Americanization of British campaigning. Leslie Smith's *Harold Wilson* of 1964 began these pious follies, a book hilariously funny for its earnest naivety. I wish the subjects of such books would do what a famous Tammy Hall Boss, Mayor Richard Croker, did when presented with such a book about himself as he was departing from New York to race his horses in Ireland: he read one page, threw it overboard into the Hudson and spat after it accurately.

The popularity now of almost any kind of biography is a sad sign of the general debasement of the political and of civic culture: we all seem more interested in personality than in ideas. Robert McCrum wrote shrewdly in the *Observer* two weeks ago about the popularity of a new literature of 'celebrity narcissism . . . the high octane autobiographical memoir'. Private exhibitionism seems to replace concern with public values. Political leaders have for long tried to personify their parties, but suddenly we begin to suspect that they are only off-the-peg personalities, not even pretending to be persuasive, speculative popular thinkers.

Nevertheless, there is a kind of well-written book about politics that often has little directly to do with analysis or advocacy of policy: I would call them political travel books. I note not entirely happily that the Orwell book prize has each year so far gone to such a book: Anatol Lieven's *The Baltic Revolution*, Fionnuala O Connor's *In Search of the State*, Fergal Keane, *Season of Blood: A Rwandan Journey*, and just now Peter Godwin, *Mukiwa: A White Boy in Africa*.

The fine writing as well as the moral integrity carried them in each case; but there were few books before us like the good old Penguin Specials. Penguin in the 1960s and into the early 1970s had three or four books a year on social problems that were political issues. Their general character was an informed and factual exposition of the problem, then a discussion of alternatives followed by a reasoned advocacy. Demand fell off. They tried again briefly in 1985, publishing eight Specials, all good, for their fiftieth anniversary; but none achieved anything like the old sales. For five or six years previously Pat Seyd and I had tried to revive that general idea in a series for Collins and then with Longman. Only John Griffith's *Politics of the Judiciary* ran strong, angering lawyers and delighting their students ('niche marketing'?). Some titles had a modest success in sixth forms; but none seemed to reach the general reader. April Carter's admirable *The Politics of Women's Rights* got many course adoptions in women's studies or politics courses, but I never met or heard of a woman who had read it outside a course, still less a man.

Now the reasons for the decline of the political book are fairly obvious. The demand is simply not there. Radio is now infinitely more venturesome and lively both in informative analysis and political advocacy than ever it was in the 1930s and 1940s. Television, after a slow start, developed likewise. The broadsheets today carry far more features and commentary than before the Second World War, even if extensive reportage, sometimes even basic reportage, has suffered. We are in a great age of the political column. But there are problems on the supply side too. Penguin tell me that they would publish more politics for the general reader if they could find the authors. Most academics write only for other academics, and even if they could write for the general reader, don't want to; there is a professional hang-up about popularizing (very odd for politics, when there are currently excellent popularizers of science, and of history too). To be fair to publishers, the calculator does sometimes get put aside in favour of the civic hunch: a number of quite unlikely houses have felt that they must have, and have chanced their arm on, a book on the Northern Ireland question – and usually lost it, or at least a bony finger or two.

If the quality media drain the market for political books, you might well ask 'so what?' – does it matter? It does matter because the complexity of social problems is hard to grasp and convey amid the diurnal galloping myopia from which even the broadsheets now suffer incurably, let alone the papers that Middle England reads. Politicians are tempted into ever greater simplification and sloganeering, 'soundbite politics' indeed, on all sides. They know the public knows no more than they do, unless some problem encounters a professional constituency. Politicians can rarely feel that a book is a political event.

There is a paradox in all this. Never fewer political books, but never more political knowledge. The social sciences have found out a lot and do have much to say. Only economists, however, seem to be taken seriously outside academia. And we are in a great period of political thought. But in both cases it is academics talking to academics. There are no incentives to talk out to the public. Partly academics are themselves to blame: the way they write in jargon, and the way in which books are composed with evidence and argument all formidably interwoven, unlike the old Royal Commission reports and the better Select Committees or public inquiries where the argument and conclusions are set out simply for all who care to read, and the detailed evidence and submissions follow in appendices.

But if too many social scientists find plain English difficult, there is also a political illiteracy among literary intellectuals. Books that should get reviewed in the broadsheets remain unknown outside academic journals like *Political Studies*, the *British Journal of Political Science*, *Population Studies*, etc. Of course space does not allow. But consider how some of the space is used (best keep off that). Even truly seminal books get missed. Too many literary editors don't know a hawk from a handsaw, just as many of my old colleagues wouldn't know a Jeffrey Archer novel from an A. S. Byatt. But no remedial attempts are made even occasionally to survey, summarize, translate what is important. *New Society* used to try. Specialists in one social science discipline writing for all others could then be understood by anyone intelligent. For a while it was analogous to *New Scientist*. But when the *New Statesman* took it over, all that vanished. Your [*Guardian*'s] lively *New Society* pages strike me as very useful for general studies in schools, but quite inadequate for informing and updating political opinion and policy-makers. Surveys of the social sciences would be possible as a regular weekly page in a broadsheet, but reading around would be a full-time job for someone with an unusual academic width and some journalistic talent.

I am glad I am now too old to be talking myself into an important and very boring job. But in any case, that is not what one really means by political writing. Rather I lament the decline or demise of the political intellectual. One meets them at dinner tables, occasionally in columns, but rarely in books.

CHAPTER 9

Political Reviewing

Long ago Walter Bagehot summed up three of his five functions of Parliament – the expressive, the teaching and the informative – as 'the political education of the nation'. He remarked that 'A great and open council of considerable men cannot be placed in the middle of a society without altering that society. It ought to alter it for the better . . .', and whether it did or not was 'matter for subsequent discussion'.

It could now be a matter for subsequent discussion whether the broadcasting of parliamentary proceedings discredits politics more than, in any sense, it educates. Certainly Parliament is a lively theatre, but that is not the point: the production (as so often in other forms of drama) is almost always so much more compelling than the meaning of the script. When people listen to the highlights they hear incredibly low level insults being exchanged, boasts and accusations, flagrant evasions of any clear question put, all more like the worst kind of domestic quarrelling than anything anyone would think a sensible way to discuss what everyone knows are intrinsically difficult national problems. If good citizens were to eschew the highlights and dutifully listen to whole debates, they would only move from moments of melodrama to agonized prolongation of tedium (as shown by the absence of MPs themselves on any but the few noisy 'great occasions'). And if most of the commentary on

---

A commentary in *Political Quarterly*, October–December 1993.

Parliament turns on the fortunes of the parties and their leaders rather than the problems of the country, this only mirrors the debates themselves and the soundbiting histrionics of leaders at the mike or on the box. Appeals to self-interest and will seem the only counters of debate: public interest and reason seem out of fashion, reasoned justifications and arguments from principle are rare events.

All this is so bad that if Bagehot's 'political education' depended only on Parliament, we should fear the worst. The worst is not, in this country, any real fear of the collapse of free institutions, but rather an increasing apathy and cynicism among the public that leaves MPs very little impeded, directed or constrained in their conduct of politics as little more than a perpetual re-election campaign. The press and the media, for all their faults, advocate, canvass and discuss alternatives at times more effectively than Parliament. They are the filter.

But let us look at one aspect of the filter. In any year there are many books and articles by academics of relevance to understanding either the practices, limits and possibilities of the political system or any number of social and economic problems. Very few of these books get noticed or reviewed even in the quality press. Only the *TLS* tries to trudge through at least the pick of the pack. But one doubts if even the *TLS* filters through to the desks of ministers and their advisers, although its present editor knows such circles better than any of his predecessors. Only *The Economist* seems aware of the need in its books section to be a bridge between specialized knowledge and informed opinion. *New Society* used to do that admirably, but heavy stuff on social policy does not attract the editors of the *New Statesman* who swallowed it. That is not for their readership. Of course not; but that is not the point. The old *New Society* used to find reviewers who would gut the heavy stuff and present the conclusions clearly but critically in accessible, non-technical terms (as we in *Political Quarterly* strive to do in everything, but only quarterly, ever since our founding by William Robson and Leonard Woolf). The *Guardian*'s 'society' pages show little sign of systematically monitoring what research and conclusions from the academy should be noted for the educated general reader.

Even the best academic work rarely gets reviewed in the literary pages of the broadsheets, dailies or Sundays. Perhaps the section editor is called the books editor, but nearly always he or she fiercely defends 'literature' against 'politics'. One sympathizes, up to a point. There is always the battle for space. Books are never given enough space, especially if one thinks of the 'diffusion of useful knowledge' (a good old phrase) as well as art and culture. But what irritates greatly is to see the kind of political books that *do* get reviewed regularly, in an inexorable yielding to editorial pressure or to long and unappraised tradition: political biographies and memoirs, quite irrespective of their literary values. And when people act out of weary cynicism their standards slip: such books are then often sent to totally incompetent reviewers, other prominent politicians, usually retired and in expansive mood; never raising, as a modern historian would, awkward questions of truth and evasions. And perhaps the favoured position of even bad biographies is a symptom of a deeper malaise in our culture: obsession with personalities rather than ideas.

Literary intellectuals often have good cause to shudder at bad writing by social scientists, and to mock methodologically laboured trivialities. But too often they use all this as an excuse not to exercise critical judgement about what to review concerning politics and public policy. If there is among some social scientists a literary philistinism, there is also a political philistinism among literary editors. Too often they appear unable to sort the grain from the chaff, and sometimes will review chaff because their idea of politics is only of strong argument, of commitment, of ideological assertion, or of Morgan Forster's 'world of telegrams and anger'. The idea seems almost lost that there is a reflective, speculative voice, an exploration of the nature of politics as concerned with moral dilemmas that may or may not be reformist. And yet this tradition is at the heart of Western culture – Aristotle, Machiavelli (the republican), Hobbes, Burke, Tocqueville; perhaps in our own time Aron, Arendt and Rawls are in this 'great tradition' of freedom and citizenship. There is a dangerous perception that 'literature' and 'politics' are antithetical. The distinction should be between bad and good writing and between shoddy or strident assertion and reasoned argument. The perception is dangerous because it marks the end, as Lionel Trilling once feared, of a unified liberal culture, rather than the triumph of professionalism, and then the surrender of politics to professional politicians.

Social scientists can hardly be helped who take no pains to write clearly and to try to reach informed opinion, too often just writing for other academics in their field with more thought of professional esteem and promotion than of reaching the public. But the fruits of the academy do deserve a more intelligent monitoring, whether by literary or feature editors. Orwell said that he wanted to make 'political writing into an art' and he practised that art in reviewing as much as in essays and books.

In *Political Quarterly* (July 1993) Mark Garnett thoughtfully raised a similar concern, what he well called the 'decline of theoretical polemic' – the tradition of advocacy based on first principles. Evidence, of course, is also important in political debate, and not all good political writing is necessarily polemical. Some of the best writing coming out of the academy in the last decade or more, in Britain and the United States, has been in political philosophy and moral philosophy. There is such a thing as a discipline of political thought, even disciplined political thinking at every level. But of that one finds next to no sign in the review pages of the quality press. The literary editors had heard of Sir Isaiah Berlin, indeed; but not of a whole generation who learnt from him and others to write well and to think sharply. But Dr Garnett pointed to an interesting paradox, that the Thatcherites came close to reviving the 'theoretical polemic', bringing an economic theory down to earth. They gained a public hearing for political and economic theory in the way that Tawney, Cole, Laski and others did in the inter-war period. Chastened survivors of the 'New Left' have a lot to answer for in that their polemics were on a level of abstraction and in a language quite inaccessible to the public (academic in the worst sense), and their only victory was the virtual destruction of the democratic socialist or social democratic tradition of Labour intellectuals. They also gave politics a bad name by their attempts to impose Marxist theory on literary and cultural values (it was, in fact, an anti-politics that they practised – only room for one truth).

Mark Garnett may be right or he may be wrong to think 'it is unlikely that the demand for theoretical polemics has dwindled', that publishers are simply uncertain of the potential market because the supply has become irregular. Certainly there are far fewer books on public issues written for the intelligent general reader than there were in the 1930s, even into the 1940s and 1950s. Academic political studies will sell, priced highly in short runs for libraries; but not real politics. The Penguin Specials are gone and the 'Counterblast' pamphlets proved a brave if misguided flash in the pan. But the tone of political debate, Bagehot's 'political education of the nation', could be raised simply if editors, while seeing Parliament, of course, as the predominant focus of political debate, also saw that there is a rich vein of political evidence and thinking there all the time, under our noses, in dozens and dozens of serious books which are neither reviewed, nor made use of in their content, by political writers in the press.

Edward Said's recent Reith Lectures, 'Representations of the Intellectual', were a good analysis of the more general problem of which book reviewing is only a small but most important part: a loss of confidence by intellectuals in their public role as critics and speculators; and of the vacuum left, now filled by so many ill winds of triviality, dumbing down and contempt for politics. And quite as important, Said's personal example, as well as his arguments, show that sharp disjunctions between literary and political sensibility (usually for the sake of a quiet life) are as unnecessary as they are harmful to any civilization based on ideas of civic freedom.

CHAPTER 10

Sassoon's One Hundred Years of Socialism

As I sat down to write I heard the sound of a pipe band. Sassenach and incomer though I am, I love the pibroch. So I went up to the street to have a look. It was an Armistice Day parade, of course, leaving the church opposite. About two hundred ex-servicemen and some women followed the band, old men and women, of course, and some of the men wore the tartan trews, dress jackets and bonnets of historic but disbanded regiments. Diminished demand, resources and modern management ideology have done their work. Some plainly mourned for the regiments as well as old comrades and all the dead of the two World Wars. As they halted in the street to dismiss, nowhere in particular, just a token march from the church, the Last Post was played, as it still is nightly at the Menin Gate of Ypres, near where my uncle lost a leg in 1914. I needed a strong coffee and a stiff whisky after that. The Last Post always tears me to hell with thoughts of needless death, both the generality and of particular relatives and friends. I was just too young for it, 'missed the war' as we used to say, just as I missed the Popular Front, the Communist Party and addiction to Marxism. Socialist tradition moves me similarly. It brought back a memory of attending my first Labour Party summer school in 1947, and being asked to take the General Secretary of the Prague Social Democratic Party to see

---

A review in *Renewal*, spring 1997, of Donald Sassoon, *One Hundred Years of Socialism: The West European Left in the Twentieth Century* (Tauris, 1996).

Windsor Castle. Years afterwards I heard that two years later he was killed by the Communists.

Reading this extraordinary achievement, what is very nearly a great book, had already put me in a mood of great sadness. For an historian of socialism it seemed like an equivalent of Remembrance Day. 'Mood', on reflection, is the wrong word. Moods come and go. Rather it is that the ceremony and the book both release an underlying sadness that some of us live with all our days: remembering lives cut off in their prime and historic opportunities missed, and lost perhaps for ever. If I had gone to the service in the church opposite me, I am sure the minister would have injected half-a-pint of fatuous uplift into his sermon, just like some political leaders. But Sassoon's service is the calm realism of not dealing in false hopes; yet the mere narrative cannot avoid a sad longing for past hopes unfulfilled. He concludes:

> The socialist design, however defined, may fade away while socialist parties survive. I do not know if the idea of socialism will weather the great chaos of the end of this millennium and the beginning of the next. Those who have sympathy for the socialist project, shared its hopes and its values, and have been impatient with the endless prevarications, the unending compromises, the stultifying hesitations of its organised parties, may well be reminded that, when all is said and done, these parties are the only Left that is left.

He sees 'the great chaos' as the unexpected speed and side effects of global capitalism while socialist parties remain trapped, as it were, in the diminished opportunities of national states. Well, straight away, 'yes' and 'no'. Capitalism is now global indeed, throughout the world. But before ever it could rampage through the Third World (or should I say 'began the development' of the developing world? – some truths are easier by definition than by difficult summaries of often contradictory empirical evidence), it arose in and dominated western and central Europe and the United States. There is a story of free trade ('prosperity and world peace!', said Cobden, Bright and Carnegie) even before the hundred years of the history under review. And Sassoon himself, within his hundred years (on my left, the founding of the Second International in Paris in 1889, on my right, the inauguration of the Eiffel Tower), constantly stresses, with an amazing and enviable width of scholarship, how the preexistent cultures of different countries made the socialist project so different in each. Fukuyama proclaimed the end of history, or rather of ideological motivation, and the universal victory of capitalism, but his next book stressed (unlike Hayek) how much capitalism was dependent on implicit moral restraints and prudential regulation by public law; so perhaps his next big book will be on varieties of capitalism (even perhaps more narrowly, I will return to this point, the market and the price mechanism). To anticipate my conclusion, and I think Sassoon's clear implication, the future will probably lie in many different and constantly changing relationships between socialism and capitalism, not head-on conflict; in relative degrees of state and local control, not ownership; and – within an international price mechanism – many different forms for compensating and mitigating the worst of capitalism's effects. For, as Orwell once sensibly remarked, 'the trouble with competitions is that someone has to win'.

'Two steps forward, one step back', said Lenin. What is the book about? Not, mercifully, another history of socialist political ideas and the theoretically correct critical perspective to adopt in writing such a history; rather it is a comparative account of socialist parties. Perry Anderson will disapprove, I hope. Raphael Samuel will be more likely to accept that it is, as the author modestly claims, history, though he will fret that many worthy and obscure English groupuscles have been left out. Norman Birnbaum, however, one of the founders of the *New Left Review* is, in the pages of *Political Quarterly*, mightily pleased, with judicious reservations, of course. Eric Hobsbawm has done what he rarely does, written a pre-publication blurb: 'vast, perceptive and encyclopaedic'; and the Professor of Modern History at Cambridge, Peter Clarke, a man who usually reserves his judgements severely, also writes on the jacket: 'I read it with unflagging interest and appetite never wishing it a page shorter. After reading Sassoon's enthralling account, glib capitalist triumphalism seems as historically misconceived as the naive socialist millenarianism of an earlier generation.'

Sassoon insists that the book 'is neither a protracted obituary of socialism, nor an optimistic "upbeat" account comforting to the remaining supporters of socialism'. And he justifies his concentration on Western Europe by reminding us that it was born in Western Europe in industrial or industrializing societies, and among 'skilled workers, not the *lumpenproletariat*' (as hard-headed

Hobsbawm, Mark 2, demonstrated to the annoyance of the dandy princes of the New Left revelling in pretend-proleishness). Time and time again Sassoon stresses that it arose in already enriched capitalist societies, not amid the wretched of the earth. That is, of course, orthodox Marxism, or rather Marx's Marxism more than Lenin's or Stalin's. And it is obviously true. Capitalism both gave the opportunity to pursue egalitarian policies that were not the levelling down or the vengeance politics of peasant revolts, and created the moral outrage at the disparity of living standards, life-chances and life expectation that defined social classes ('the shame of poverty amid plenty', as we used to say on every platform). Sassoon could well have recalled Tocqueville's great insight that revolutions only occur during economic upturns: the depth of depressions conditions feelings of hopelessness not hope. But Sassoon also hints, as Clarke sees so clearly, that capitalism might never have survived politically if it had not had to respond, however grudgingly and inadequately in different times and places, to the political challenge or even the distant threat of socialism. Bismarck and Disraeli both feared revolution if nothing was done for the welfare of the masses, perhaps more than some socialist theorists actually expected to see it. And socialists and reformers have, indeed, saved capitalism from itself – consider FDR's New Deal, for example. Capitalists did not unite in any unconstitutional, undemocratic, violent way to remove Scandinavian or British social democratic governments. In Germany the situation was infinitely more complicated by the defeat in war, hyper-inflation, the rise of the Nazi Party and the more immediate threat of Communism. Even so, it was dogmatic Marxism, not true history, to see Nazism as capitalism *in extremis*.

So that is what the book is about. A critic in the *TLS* was wide of the mark to imply that a history of socialism without the Soviet Union is like *Hamlet* without the prince. Sassoon by no means ignores the constant presence of the Soviet Union throughout most of his period, both as threat and, in some respects, model. Think of the well-meaning folly of the Webbs in their old age, believing both that there was such a thing as scientific planning and that the Soviet Union exemplified it – wrong on both counts. But he makes a very important point about Communist parties in Western Europe (indeed throughout the non-Soviet world), now so obvious but before 1989 hard to grasp: that they were hopelessly handicapped by being run from Moscow, almost completely powerless to act politically in the sense of adapting to local conditions, reacting pragmatically to the initiatives of other parties – in a word, unable to act politically.

Socialism is a Western European phenomenon. To attempt the enterprise in a vast and backward pre-capitalist economy was, indeed, fatal. But in telling the story of socialism in so many different countries at length it is sometimes easy to forget, as perhaps the author does at times, his clear understanding at the beginning and end of the book as to how much the strategic freedom of action of European socialist parties has been limited by the need to keep the capitalist connection, as embodied in the American connection (both for prosperity and defence), and to keep a distance from Soviet communism. Before 1917 it was in some ways easier. The German SPD was the largest and best organised party of any kind in the world. Though its theorists could sound arcanely Marxist, in fact, Sassoon argues well, its pre-1914 motivating ideology was a more simple, comprehensible and plausible 'vulgar Marxism' comprising three (of course) essential propositions: (i) that the wage system of capitalism was unfair to and exploitative of the real producers of wealth; (ii) that history proceeds through necessary stages, socialism following capitalism; and (iii) that workers are fundamentally an homogeneous class. Sassoon, again like Hobsbawm, regards the third proposition as a mental construct, not an historical reality. One can make what one will of the other two.

In fact the actual programme of the SPD was severely practical, so perhaps what angered German Marxists about Bernstein's revisionism was not its programmatic implications, but that he exposed much of Kautsky's orthodox theory as intricate hot air. Sassoon is particularly good at showing the 'operating ideologies' behind the rhetoric. It was said of Kautsky 'the verbiage breathes fire; the tactics are tame'. Classic social democracy, it seems to me, never worked out any theory of time and stages. What kind of objectives can be realized in a particular society in what kind of time-scales? What can immediate legislation do, what must wait on education? There was a theory waiting to be written to explain how Shaw and Morris could see themselves as allies on many things, and how the very Fabian Webbs of the 1900s, practising permeation and believing in 'the inevitability of gradualness', could regard the seemingly absurd Shaw – provocatively arguing for literal equality of incomes – as their propagandist. Perhaps persuasive polemic, unlike theory, often does have to go over the top, to catch attention, to force people to think at all. You know they don't mean quite all that. (If only the modern spin-doctors were not so incredibly literal-minded and dismissive of popular ability to take everything with a pinch of salt, so long as there is something clear and morally moving being said.)

I said that this was a 'nearly great book'. The author must be sick of hearing this, but it is odd in nearly 800 pages of text for only 83 to tell the tale up to 1945, albeit the compression of Book One, called 'Expansion', would that it were, is brilliant for the pre-1914 period. The whole past so much conditions the present. It is the inter-war period that is oddly skimped. Yes, this is a history of socialist parties not of ideas alone, but it is not helpful to the modern, new reader to stress the moralism more than the Marxism of the British Labour Party, and how much its origins were trade union rather than a socialist party at all in the then German sense, without, however, even mentioning R. H. Tawney. I share Sassoon's lack of belief, but he has a blind spot to the effect of Christian belief on socialism, to Christian Socialism specifically (even in its secularized form). He recently mocked in the *TLS* what sounded like a thoroughly bad book on English Christian socialism; but did not seem to think that a better one was worthwhile. Once upon a time one got sick of the constant reiteration of the one recorded aphorism of Morgan Phillips (secretary of the Labour Party in Attlee's Day) that the party owed more to Methodism than to Marxism, but to ignore that dimension entirely in a history is a gross mistake. This is not just the history of ideas, it is part of the history of the party. There may not have been a theory, but by God there was an ethos (still is in the North and Scotland).

Nonetheless, this book is a small masterpiece. It is vastly informative on the post-war scene, and it is wise in its conclusions, or one might say its 'inconclusions'. National cultures count for a lot both in modifying 'pure' capitalism and the 57 varieties of 'pure socialism'. But where there is no socialist tradition or labour party to restrain capitalism, whatever the names, or new name, the result is the United States: one of the richest countries in the world with a huge underclass that it has now written off; conditions worse than anything in Europe. Americans, like middle class Indians, are just conditioning themselves not to notice, or else the pain and guilt would be unbearable.

Sassoon shows that capitalism has encircled the globe but that socialism remains anchored to the nation state. Is this necessarily a bad thing? And is it really the case that 'capitalism' appears to have 'won', or rather a new realism that there is no other way of pricing goods in large-scale societies other than by the price mechanism? It was not the lack of 'capitalism' that led to the collapse of Communism, but lack of a market mechanism to determine relativities and create entrepreneurial and work incentives independent of loyalty to state or party. Yet within a national culture, part of an international price mechanism, there are very wide opportunities for different kinds of public law, different kinds of tax system. Having got rid of the shibboleth of ownership, democratic socialist parties have more room to play and to think seriously about justifications and criteria for control, the true aims and means of welfare and about rational and acceptable taxation policies. People do want better public services than they seem willing to pay for. There is a widespread feeling by people who have no sympathy or taste, indeed, for socialist rhetoric that privatization has been pushed dogmatically far too far, and that public values as well as services have been run down by the state itself; but people are puzzled where and how to draw the line, and want sensible discussions on it. The old socialist movements were not frightened of trying to change public opinion, sometimes successfully, sometimes not. And we had some theories on these matters, not all refuted or outmoded, if always needing to be recast. All these are political questions which neither capitalism nor the market can remove, only limit. Whatever name we trade under, we should not be frightened of raising the level of public debate.

CHAPTER 11

Goldhagen's Willing Executioners

Rarely has a book on any subject so divided expert reviewers from what I will call in a politic way professional reviewers (to say 'journalists' would lump together those whose only knowledge of the subject is that it is important, terrible and always compelling, with those who read serious books on 'the Final Solution'). The difficulty is that here is a book by an assistant professor of government and social studies at Harvard which is based on an extraordinarily ambitious PhD thesis that gained the American Political Science Association's Gabriel Almond prize for comparative politics; and a book, moreover, that by size and footnoteage (almost 150 pages of apparatus) looks overwhelmingly scholarly, but is written with polemical anger and presented by both author and publisher as if it is intended to be a best-seller, which it has become on both sides of the Atlantic, showing the public, says the jacket, 'that none of the established answers hold true'.

Let me just say at the beginning that this is, indeed, as many academic and specialist reviewers have already said, an arrogant claim. Arrogant for the simple reason that if 'none of the established answers hold true' it can only be because some of them are also theses of a single cause, a single explanation. Indeed the claim is

A review in *Political Quarterly*, January–March 1997, of Daniel J. Goldhagen, *Hitler's Willing Executioners: Ordinary Germans and the Holocaust* (Little, Brown, 1996). First published as *The Politics of the Holocaust*.

false in that most of them do make some useful contribution to understanding and explaining an event that plainly had no single cause and can have no single explanation. The publishers further claim that this is 'A work of the utmost originality and importance – as authoritative as it is explosive – that radically transforms our understanding of the Holocaust and of Germany during the Nazi period.' Most historians reviewing the book have taken the view, in the words of Wolfgang Mommsen, that it 'sets Holocaust studies back twenty years'. For it revives a view dominant after the Second World War, even among the guilt-ridden and self-flagellating new generation of German historians, that the Holocaust was the product of the long history of German anti-Semitism, or crudely 'the national character', more subtly of 'the special course of German history', the *Sonderweg*, its exceptionalism in the European tradition.

If the 'overall objective of this book is to explain why the Holocaust occurred', then Daniel Goldhagen right from the beginning, and then with endless, angry and passionate repetition, through every source and every atrocity he analyses, argues that it must be found in the nature of German society and beliefs. The conclusion of this book is that anti-Semitism moved many thousands of 'ordinary' Germans – and would have moved millions more, had they been appropriately positioned – to slaughter Jews. Not economic hardship, not the coercive means of a totalitarian state, not the psychological pressure, not invariable psychological propensities, but ideas about Jews that were pervasive in Germany, and had been for decades, induced ordinary Germans to kill unarmed, defenceless Jewish men, women and children by the thousands, systematically and without pity.

The subtitle of the book is portentous, a direct rebuttal to Christopher Browning's *Ordinary Men: Reserve Police Battalion 101*. A strength of both books is that they both examine not just the camps but also the far more open and less secretive killings by soldiers behind the lines, probably as great in extent as that in the gas chambers if Russians, Slavs of all kinds, Poles and gypsies and other *Untermenschen* are added to the arithmetic of death; but this Goldhagen never does: the book is remorselessly, myopically, obsessively about Jews and Germans. Browning's book was a case study based on records and interviews with survivors not of an elite formation but of Police Battalion 101, middle-aged conscripts from Hamburg (notoriously, to the Nazis, a Social Democratic town).

They obeyed orders to kill thousands of Jews, Poles and captured partisans. Browning finds initial revulsion and reluctance, then a gradual and disgusting brutalization. But Goldhagen, going through the same material as part of his much wider study, finds a willing acceptance of the task as 'all for Germany' and as the logical culmination of their anti-Semitism. Browning thinks that 'ordinary men' are capable of being active agents in genocide in circumstances of total war. This view of the importance of war as such, brushed aside by Goldhagen, is shared by the Israeli historian Omer Bartov when he speaks of 'the reality of acclimatisation in war' (and I think that is what Pat Barker's recent trilogy of novels about the First World War is about – how decent men can commit inhuman deeds). Goldhagen, however, thinks that only Germans were capable of the Holocaust, and the war was only the opportunity; and he assumes, rather than argues, that the Holocaust was a unique event, quite unlike any other genocide (almost as if, as one Israeli historian has said with terrible irony, 'it is a Jewish possession').

Goldhagen sees his 'first task' to be 'restoring the perpetrators' to their proper name 'by eschewing convenient, but often obfuscating labels like "Nazis" and "SS men", and calling them what they were, "Germans"'. He even makes, in a tortured footnote, a 'terminological problem' of how to refer to German Jews, because, he says, 'Germans' when contrasted to 'Jews' seems 'to imply that the Jews of Germany were not also Germans'. Therefore 'I have, with some misgivings, decided to call Germans simply "Germans" and not to use some cumbersome locution like "non-Jewish Germans". Thus, whenever German Jews are referred to as "Jews", their Germanness is implicit.' It is as if it physically hurts him to write or say, 'German Jew'. (His father, to whom the book is dedicated as 'father and teacher', was not German Jewish, it is fair to remind, since he was in a class I tried to teach long ago at McGill, but a Romanian Jew who somehow survived Treblinka.)

Now there is no possible doubt about the extent of virulent anti-Semitism in old Germany, even if there is a good deal of doubt whether it was inherently, somehow immanently, 'exterminatory', or as he sometimes more cautiously says (without appearing to notice a rather important distinction) a deeply rooted desire to 'get rid of the Jews'. So Goldhagen has some trouble comprehending why so many German Jews who could have left hung on so fatally long, even after the *Kristallnacht* of 9 November 1938; why they thought that violent anti-Semitism was a Nazi aberration and that enough good Germans remained to protect them with good values, which they, the assimilated Jews after all, fully shared. Several of my best friends are the children of – to Goldhagen – such fools. He is, of course, wiser than they (after the event). But in any case it was a German culture that the exiles, those who did get out, preserved.

The strength and challenge of the book is its range. He takes the camps almost for granted. He even admits, assumes or implies, that there are plenty enough good scholarly accounts of their workings, let alone the literature of the survivors. But he has four chapters on that one police battalion, and has no difficulty in showing by many references that these 'ordinary Germans', to him 'willing executioners', were unlikely to have been exceptional. He has three chapters on the relatively neglected 'work camps', arguing plausibly that any idea that bureaucrats had that these camps could be efficient and useful for the war effort were hopelessly compromised not just by anti-Semitism, but by his continual *a priori* assumption of an 'eliminationist anti-Semitism'. Therefore debilitating and destructive punishment, not production was the operating ethic.

Two chapters on the final death marches, when camps were abandoned in the face of the final Soviet advance, show that the crazy hatred reached new heights of irrationality: the guards marching their charges nowhere until most dropped dead from starvation and exhaustion, instead of, with a rational prudence, abandoning them and losing themselves in the floods of German refugees. He makes a strong case that the skeletal Jews were mocked by many ordinary civilians as they were marched west, and a still stronger one that most bystanders did nothing: they threw no stones but they gave no crusts.

He brings to the attention of the general reader what has long been known to scholars: that knowledge that the concentration camps were in fact extermination camps was far more widespread than early studies had suggested. Granted that, he prejudices the reader towards that conclusion by dealing first with the letters to mother, with accompanying photographs of Jews being hung or shot, that ordinary soldiers had sent home from the Eastern Front. It was, indeed, presented as a race war and fought as a race war against Slavs as well as Jews. But nonetheless, he makes a real point about civilian knowledge of the camps too, even if many established scholars of the Holocaust are greatly divided about how widespread was such knowledge. I read the consensus among historians that the true purpose *was* known outside the wire, but only locally; and even within the party and the bureaucracy, only on a 'need to know basis', even if the organization and resource demands of the 'Final Solution' made that need more widespread than first studies had supposed. But no one doubts the almost universal guilt of 'not asking' what had become of neighbours and fellow Germans.

This almost universal guilt as sin of omission is, however, not enough for Daniel and Erich Goldhagen. Three summary chapters begin the book with a very familiar, if highly contentious and simplified, intellectual history of nineteenth- and twentieth-century Germany. The section heading says it all: 'Understanding German Anti-Semitism: the Eliminationist Mind-set'. What needs proving he simply assumes from the beginning, so that by the final section, 'Eliminationist Anti-Semitism: Ordinary Germans, Willing Executioners', he has accepted his own initial assumption as proof and, therefore, the only explanation needed of it all.

An historical debate rages between 'the intentionalists' and the 'functionalists' to explain the Final Solution: was it Hitler's original intent which he could not realize except in time of war? Or was it a ghastly but largely unpremeditated side-effect of ridding Europe of Jews but finding nowhere to put them – the Battle of Britain had made the Madagascar fantasy totally impossible, and the stalemate on the Moscow front removed the Siberian option from the drawing boards – as well as policy-makers grudging enough resources to feed them? Even when social anti-Semitism had become crazily and wickedly exclusionist, there is still a chasm of explanations to be crossed to reach the final horror of genocide, even within the mentality of some party members and state officials, let alone most ordinary Germans.

Goldhagen, of course, regards functionalist and contextual arguments not just as nonsense but as a modern German evasion, special-pleading, distancing, obfustication. And he ignores the reasons why some American, British and Israeli historians, not just German, have pushed, in different ways and to different degrees, in that direction. He radiates scorn and contempt on those who would think that any true account must contain important elements of both, such as Christopher Browning in his *The Path to Genocide: Essays on Launching the Final Solution* (CUP, 1992), or David

Cesarani's painfully judicious introduction to the scholarly anthology he edited on the controversy among historians, *The Final Solution: Origins and Implementation* (Routledge, 1994).

The Goldhagens, like all polemicists, seem innocent of any acquaintance with 'the fallacy of the excluded middle', or the more general opinion of historians that great events seldom have a single cause. Not merely is the eliminationist intention of Hitler clear to them right from his first speeches and writings (which is at least highly plausible – how sick at heart one is to recall A. J. P. Taylor and many others dismissing all that as mere rhetoric), but also that he was preaching to the converted.

This book is a sadly clear case (of a kind discussed in the late Ivan Hannaford's *Race: The History of an Idea in the West* – see Chapter 12) of falling into the same concepts as one's enemy: a racial account of a particular racism, indeed what Omer Bartov called in a review 'a bizarre inversion of the Nazi view of the Jews as an insidious, inherently evil nation' (*New Republic*, 29 April 1996). That is a harsh thing to say, though other reviewers have hinted this more delicately. But to attach eliminationist anti-Semitism uniquely to Germany is to be anti-German to an unpardonable and irrelevant degree. What of the Lithuanians, the Ukrainians, French and Belgian fascists even, and many others who did their squalid bit? So many of the *Kapos* were from the lesser breeds within the law. Certainly 'the Jewish Question' dominated the Nazi theory of race, but by God it was a comprehensive theory. It graded most of humanity in ranking order, many other groups were classed as degenerative and better off for us to be without. And if the Holocaust was unique, genocide is not unique. A lot of the author's historical argument depends on an assumption that Germans are specially prone to it and good at it. He might have spared a casual word for the Croats in those happy times, or the Serbs yesterday; or the Congo in good King Leopold's golden days, etc., not to mention Pol Pot. Rousseau once wrote that when he thought of Nero and Caligula he rolled on the floor and howled to think that he was a man.

It is truly astounding that this book in its thesis form could have got the American Political Science Association's prize for 'comparative politics', for there is no sustained comparison in it whatever! Thus its methodological claims are doubly fatuous. They are fatuous in terms of empirical political studies: the book simply ignores evidence contrary to his long discredited hypothesis. And they are fatuous in terms of the modern history of political ideas: Goldhagen has no grasp of how complex and subtle the debate has become on distinguishing rhetoric from real intention, and about the many possible relationships there can be between values (good or bad, explicit or implicit) and policy. He is an angry bull in a cluttered china shop.

The questions arise of 'why the award?' and 'why the best-seller status'? Well, there are few PhD theses of such a scale, so many footnotes, so much moral intensity and making such sweeping claims to importance. Perhaps there was some nervousness about what would be thought if they did not make the award. But with deliberate bathos may I remark that the Government Department at Harvard and the APSA in their turn should have had a subject specialist as one of the examiners, even if it meant crossing disciplinary lines for an established historian of the Holocaust (except that he has attacked nearly all of them).

The best-seller status is due partly to the super-hype of its American launch by Knopf, but this blitz depended on the real need of each new generation for a popular book on the Holocaust. In fact this is a very demanding book; but it is presented as if it is popular. Actually, when the general reader reads it, or more likely dips into it, he or she will find a more balanced account of the whole killing of Jews than in those many books for which the Holocaust means the extermination camps alone, not also the atrocities in the field, behind the lines, in the work camps and in those final death marches. All that is badly wrong is his simplistic explanation of *why* it all happened: a unique German eliminatory anti-Semitism.

Finally, two rather different, but equally difficult, issues worry me about the book's publicity and popularity, although I am the last to want to throw stones at any author who tries to reach both a popular and an academic audience. One must doubt if most American readers, including Jewish readers, are as anti-German as Goldhagen appears to be, or take his main thesis as seriously as he would wish. Germany has become, after all, a favoured ally of the United States. Most Jewish readers may have had other thoughts in mind. Some publicists and organizations are, after all, notoriously trigger-happy to assert that any criticism of the State of Israel is anti-Semitic, or that any criticism of a book by a Jew on the Holocaust is really aimed at the State. By now the old issue of

German or Nazi guilt is almost an irrelevance to Jewish opinion; but memory of the Holocaust is, of course, understandably and properly important in maintaining Jewish identity, especially the identity of the non-religious, in a more or less secular but nonetheless semi-Christian and still not always fully welcoming society. So passionate remembering achieves a kind of transference into the defence of the State, making criticism of Israel's Palestinian policy untouchable.

My other worry is that the common reader, Gentile as well as Jew, will probably skip the intellectual history anyway and go for the vivid accounts of the horrors and atrocities. In the culture of our times the existence cannot be denied, in cinema, television and newspapers as well as books, of voyeuristic attraction to horrific violence. Truths about terror need handling so delicately. Those to whom accounts of the horrors are already familiar must surely yearn for a balanced popular exposition of the many causes and conditions that led to the Holocaust, and the scholarly debate about their overall relative importance. Browning's *The Path to Genocide* has come closest to what is wanted. But, alas, most scholars of the Holocaust are no better than other historians and social scientists in writing mostly for themselves, not thinking of the reading public. So they get the Goldhagens they deserve.

Every decade needs a Holocaust book, and this one may perhaps, in the publisher's 'mind-set' (whatever the author's intention), have ridden on the back of *Schindler's List*, but with the twist (so good for controversy and publicity) not of one good German but of all Germans bad. But this raises other large questions about the relationship of learned books to popularization, and the differences between the culture of university presses and trade presses – issues of moral responsibilities as to method, manner, motives and market.

CHAPTER 12

Hannaford on Race

The transmission of scholarly knowledge to the public is a fortuitous process at best and always involves long time lags. Critical history usually only makes small, slow gains, despite its weight of learned armour, against popular resistance fuelled by widespread nationalist myths. Sometimes the 'revisionist' historians (now more often a term of abuse than one of praise) are reviled by political intellectuals and the press as unpatriotic troublemakers. When it is grudgingly conceded that what they say may, in part, be true; then it is labelled as most unhelpful to current social purposes. And, anyway, it is all a matter of subjective opinion, isn't it? That is the populist basis of high-brow academic post-modernist deconstructionist ideology.

Intellectuals might be supposed to be a bridge between the scholarly and the public mind, especially when matters of understanding are of great political and social importance. But I read and encounter so many intellectuals who assume that nationalism is a perennial human phenomenon, and seem quite unable to imagine any other ties of obligation by which societies were bound together under government (such as religious belief, dynastic loyalty, tradition, fear, self-interest, civic patriotism, desire for law and order) before the invention and diffusion of nationalist

A foreword to Ivan Hannaford, *Race: The History of an Idea in the West* (Woodrow Wilson Center, Washington, DC, and Johns Hopkins University Press, Baltimore, 1997). First published as *The Idea of Race*.

ideology in late-eighteenth-century Europe with, arguably, some few premonitions or preconditions in the previous century. Certainly there is no turning the clock back, whether one considers nationalism a curse of modernity or a unique blessing (or more sensibly, thinking for once of the 'fallacy of the excluded middle', if one takes a score of plausible positions appropriate to widely differing circumstances).

The case of 'race' is even more muddled and confused. Many people denounce 'racism' nobly and boldly, sniffing it out in the most unexpected contexts, yet attack ideas of racial superiority by asserting the equality of races, rather than the equality of men and women. Even those who concede that no biological definition of race can possibly serve as a general theory of history and an explanation of individual human characteristics, capabilities and worth, even those who accept that such pseudo-explanations are invented ideologies, still cannot imagine a world in which such a comprehensive ideology or myth did not exist; or if the idea existed at all, then highly marginal and speculative, no guide or clue to understanding social organization. So people conclude that racial identification while it must always be mediated can never be rejected fully. Even if the Greeks and the Romans, the Celts and the Saxons, were not strictly speaking races, did they not believe that they were? Ivan Hannaford's long laboured researches give the unusually clear answer, 'No'.

Most modern scholarly writing on race by social scientists and historians is concerned to combat the idea of racial prejudice and to reveal the sad extent of discrimination. But Hannaford reminds us that there is a double prejudice. The belief that there has always been such a real and socially important thing as race precedes modern (or any other) race prejudice. I add this caveat 'socially important' for Hannaford is simply not concerned with assessing the amount of heat and light generated by claims that there are small differences of intelligence (however defined) between groups perceived as races. Even if that were true and the assumptions of such research sound, those small alleged differences (I tread every step carefully in this fought-over minefield) could not possibly carry the explanatory weight that racial theorists and even eugenicists (once) would attach to them in explaining different formations of culture. Many, many other factors are involved: class, law, tradition, education, etc., say generally context and environment; nor could such factors validate moral judgements. Hannaford, however, is vitally concerned to show that the existence of racial thought in the ancient and medieval worlds is almost entirely an invention of nineteenth-century historians and pseudo-historians (such as enlightenment biologists and zoologists constructing huge *a priori* schemes for the universal classification of species). He demonstrates by leading cases how this invention gave itself the authority of ancestry only by mistranslating ancient texts, either from ignorance or deliberate tendentiousness, or more subtly and respectably by an unhistorical and anachronistic use of new concepts of the translators' times to translate somewhat similar ancient terms. If one is completely seized with a new big idea one usually can find what one sets out to find in old texts. Heinrich von Treitschke's now little read histories of Germany were once the great texts of 'respectable' racial theory. The 'Anglo-Saxon destiny' historians like John Fiske in the United States or Sir John Seeley in the United Kingdom looked up to him, but none of these gentlemen went on to advocate ethnic cleansing, even though they created an intellectual precondition for people to believe that that would be helpful. But Treitschke's use of medieval and classical sources, while it looked scholarly, would fail badly modern standards of translation, let alone of scientific method. Scholarly intellectual history has made real advances in our time. Texts and concepts within them are now examined in the context of their times to gain their contemporary meaning, often very different from ours. Only then can we come back to the text. Thus I summarize with savage simplicity the interpretative doctrines of 'the Cambridge school' of the history of political ideas (Cambridge, England, but common to most present-day American and German intellectual historians).

Hannaford employs these methods meticulously in what is astonishingly the first scholarly history of the idea of race. There have been some highly unscholarly ones, in both a racist vein and an anti-racist vein. The difficulty of a history of race, it soon emerges, is that no pre-modern author believed that culture was a product of biologically determined factors. Eric Voegelin in his monumental volumes, *Order and History*, sees the symbol of blood and the blood relationship as universal, but only important as a mass ideology, rather than as an ancient esoteric mystery, in the modern world. There were and are so many other different explanations of how cultures are constituted, continue and change or evolve, not all of them mutually exclusive by any means. Aristotle, for instance, attributed physical differences between peoples to climate, but some modern translators say that he was using that as an explanation of race – a concept he would not have understood. But so deeply rooted is the belief either in the objective existence of racial determination or that people held this fallacious belief, that Ivan Hannaford felt the need to perform the great service in Part I of this book of re-examining not merely the classical texts used by the modern progenitors of racial theory but also esoteric, cabalistic, astrological and occult texts which have influenced popular thought (what Hannah Arendt once loftily called 'the metaphysics of the gutter'). He approaches an astonishing range of literature with great empathy, and from the beginning of his work he quite expected to find, so strong were the modern pointers, what he did not find: racial theory. Perhaps never has so much ground been covered to reach such a negative conclusion, but it is an extremely important negation. One does not have to be a Popperian (though I think we are both a little Popperian) to see that knowledge advances both by refutation and by assertion. But to turn the negative assertion of Part I on its head, the positive assertion is that racial conditioning is not part of the human condition.

Among groups subject to racial prejudice the defence can be developed that they are a race as good as any other, or even in some respects better. This is a defence that is as dangerous as it is unneeded. To use the rhetoric of the enemy to fight the enemy is often to become the enemy. For it is at most a culture that needs defending and asserting, not a race; and, of course, human rights. Reading Hannaford makes me (though I now go beyond his argument) even more worried about attempts to invent and assert legal doctrines of group rights. Individual civil rights are good enough to do the job. The difficulty with asserting group rights (whether based on racial or religious identifications) is that if those identifications are held to be legally and morally superior to individual rights, then it follows that these groups have rights, or will feel that they have rights, not merely against detractors but over all the individuals who are members of the group – not to act differently, not to leave the group, not to marry or have sexual relationships outside it. This is an entirely different matter from making deliberate political concessions when necessary, when desired, when generally acceptable, to groups who suffer discrimination. Hannaford does not make a case for an atomic individualism, we are all both individual and social beings; but we are social in relation to a plurality of groups, none of which alone determines our identity or can claim our exclusive allegiance; and even among those groups formed by racial stereotyping, race can be but one attribute among many.

The second part of this profound and challenging book seeks to redress a general, almost complete ignorance (I speak for myself before I had read the manuscript) about who were the progenitors of racial thought. The confusion of the biological with the social, typical of racial thinking, leads the author into largely forgotten byways of the history of science as well as of social and political philosophy. Few now can claim to grasp even the outlines of both, as thinkers of the eighteenth and early nineteenth centuries still claimed, often rashly. We should now be able to be more clear in distinguishing fact and value, and empirical generalizations from moral judgements. Because members of every labelled human species can in fact copulate together and procreate, the racial theorist has to ascend or descend to the dubious psychology of intelligence-testing in order to attempt to validate a naked moral judgement. But even that does not work perfectly. Had I been both very, very intelligent and very market-orientated I should have mated with a dim but strong, healthy, lithe and muscular (perfectly stereotypical) non-white mate in order to breed the most sought-for football or tennis super-hero of our times. Of course, like the story of George Bernard Shaw and Mrs Patrick Campbell, it might not have worked. But racial theorists invariably employ an outmoded concept of causality that has difficulty with statistical probability.

Most of those who believed in racial theory, or still do, up to a point, of course, are not racist in the sense that they advocate, from the time of Houston Stewart Chamberlain, compulsive cleansing of the good bloodstock and the elimination or segregation of the bad. But racial theory, if not a sufficient condition for active racism, is a necessary condition. Mere dislike and fear of strangers, literally the 'outlandish', is common to most cultures at most times (and is what some historians have sometimes innocently confused with racial reaction); but never before this century did it reach the extent of deliberate state policies of genocide, compulsory sterilization of the feeble-minded or legal apartheid. Examples of large-scale elimina-tion of heretics and infidels can be found before the modern era, but these were religious matters. Even then conversion saved many a life. Also ethnic prejudice only shades into racial prejudice when the belief that a culture is an extended family with blood ties also seeks to prohibit and punish marriage in or out of the *ethne*. I must admit, picking a small bone with Hannaford, that some ultra-orthodox religious beliefs can at times seem to me remarkably like racial beliefs, both in dogma and behaviour; but his answer would be, I well see, that precisely by the nature of those beliefs they are not for universal application or emulation. We cannot all be among the chosen, whether Jewish or Calvinist.

Arendt has said that our times have seen only two ideologies – in her special sense of a comprehensive set of ideas purporting to hold the key to history. They are economic determinism (whether of the Marxist or the market kind) and racialism. Eric Voegelin pointed to the unique dangers of political religions taking on a racial dress. Hannaford has traced for the first time the aetiology of this damnable but pervasive term, and in showing that it is uniquely modern, not universal, has not so much landed us with another possible guilt and 'burden of our times', but gives us clear ground for hope that what is culturally created can be culturally – in a common-sense sense – deconstructed. And the alternative? Well, he reminds us that before the determinism of either race or the market there was a long established Western tradition, honoured and remembered even when it could not be practised, that human societies were self-made creations of citizens. Loyalty was given not to myths of race but to civic institutions that were worthy of loyalty. I am honoured to write this since he invokes my *In Defence of Politics* as an advocacy or remembrancing of this great tradition that has no place for racial barriers nor ethnic crutches for explanation; but we both merely echo, above all, Aristotle, Machiavelli, the political thought of the *Federalist Papers* and, in our times, Arendt. Hannaford sadly but memorably asserts that after the time of Darwin:

> it was generally agreed that classical political theory had little or nothing to offer Western industrial society . . . The tests of true belonging [to a state] were no longer decided on action as a citizen but upon the purity of language, colour and shape. And since none of these tests could ever be fully satisfied, all that was left in place of political settlement were ideas of assimilation,

naturalisation, evacuation, exclusion, expulsion, and finally liquidation.

May I add a supererogatory word about the author? I have not called him Dr Hannaford nor Professor because he was neither when he wrote this, although recently he received an Honorary D.Litt. He came to the LSE as a part-time mature student, taking a master's degree in political thought under Michael Oakeshott while teaching a great many hours and students at one of the former British polytechnics, now Kingston University. But his talents, common sense and ability to grasp large issues calmly (all of which show in this work) soon saw him dragged out of teaching into high administration, although, he tells me, 'to retain my sanity I taught clandestinely'. More to the present point, he became deeply intrigued by a suggestion that Oakeshott had made to him that the story of Ham's delinquency was similar to that of the tower of Babel. So for over twenty years he worked in his spare time on this history, originally uncertain what he would find, and as surprised as the reader at what he did not find as well as what he did. Only in the last few years did a few of us become aware, through a paper he gave at the annual Political Thought Conference at Oxford, of how important this work was. Rumour could make it appear obsessive and eccentric but the reading of it showed it to be sound scholarship, bold in its extent but cautious and trustworthy in method and tone. Some who heard the paper were able to steer him towards two fruitful, if belated, periods of working leisure at Wolfson College, Cambridge, and then at the Woodrow Wilson Center. Struggling with motor neurone disease he was just able to read the proofs of his book, but never saw a bound copy before his death. Although my bread has come from the university all my life, I take a sad and sardonic pleasure in seeing this book as an outstanding proof that private scholarship is still possible when the will is there and the importance of the subject possesses the author.

CHAPTER 13

Multiculturalism

In order to produce a government strategy to affect public attitudes towards ethnic communities in the UK, it is important to know what these attitudes are and how they have changed since the 1950s when substantial numbers of immigrants began to arrive from the ex-colonies. Indeed, no comprehensive survey has been conducted since Rose and Deakin's seminal *Colour and Citizenship* of 1966, despite all the huge bibliography one can find under 'race', 'colour' or 'ethnicity', words which are not synonyms (would journalists and students please note), still less are to be lumped together under the label 'black' except in the rhetoric of both racists and of too many anti-racists. So IPPR commissioned two surveys in 1997. The first was a quantitative survey from NOP to find out the attitudes of white people by age and class towards Asian, Afro-Caribbean and Jewish peoples; and the second was a qualitative study by Opinion Leader Research to explore the reasons behind these largely negative attitudes. For instance, 94 per cent of whites believed that there was at least a little prejudice, with 46 per cent seeing it strong. Prejudice against inter-marriage remains strong in all groups, actually stronger in the minority groups; but less strong among the young. The most common reason given for prejudice was economic

A review in *Political Quarterly*, October–December 1999, of Yasmin Alibhai-Brown, *True Colours: Public Attitudes to Multi-Culturalism and the Role of the Government* (IPPR, 1999).

and employment uncertainty – 'they take our jobs', etc.

That is just a taster. The author collects many other polls and surveys, and did some brave in-depth door-stepping research in trouble spots. The book is a solid compendium of up-to-date knowledge. But it is far more than that. What is truly impressive is the tone both of deep moral commitment and thoughtfulness, going together with, which is all too rare, a concern for practicality by setting down carefully, cautiously and sensitively, without rhetoric or hyperbole, what is known of the facts of the case. This is so unlike the perpetually strident tone of some leaders of anti-racist groups who, as if drunk with the righteousness of their cause and inflamed by flagrant, real injustices, lose all sense and perception of how to persuade those who need to be persuaded; at best they give fleeting comfort to their own communities, at worst their effectiveness is too often only that of leadership and institutional politics within their own communities. Was it Orwell who said to Koestler, or Koestler to Orwell, 'Know thy enemy as thyself'? Polemicists all too often either speak to the already saved or speak simply to cheer their own. This author explores how to persuade the prejudiced, and to arouse the indifferent.

She has no doubt that government itself must take the lead. Negatively, it must avoid making statements 'based on the assumptions that good race relations depend on tough immigration policies', and inflammatory language like 'bogus' and 'abusive' when characterizing those ineligible for refugee status under the strict enough criteria of the Geneva Convention. Contradictory messages are common from different departments of government (that question of 'joined up handwriting', as ever). Positively, the resources of government, so well developed to spin good news of the economy, the health service and education (sometimes a little ahead of hard truth) could be far better mobilized to spread news of positive achievements by groups and individuals in the minority communities, or of how proud we should feel to have given succour to refugees from persecution. (Photo-opportunities for ministers; but the refugees might be a bit angry when they eventually emerge in the clear.)

She is not hesitant to reiterate Roy Jenkins' 'momentous speech' when Home Secretary, which said that integration was the goal but that it did not mean:

the loss by immigrants of their own national characteristics and culture. I do not think we need in this country a 'melting pot' . . . It would deprive us of most of the positive benefits of immigration which I believe to be very great indeed. I define integration, therefore, not as a flattening process of assimilation, but as an equal opportunity, accompanied by cultural diversity in an atmosphere of mutual tolerance.

It happens that as I write this review I am thinking anxiously about a clause in the proposed new statutory curriculum for citizenship which is out for consultation: 'Pupils should be taught about . . . (b) the origins and implications of the diverse national, regional, religious and ethnic identities within the United Kingdom and the need for mutual respect and understanding.' That is one of seven 'should-be-taughts' under 'knowledge and understanding' for 14–16-year-olds in maintained schools. By the time this is printed it may or may not have survived strong and well-meant lobbying (from within government as well as without) to state instead an explicit duty to teach 'Anti-Racism' – multiculturalism is not enough. But the thinking behind the multiculturalist approach of the draft order has, I believe, two strong grounds, which the thrust of Yasmin Alibhai-Brown's argument shares, quite apart from her seeing that the priority must lie with an example set by the government and prominent public bodies. The first is that explicit attacks on racism or teaching anti-racism full frontal can prove inflammatory – just what the racist white lads will look forward to in classroom discussion, or disruption. Indirect approaches about fading but once real national (take the Irish, for instance), religious (take anti-Catholicism of yore) and even regional prejudices (take accent, for instance) may prove more effective. Significant and hate-filled diversities are not all racial. Northern Ireland reminds us of that. The second is the uncertainty principle: that we know little in general about what effect explicit strategies have and what training is needed. Some evidence suggests they can be counter-productive if applied to all the very different circumstances of each school's locality. And I have a third worry: that too often the discourse of *racial* prejudice perpetuates the fallacy, no older than the late eighteenth century, that mankind is divided into clear-cut races and that character, intelligence, morality, behaviour patterns, etc. are genetic racial products. Well, we are stuck with the word in popular discourse and well-meaning people argue for the equality of races rather than of man; but we can only really mean 'ethnic prejudice', perceived cultural differences. Ethnicity is real, and people kill because of it; but unlike the belief in race shared by racists and early 'human zoologists', it is not immutable. One can share, cross and even change cultures in a lifetime. Education should try to get this distinction across. I go beyond the author's argument, but books like this help mightily.

I have only one difficulty with the argument of this most judicious and ethically well grounded book. It urges government to stress 'respect and acceptance rather than tolerance'. Charter 88 takes this line too, objecting to 'toleration' being held up as a basic value of citizenship because it is 'condescending' to tolerate anyone. This view is common among the anti-racists and minority lobbies. However, we must distinguish. No one accepts everything and everyone is in every respect equal. We must discriminate, indeed, between good and bad, between practical and impractical policies. To discriminate as such is not wrong, only if for bad reasons; to tolerate is not to condescend, only if out of a false assumption of moral or social superiority. To tolerate is to recognize genuine differences, even to feel or state some disapprovals, but to limit one's reactions. Certainly I do not tolerate people because of their colour – colour is morally irrelevant; I try to judge everyone as people, and their actions as good or bad, rarely wholly good or bad. But I do have to exercise toleration (that is to limit my disapproval) of some people's religious and ideological beliefs, and of some of the practices that follow from them. I both disagree with them and disapprove of them, and of some other cultural practices too; but I restrain my behaviour while not abandoning my beliefs, nor expecting others to abandon theirs. I 'respect' differences in a practical, peaceful, law-abiding way (I hope). 'Respect' cannot mean that we think all sincere beliefs are equally true, or their consequences equally acceptable to all others in a society. Ernest Gellner once said that it is imperative to be socially tolerant always, intellectually tolerant never. We should not be ashamed of toleration as a prime value of freedom and civilization. Total acceptance would be the end of what we all are, significantly different as well as having rights, mutual dependence and humanity in common. We should be far more conscious of being a multicultural society and a multinational state, but not with a multiculturalism, she argues, that locks people (especially women) into traditional communities. To demand full acceptance rather than toleration is to demand assimilation rather than integration, a single common culture rather than, what we have long had, a pluralistic society. But it is the practices of a common citizenship that can hold together to mutual advantage real differences (important to both minorities and majorities) of national, religious and ethnic identity.

She argues, here and elsewhere, that we need to move beyond multiculturalism. That is one way of putting it. I would rather suggest we stress that a recognition of multiculturalism needs always to be seen in the overarching context of general laws, human rights and practices of free citizenship. I wonder if we really differ?

CHAPTER 14

Talking to the Loyalist Paras

It is easier to take seriously irrational ideas when we can study them historically than when they stare us, or hit us, in the face. However, Steve Bruce, who is Professor of Sociology at Aberdeen, had the good sense when he was for many years at Queen's, Belfast, to act like an old-fashioned social anthropologist or field zoologist and spend much time observing the wild animals all around him, rather than be fused to a computer terminal, aggregating data from distant parts. The result of earlier forays was a unique study of the most famous of the Great Bulls of Ulster, *God Save Ulster! Religion and the Politics of Paisleyism* (1986), followed by an equally challenging study of a herd rather than a sect, *The Red Hand: Protestant Paramilitaries in Northern Ireland* (1992).

In both studies he took the ideas of the loyalists seriously and concluded that they said what they believed and believed what they said, a conclusion abhorrent equally to 'Quaker ecumenicals' (the 'look at what they *really* have in common' brigade) and to both Marxists and Freudians (to whom what people say is always a false clue to what they really mean). Normal, pragmatic politicians also found it hard to take Paisley's theology seriously. I was once in a closed room when a permanent secretary of the Northern Ireland Office, experienced in the politics of the Trucial Sheikdoms, asked

---

A review in *Bulan*, winter 1994, of Steve Bruce, *The Edge of Union: The Ulster Loyalist Political Vision* (Oxford University Press, 1994).

how Paisley could be bought. His senior advisers mimed pretend-shock at such plain speaking, but then looked cross when the two academics present opined that he couldn't be bought, that he really believed all that 'seventeenth-century stuff' about the Pope as Anti-Christ and, in any case, lived for the storm, indeed the *Sturm und Drang*, not for a hard bargained or gently induced settlement; but the field officers backed us, adding that his own people would probably kill him if he appeared to compromise or falter. Bruce later gave chapter and verse to show how much more important was the church of Paisley's original foundation than the party of his latter-day creation. Reading *The Red Hand* should convince anyone that those fellows mean it when they say that at no price could they be reasoned or tricked into peacefully entering what John Hume cautiously or casuistically used to call 'some form of unity in an Ireland of the future', a formula that might have left the fur of Carson's orange cat reasonably unruffled. Those with 'a solution to the Irish question', whether nationalists or *politique* half-way-housers, have spilt a lot of ink trying to deflate or discredit Bruce's irritating conclusions. What was irritating was the scholarly care, detail and empathy he employed in his work. Our refusal to face reality, masked as critical scepticism, has driven Bruce back into the field again, drawing together the threads of both previous books, and may also account, as he himself notes, for a tone of anger in some of the key passages. He hates the folly and self-deception (unhappily deceiving others too) of those who will take seriously both the aims and the power of the IRA but not the awful authenticity of the beliefs and values of loyalist militants. This exasperation does pull him off the fence to say at the end, as his critics always suggest he wanted to say from the beginning, that if one is to prescribe after painfully describing, no settlement can by-pass the loyalists, whatever demography holds in store.

Well, isn't that almost what the two governments are now saying following the Joint Declaration? But they say it as if dealing with people open to and used to bargaining, gradual persuasion, political compromise, not with the strong passions, hatreds, suspicions, fears, myths and ethnic pride that Bruce so patiently and fully sets out.

This new study is based on interviews and conversations with what he sees as the two extreme polar groups of unionism: the mainly rural evangelicals and the mainly urban loyalist terrorists. Too many social scientists, he suggests, would try to understand loyalism and unionism by putting in for large grants for structured social surveys, and if these are not forthcoming then would try to knit together loose ends of responses to different questions from opinion polls taken at different times for different purposes. Even the best of surveys, he believes, can only offer stock responses to pre-set alternatives, simplifying complex situations and treating all respondents as of equal value. This makes it hard to grasp a popular ideology as a whole composed of inter-active and not always consistent elements. And it is still harder to get beyond what people say they want to some feeling of what they may accept, put up with or come to stomach at a pinch or squeeze.

CHAPTER 15

Rethinking Unionism

When I was a student in London in the late 1940s I was much impressed by Harold Laski's love of Seeley's dictum which he worked into nearly every lecture: 'History without politics has no fruit, politics without history has no root.' To an historically minded student of political theory, it seemed so clever and apt. And over the years one began to see that often the most relevant political philosophy (then supposed to be dead or dying) was found in the debates about historiography. Hexter said so quite clearly. Elton and Namier pretended to be above the battle, but looking at their presuppositions (*pace* Collingwood), it was clear that they weren't: their method yielded the result each wanted. So to read twenty years later the Irish revisionist historians was not so much a surprise as pure intellectual pleasure. The old debate about partition had been lifted onto a higher level. Even those who took the view that scholarly (or scholarly looking) history should, or must inevitably, serve the purposes of nation-building, *and* that the nation in question must be coincident with clear maritime boundaries, had to brush up their act and spend more time in archives.

Now something similar is happening with Unionism, and there

A review in *History Ireland*, spring 1997, of Richard English and Graham Walker (eds), *Unionism in Modern Ireland: New Perspectives on Politics and Culture* (Gill & Macmillan, 1997) and of Norman Porter, *Rethinking Unionism: An Alternative Vision for Ireland* (Blackstaff Press, 1997).

is something to be said for a late start. The standard of debate is then higher. Not, of course, by Unionist politicians, a sorry lot who do their people no favours in how they present their case to the outside world (and some of them do care), but by historians and political scientists who show some understanding of their cause, or the cause of their fears. If hitherto Unionism has been lacking, with few exceptions (A. T. Q. Stewart obviously and honourably) in the kind of justificatory history and literature so abundant in the nationalist tradition, yet in the last few years a remarkable recrudescence of justifications of Unionism (always 'up to a point', of course) have appeared, not seen since the 1900s and Dicey's *England's Case Against Home Rule*. I count as justifications not so much books stridently stating the case for Unionism (there are very few of these, as very few Loyalists can run to even the appearance of a scholarly book – or would read them if written), but serious studies of Unionism and Loyalism, all of which at least make clear the extreme political difficulties of ignoring it.

Northern Ireland is plainly a pill too big and bitter for the Republic to swallow whole without fear of poisonous eruptions, whereas the majority in the North have been able, however painfully and roughly, to hold down the bitter pill of nationalism. The IRA has not proved successful in breaking down government, and most nationalists (I simply mean people who feel themselves wholly Irish, or more Irish than British) have made some sort of accommodation, or at least (the opinion polls tell us) want to look very closely at what is in any package labelled organic unity. A large number in both communities now favour what no political doctor wishes to prescribe: joint rule.

Alas, the title of this book promises more than it offers. All anthologies are uneven, just as the true and good intent of this anthology (like the famous curate's egg, 'good in parts') is to show that Unionism is not all of a piece. The editors of *Unionism in Modern Ireland* say that they wish to build on foundations already laid in the field by figures such as Steve Bruce, Alvin Jackson, Arthur Aughey, Paul Bew, Henry Patterson, Jennifer Todd and Peter Gibbon, and they pay tribute to the earlier work of Alvin Jackson. Perhaps we should add George Boyce and Paul Arthur who, if he has not written on Unionism *per se*, yet speaks for many Northern Catholics who have developed a deliberate empathy, not so much in the name of true history, but of political conciliation.

However, eight of the thirteen contributors are at Queen's, and I sniff that some of the others began adult life there. Anthologies are strange beasts. If you go for the best eleven possible, you wait for ever and nothing gets done. House products have some advantages (apart from chalking up research funding points). It is good to offer 'exciting, fresh and wide-ranging work by young scholars at an early stage in their career'. But not all the young are either fresh or exciting. Some are born old and dull.

To kick off, there is a brilliant historical essay on 'Ulster and the British Problem' by Ian McBride, a Junior Research Fellow at Corpus Christi, Cambridge, teasing out several different strands of Unionist identity, showing how complicated they are (no less than Irish identity), and that the very 'British' identity to which they also wish to belong is, to coin a phrase, an essentially contestable concept. But there is a study of football and politics, by one Scott Harvie, '17 November 1993 –A Night to Remember?' that charts the background to the outrage in the nationalist and Irish press at the crowd behaviour at that Ireland–Northern Ireland match. I had forgotten about that, so read all his preliminaries, listing the terrorist incidents that happened to precede previous internationals, as if there were causal connections and bloody doom was about to strike; but all that happened was foul sectarian abuse. It strikes me as amazing that nothing worse happened and that such games have been able to take place at all. For the sake of political science, I formally accuse Dr Harvie of lack of comparative method (a heinous charge). Has he even watched a Rangers–Celtic fixture, a Manchester United–Chelsea game, or heard the unanimous and considered views of West Ham supporters when a black visitor scores? His ear is not good. He talks of a 1988 European Cup game where English fans indulged in 'sectarian' abuse against Ireland. Highly unlikely. My fellow English yobs wouldn't know a Prod from a Taig. Their forte is strictly racist and nationalist abuse. That is one of the things that drives Loyalists mad when they visit or work on the mainland. The English worker cannot tell an Ulster from a southern accent. Irish ears are far more acute, for obvious historical and prudential reasons.

Studies of popular culture are important. A study of attitudes to 'the Crown' from Thomas Hennessey is important, and one on Armistice Days and Remembrance Sundays in Dublin, 'A Twinge of Memory' by Jane Leonard, is poignant and interesting. But it is odd and misleading that the new or revived Ulster literary movement, consciously cross-denominational and secular, finds no place (the Longleys will be cross) – only Patrick Maume's laboured disinternment, 'The Ulsterman of Letters: the Unionism of Frank Frankfort Moore, Shan Bullock and St. John Ervine'. There is no study of the Orange Order, nor even of the UDA. The book is simply not a planned whole, just a gathering of what colleagues, friends and former students happened to be working on, or have worked over. Richard English makes a brave editorial attempt to pull it together at the end, very much worth reading on its own: 'The Same People with Different Relatives? Modern Scholarship, Unionists and the Irish Nation'.

There are some good parts to this curate's egg, each of which could grace a journal, even if they do not make a comprehensive book. For instance, the editors say that 'surprisingly some of the strongest arguments in favour of cultural pluralism and and citizens' rights' have come from David Ervine and Gary McMichael (of the UDA). True, if there had been a study of the UDA it would not then have forgotten that Glenn Barr was with William Craig's Vanguard Unionist Party in 1974 when they struck a deal with Hume and the SDLP in the Northern Ireland Constitutional Convention for 'power sharing for the emergency' (that would last, they used to joke over the glass, 'until the Thursday before the second coming on a Friday'); a deal only wrecked by the jealousy of Paisley and Harry West. A decade later the New Ulster Research Group (which I called 'the spiritual arm of the UDA', a joke they enjoyed) were talking to Gerry Fitt, Paddy Devlin and to some anti-Provo old IRA about a power-sharing working man's Republic of the North. Moonshine perhaps, but well meant and a helpful factor in the future cease-fire. The UDA too had an aspiration to have 'an Armalite in one hand and a ballot box in the other'. Even McMichael *père* had talked that way speculatively. That part-time gangster summoned me for a working lunch on the nature of pluralism, as his bodyguards stood by; and I then received a Christmas card from him; unhappily a few days after he was killed.

Norman Porter's book also discusses the nature of pluralism. Never before has the hermeneutic theory of understanding and the phenomenology of Jürgen Habermas been applied to the Northern Ireland problem. The people who should read this book and be convinced by it will, unhappily, find it almost incomprehensible. I had to work hard, but was richly rewarded. Just as there are poets who write only for poets, musicians for musicians, so he is writing for all historians and political scientists who would write about Northern Ireland in the problem-solving mode. He takes some kind of unionism for granted as an expression of culture and history, and he is a Unionist in a moderate, minimal but irreducible political sense. He argues profoundly that human identity is always complex, never simple (except for passing moments, crises or ceremonies), and that for *both* communities in Northern Ireland a distinct identity is not dependent on a sovereign state, nor does its peculiar richness depend for preservation on perpetual antagonism. Identities in these islands are especially complex. Scots have been Scottish without a state for almost 300 years, but are still very Scottish (in somewhat different ways). If they want a parliament or even a state, the best argument is democratic (because a clear majority want it, and mean no harm to others), not because of ethnicity or because identity is held (as in nationalist doctrine everywhere) to depend upon having a state.

Porter sees the tragedy of a sense of Britishness that is incomprehensible to mainland Brits. However, to think of Northern Ireland as 'a place apart' is to chasten nationalist historiography but also to encourage parochialism. He prefers Edna Longley's metaphor of the North as 'a cultural corridor' open at both ends to a flow of Irish and British traffic. Those who have too fixed and rigid a construct of identity are unaware, he argues, how much that identity is itself shaped by those whom they believe threaten their identity. So he argues for a civic unionism, to recognize that the practices of civic republicanism are quite as important as the formal constitutional framework. He argues for a 'rethinking of Unionist orthodoxy . . . to hold out against despair, constrained visions and stalemate . . . to insist, in the rich language of civic republicanism, that politics matters'.

He might well pounce, as I now do, on an ambiguity or confusion in Richard English's otherwise shrewd concluding essay in the Queen's anthology on scholarship and nationalism. English quotes from an essay of Kirby Miller, 'Revisionism Revised': 'For statesmanship to be constructive . . . the equal validity of the cultures, traditions and interests of all parties must be acknowledged.' But he says it is difficult to sustain an argument that traditional nationalist and unionist readings of the history of Northern Ireland are simultaneously valid, given that each depends on a denial of the truth of the other. Indeed, but 'statesmanship' was Miller's word and concept, not true history. This is where history and politics have different perspectives, and hermeneutics can comprehend the gap. If there is to be political conciliation, the statesman has to act *as if* both traditions are equally valid – legitimate might be the better word. I got into trouble in South Africa once for incautiously saying, or appearing to say, that the Afrikaner and the ANC cases should be *treated* as if equally just. But, in the end, the traditions were so treated – the only way out or forward. Norman Porter more subtly suggests that 'parity of esteem' can only be reached through 'due recognition'. Knowledge of the other tradition, including the tendentious histories, is a necessary condition for moral goodwill or for a trust strong enough at least for peace.

CHAPTER 16

Gellner and Postmodernism

Ernest Gellner will remain one of the greatest voices for truth and reason within the academy of our times. He was little known outside the academy (largely due to the ignorance of most literary editors in the quality press, even though his work is aimed not at subject specialists but at anyone interested in ideas), but within it he ranged and often raged free. Original research and thinking in anthropology, original thinking in philosophy and sociology gave him the solid basis for critical assaults and judicial ridings far beyond. Are we not all voices for truth and reason, according to our abilities and opportunities? He thought not, and – if one can face it – he was right: so much in social thought is fashion, professional opportunism and an easy tolerance of other meanings and discourses, a tacit avoidance of questions of truth and moral judgement, or as he tersely puts it: 'Total permissiveness ends in arbitrary dogmatism.'

The permissiveness to which he refers is, of course, not not knocking your neigbour's spouse, smoking hash or encouraging single women on welfare to have babies, but is intellectual permissiveness. In one of his earlier gatherings of essays he propounded a modern categorical imperative: 'social tolerance, always; intellectual, never'. So the main target of both these books,

A review in *Political Quarterly*, April–June 1996, of Ernest Gellner's last two books: *Postmodernism, Reason and Religion* (Routledge, 1992) and *Anthropology and Politics: Revolutions in the Sacred Grove* (Blackwell, 1995).

the one his sixth collection of essays, the other a long essay printed as a book, is 'relativism'. Relativism may seem a surprising target for a polymathic socially tolerant man who found, indeed, nothing human uninteresting.

The argument goes like this: the world dominance of the West in the last century was a product of science, technology and industry, caused at least partly by a new type of secular reasoning in the previous century usually called 'Enlightenment'. Hardly surprisingly paternalistic, condescending attitudes were formed towards traditional or undeveloped societies. So, properly if not inevitably, a reaction followed by thinking and often guilt-ridden Western intellectuals. Anthropologists discovered relativism. Irrationalities and superstitions have a meaning and work within a social system. Values and beliefs function as self-contained systems. Science becomes a Western set of values (however much everyone wants and uses it, he adds).

Long ago Gellner pointed out that this is all very true, up to a point: the point at which some beliefs – prayers and sacrifices do not bring rain to arid land or fertility to women, for instance – hinder the survival or betterment of many communities, let alone shutting them off from such ethnocentric, liberal, neo-colonialist namby-pamby stuff as notions of universal individual rights to life, liberty and happiness. (I stumble into Gellner's kind of brutal irony, which is not always noticed by his more wounded readers.) So extreme has this reaction to Victorian ethnocentricism become that it now seems that 'anything goes' so long as it is a coherent system of meaning, or even if incoherent (for coherence entails much sweat), then an authentic utterance of a liberated individual. That is why postmodernism comes in for lethal side-swipes. In the last essay, 'The Coming *Fin de millénaire*', he quotes a marvellous passage from Musil's *The Man without Qualities* about the revelling in 'new everythings' in Vienna of the 1890s. That was fun, he sagely comments, but

> This time round, however, it is not obvious that there still are any certainties to be undermined. Scepticism or the overturning of truisms by now has an inverse or boomerang effect: by undermining the criteria of all rational criticism, it confers *carte blanche* on any arbitrary intellectual self-indulgence. Total relativism ends by underwriting cheap dogmatism. If anything

goes, then you are also allowed to be as utterly dogmatic as you wish: the critical standards, which might have inhibited you, have themselves been abrogated. What can there be to check you? He who tries to restrain you, in the name of fact or logic, will be castigated as positivist, or imperialist, or both: after all, objectivism was at the service of domination. Total permissiveness ends in arbitrary dogmatism.

The *fin de siècle* was liberating, the *fin de millénaire* may be wilfully destructive.

Relativism is one of three views that he sees as the main contestants for legitimate belief in the modern world. The other two are religious fundamentalism and what he sometimes calls, with a self-deprecatory irony, 'rationalist fundamentalism' or else 'Enlightenment rationalism'. His explanation of why Islam sees a revival of fundamentalism has been hotly debated, but to deny the facts hopefully and accuse him of 'orientalism' does not seem very helpful. His sympathies are with those who suffer because of fundamentalism, but its dominance in modern Islam compared with the 'facile ecumenical relativism' of most contemporary Christianity is obvious. It refutes the 'inevitability of secularism' thesis, he says, however much we might wish otherwise. He does not favour living our lives according to 'claims for localised cognitive authority, known as Revelation', confessing himself to be 'a full-blooded, committed believer and an intellectual adherent of Enlightenment doubt'. For doubt, discovery and test are the methods of science. The commitment to truth in this perspective is a commitment to unfolding truths, no final truths as in these 'local revelations'. But these local revelations gain in strength amidst modernity and relativists must accept them as a package.

Science, however, he reminds us with brusque common sense, is a universal phenomenon, 'doubly transcendent' indeed. First because its laws of nature work throughout the world, second because they appear to work in the universe. But it is a commitment to procedures, *not* to substantive values. Values are relative, up to the point that they do not deny or obscure cognition (or, I think he might have added explicitly, threaten other cognitive beings). Relativism is perfectly appropriate to how we choose the wallpaper and furnishings, but if the house is not built according to scientific principles it will fall down, or at least not last as long as those that are. Life is, of course, a series of compromises between the constraints and opportunities of material nature and the relative choices of society; but viable compromises must recognize this duality, indeed a hierarchy within it with reason on top. Following Gellner, I see it this way. A child challenges an injunction by saying, 'Well, that's what *you* think'. Rationality begins when the parent demands 'What if everyone did that?' and didactically points to the likely consequences of pursuing such a course of action as a rule, or even 'just when I feel like it'.

Gellner is at pains to stress, very much as Karl Popper did, the tentative nature of knowledge. No two accounts of scientific method agree, but there is usually a consensus among scientists as to what is knowledge. The only rules are procedural rules, *how* to procede. Unlike revelation they do not beg the question of *where* we are going, nor like the relativist say it is all a matter of taste or chance. At this point one might expect him to have related this to the thoughts of his 1994 book, *Conditions of Liberty: Civil Society and its Rivals*. Popper had, after all, made a very serious attempt to tie the experimental method of science to a procedural rather than a substantive theory of democracy. But surprisingly he doesn't. It would have taken only a paragraph. Did he take a lofty and impatient 'done that' view – let the reader do some work? Or would it have taken only a paragraph? For there is a big problem that he never faced. It would not affect his moral stance but would modify his sociological account of modernity: that the political, republican tradition *preceded* modern science, industry, enlightenment – Aristotle, Cicero, Machiavelli, the city states and all that. Science and republics? As Yeats remarked, 'Which the rider, which the horse?' And is not the idea of constituting a social order to make decisions politically by public debate as much 'Western' as science, and as capable of export?

Of course, unusual among social scientists, his favourite form was the essay, not the would-be definitive monograph (too often definitive by crushing its borders drastically): so speculative, open-ended, stimulating, critical and shameless in crossing borders, at times a little self-indulgent (but then that warns the reader that he or she is joining in an argument with a person who thinks ideas are of the utmost importance, not a sermon to others), at times too fond of paradox (as if Bertrand Russell trying to be G. K. Chesterton), but also at times just a little hasty, a little too impatient to be on to the next big theme to bother to consolidate and relate his positions. Others may now try. Two more books, it is said, are in the press. So no final statement, even from those, of course. There are no final statements, there is only the life of reason (or perhaps better, of reasoning). He led that life to the full to the enlightenment of so many of us.

CHAPTER 17

Hannah Arendt and the Burden of Our Times

Many have written more clearly about the dynamics of the concentration camps in both Germany and the Soviet Union, and about the fundamental conditions of European civic republicanism and its seeming decay into individualistic consumerism. But no one other than Arendt has tried so hard to see the links between these different phenomena and to set up a mirror by which European civilization can recognize its faults and perhaps seize a last chance to set its house in order before some other great disaster, or at best a gradual decay of civic spirit and public values, a privatization of all concerns. That is, if this has not already occurred: what does it bode for the future that the massacres in Bosnia were allowed to rage so long, let alone in 'far away' Rwanda and Burundi; or that the former Soviet Union has been left to rot, as no immediate danger, rather than helped to the hilt to establish and stabilize free institutions?

However, until at least a decade after her death in 1975 Hannah Arendt's reputation stood far higher in the United States than in Great Britain. Perhaps this is due to the greater openness of American higher education to thinkers who do not fit easily in the Procrustean beds of academic disciplines, thus the greater interchange there between academia and quality or intellectual journalism, and also to the greater openness of New York than the Oxford–Cambridge–London triangle to the ideas of the refugee

From *Political Quarterly*, January 1997, in a series on 'Reputations'.

generation from Germany. So in the USA there have for a long time been more people willing and able to cross what here in the UK is still the great editorial divide (despite Orwell, or why some still dislike, distrust and resist Orwell) between politics and literature, not to mention a certain lingering intellectual parochialism. Consider that in New York her closest and most understanding friend, literary executor indeed, was the late Mary McCarthy, novelist and critic, and W. H. Auden knew and admired her too (bizarrely he wanted to marry her, presumably wanting a nanny with intellectual and cosmopolitan class).[1] Only recently have Arendt conferences broken out here – in the States they have been legion,[2] and probably the best of many books and symposia about her has come from an English academic author, Margaret Canovan, certainly the best for clear exposition and good judgement.[3]

The first British edition of her famous *The Origins of Totalitarianism* (New York, 1951) was titled *The Burden of Our Times*. That title could hardly have seized the attention of historians and political scientists, nor was the publisher, Fred Warburg, known in academic pastures. Secker & Warburg had sprung to prominence and prosperity as Orwell's last publisher, and as having the English rights of Thomas Mann and Kafka. Warburg was surely at least half right to see Arendt in such company, must have seen Arendt as keeping such company: deep-thinking writers who are probably more influential in shaping the concepts by which we perceive the world than are social scientists and historians.

So the book, as well as being long and difficult and by an unknown author, appeared here with a title of ambiguous connotation, even if in some ways 'burden of our times' made better sense than 'origins of totalitarianism' – but only when one had got into the book. Only a literary reviewer, Al Alvarez, was fully perceptive as well as unreservedly enthusiastic about what she was trying to say. She was writing, indeed, about the dreadful burden of guilt and horrified astonishment of our times. *How* could such things be done at all that were done so deliberately and in such cold blood in the camps? After all, most people in the wartime USA and UK, hearing rumours or reading dramatic underground reports of what was happening, simply did not believe them; and it is facile to attribute this unbelief simply to anti-Semitism or scepticism about Zionist propaganda. Few people believed that human beings could do such things to other human beings, deliberately, cold-bloodedly, *en masse*.

Arendt was not writing primarily, as historians and some sociologists thought (and then faulted her because of this thought), about *why* this happened, thus to be read as an empirical, historical, account of the causes of totalitarianism, but rather as a detailed speculation about how it could have happened at all. Many were, indeed (and still are), sceptical about the very concept of totalitarianism that then appeared to be, following the American title, the subject matter in all subsequent editions and revisions.[4] I know of no British political thinker who reviewed the original *Burden of Our Times*. When political theorists did come to look at it, the then prevailing tone of logical positivism or linguistic analysis would have shared Isaiah Berlin's *ex cathedra* judgement. He once said to me, *à propos* of kind words about my *In Defence of Politics* (the second edition of which carried an explicit acknowledgement, or dawning recognition of Arendt's influence): 'We seem to agree on most things except your admiration for de Jouvenal and Miss Arendt. Could you summarize either of their arguments for me in brief propositions?' 'That's a tall order.' 'Indeed, can't be done. Sheer metaphysical free-association. Fairy gold, Bernard, fairy gold, I beg you to notice.' But I still beg to differ. She irritated him mightily for when the *Observer* some time back in the early 1960s had a naughty one-off feature, 'Most Over-rated Authors of the Year', Berlin contributed not with a paragraph of more or less reasoned denunciation, but with two words: 'Hannah Arendt'. *Ipse dixit*.

There are things to irritate. She could be both verbose, repetitive and eager to say everything at once, and every time; as if, when she started writing in different journals, she was unsure, under-standably, whether she had a continuing readership. I think she was primarily an essayist and a speculative, contemplative thinker. *Between Past and Future* (1968), *Men in Dark Times* (1970), *Crises of the Republic* (1972) were, indeed, all collections of essays. I think her least successful books were when she tried to be a fully systematic thinker, as in her final and unfinished purely philosophical volumes *The Life of the Mind* (1978). Even her most elaborate book, perhaps even her most important book, *The Human Condition* (1958), while it looks systematic, is more like a set of variations on two great themes, some harmonizing well, others discordant and thus 'unsuccessful', but all provoking what she valued and gave us above all, active thought. Even her two most contentious books, *Eichmann in Jerusalem: A Report on the Banality of Evil* (1961) and *On Revolution* (1963) are only essays, far from monographic and comprehensive treatments. Only her short book, *On Violence* (1970), achieves the symmetry of form and content of great political writing. Berlin, who writes as well as Conrad, might have made some allowance for the difficulties of writing philosophical English as a second language in maturity. So in the image that he popularized, she is a supreme example of fox appearing to be hedgehog. With Berlin I think that the story of human freedom is one of many foxes, the plurality of thoughts and thinking in a civilized, civic context, rather than invocation of one or other of those hedgehoging, all-consuming big thoughts; but I longed to persuade him that she was a great fox for freedom, if her more than occasional vices of exposition can be forgiven and the reasons for her inconsistencies understood. Her pretensions can at times irritate: she has a bad old Germanic habit of appearing to think that through philology the original meanings of concepts should be returned to – in fact she knew better but liked to parade her erudition; pretending to be a hedgehog. And it took a long time before those in the British empiricist tradition could see that her existentialism, taken pure from Jaspers and tainted for a while by Heidegger, was more than the card-castle of neologisms that passed for philosophy in Sartre, was closer to the humanism of Kant (for ever moving between Newton and Rousseau ('the wonder at the starry heavens above *and* the moral law within').

Return to *The Origins*

One step forward, two steps back. *The Origins of Totalitarianism*, her first published book, looks the most systematic, but it is not. Part One on 'Antisemitism' and Part Two on 'Imperialism' are somewhat loosely connected to Part Three on 'Totalitarianism', which contained her basic concern, our common burden of failure and guilt: how the Holocaust could ever have happened. She saw this as not necessarily a unique event over the whole sweep of human history in terms of numbers (she was irritated at arguments that treated it 'as a Jewish possession'), but as unique horror and shame for our times in that it negated, came near to destroying, the liberal hopes of progress ascendant in Europe and America before the First World War. Not that she thought these liberal ideas unflawed, as we will see, even if they could not be held responsible for what happened in the camps simply because of their alleged 'emptiness', or by their deification of the self-contained individual (in some strained sense 'lonely' or 'anomic') – as some conservative and even a few socialist theorists maintained. Her explanation begins with the breakdown of liberal expectations of a rational and peaceful international order. The First World War, she argued, smashed the old system, whatever its causes, profound or contingent. The idea of total war could become applied to social change. And the Great War released two irrational demonic-like forces destroying civic structures and rational expectations, especially in Germany: mass unemployment and hyper-inflation. The peace settlement was based on nationalism rather than constitutionalism and, in turbulent conditions, nationalism could easily turn to racialism as scapegoats were sought for economic and political failure. Racialism and anti-Semitism explained much (not all) of what then happened, why there was the drive to exterminate hated and scapegoat minorities, and one particularly large minority, not just in Germany.

Part of her bold explanation has led to misunderstanding. She was not saying that English, French, Belgian or even German imperialism was a direct cause of Nazism, but that, first, the dream of an imposed universality created a new type and scale of thinking (she quoted Cecil Rhodes, saying that he 'dreamed in centuries and thought in continents'); and, second, such incidents as the Congo massacres and exploitation to death showed that a contempt for human life could coexist with modernity, or more subtly and terribly, that such lives were thought not to be human. It then became 'proved' to the Nazi racialists in the extermination camps (no longer mere concentration camps) that Jews were not human: for they did not revolt, they dug their own graves, and individuals when degraded and rendered utterly desperate lost all mutual care and sociability which, to her, is the very mark of humanity.

Part of the 'totalitarian thesis' was, of course, the perception that there was something grimly in common between Hitlerism and Stalinism. She was not the first to have this thought, and was a little cavalier not to have noted (or even noticed perhaps) that certain intellectuals and political writers, all outside the academy, had had this dark thought even in the 1930s: notably Borkenau, Gide, Koestler, Malraux, Orwell and Silone. Certainly the book is gravely unbalanced between a detailed treatment of Germany and the generalized and sketchy treatment of Russia. But the thesis was sound in one vital respect. She could deal with the seeming rationality of the irrational by invoking, in a special sense, the concept of ideology: how crazy ideas of the gutter or the library desk-top could become state policy in both regimes. Never before had two sets of ideas which claimed to be comprehensive and predictive explanations of all human conduct become state policy. And there were only the two ideologies, both modern: the ideology of racial determinism and of economic determinism. All other purported ideologies (better to use another word, say 'doctrines') were in fact, however good or bad (thank God, or common sense), partial. Some reject this 'partiality', others accept it as part of the good plurality of existence. As she wrote in the first edition:

> While the totalitarian regimes are thus resolutely and cynically emptying the world of the only thing that makes sense to the utilitarian expectations of common sense, they impose upon it at the same time a kind of supersense which the ideologies always meant when they claimed to have found the key to history or the answer to the riddles of the universe. Over and above the senselessness of totalitarian society is enthroned the ridiculous supersense of its ideological superstition. Ideologies are harmless, uncritical and arbitrary opinions only as long as they are not believed in seriously. Once their claim to total validity is taken literally they become the nuclei of logical systems in which, as in the systems of paranoiacs, everything follows comprehensibly and even compulsorily once the first premise is accepted. The insanity of such systems lies not only in their first premise but in the very logicality with which they are constructed. The curious logicality of all isms, their simple-minded trust in the survival value of stubborn devotion without regard for specific, varying factors, already harbours the first germs of the totalitarian contempt for reality and factuality.[5]

Both Margaret Canovan and I have argued that *The Origins of Totalitarianism*, for all its faults, and its bold but discomforting and alarming – not only to the empiricist – leaps from history to sociology to philosophy, and its mixture of factuality and speculation, is still her key work, possibly her master work. It is a magisterial if untidy mixture of deep passion and cool analysis;

and many or most of her other works are like huge footnotes to resolve difficulties left behind in the post-war urgency and immediacy of its exposition.[6]

Political man

The Human Condition is then the clearest account of her political philosophy, of how political action is the absolute antithesis of totalitarian systems. But it is also an account of the decay of that tradition. Once there was the Greco-Roman idea of citizenship as the highest attribute of human excellence, free men acting together in concerted policies reached by public debate. (And in our times women too, of course; but she did not labour the point, nor see the source as tainted by the age-old gender ostracism.) To her the essence of the human condition is the *vita activa*, where citizens interact, not the *vita contemplativa* of the philosophers or the religious, still less the view of man as *animal laborans*, the mere creature of necessity. We must *labour* to stay alive, but there is *work* too which she defined, leaning too much on a special definition which, if it works at all, only appears to work in English and German, as things that we make with our hands to last as if for their own sake, not simply to consume out of biological necessity. This distinction is far from clear. Works of art can obviously both be made and certainly traded as consumer goods, and can go out of fashion very quickly. Think of what Thorstein Veblen once had to say about 'conspicuous consumption' and class differentiation. But the important thing is that she saw political action as part of the *vita activa*, not of the necessity of labour. Political acts are free acts, they are spontaneous interactions, their values lie in themselves. To act freely is good in itself, keeping in mind that political action is always in concert with others. And her sharp distinction between labour and work enables her to see (whatever words are used) that both Marxism and *laissez-faire* economics are variant restless and illimitable forms of worship or sanctification of labour for its own sake, rather than limiting its space to what is necessary for a fully human life of action in the public realm, creative work, friendships and contemplation – all higher values than mere labour. (In terms of her definitions, the present British Conservative Party could well be called the Labour Party, except that New Labour might see no need to change its name either.)

She attacks modern liberalism for overvaluing the realm of privacy as against the public realm, just as she spoke carefully of civil rights rather than individual rights. To be protected by law from state intervention never lasts unless individuals are willing and able to busy themselves in the making of those laws. Her *Eichmann in Jerusalem: A Report on the Banality of Evil* angered her fellow Jews partly by a misunderstanding that she meant that evil was 'banal', rather than that evil men acted not flamboyantly but in a bureaucratic mode to organize mass killing; but also by making sadly the historical point that there was virtually no tradition of political action in the stateless people that might have led to resistance, and her seemingly heartless view that while resistance was impossible it should have been attempted precisely to demonstrate human freedom and dignity in defiance even of necessity, somewhat as the stoic faces death. She recounted that Cicero held that a free man if captured and enslaved with no possibility of escape, then should commit suicide – the last free action possible, when possible – rather than see his humanity inevitably debased. The religious may say that there is a always a soul that should not take its own life, though a rationally calculated sacrifice likely to save another is always permissible. But Arendt's free-thinking or even pagan existentialism saw our very sense of unique and individual human existence as being in social relationships: how we interact with others, others with each of us. If these conditions of sociability are removed, we cease to be human. So we should at least assert our freedom while we can, even hopelessly, perhaps to set an example; but we cannot ask to be sure that the brave example will be remembered, therefore honoured or possibly even effective in the future. She was not a utilitarian. It is a hard doctrine to swallow, or for many to understand. But to try to make an ethic out of the contrary is even harder. Any moral duty of action or resistance that depends on guarantees of probable success is a poor defence in desperate times.

Thus though she is often thought of as a modern Aristotelian, she rejects his teleology: even a polis with well-ordered institutions will not necessarily increase in betterment, so much depends on free human action (and sometimes accident, Machiavelli would add – say Caesare Borgia's sudden death or, for example, John Smith's); and she rejects what is perhaps his instrumentalism: that free political action in the long run ordinarily succeeds (he might have noticed,

under the pikes of Macedonia, that it didn't). She astonishingly sees
political action as valuable in itself. Quite simply I think we should
live with that astonishment of delight, as when faced with works of
art. We do not always say 'what for?' or 'how much is it?'[7]

So she stands in a tradition of classical republicanism but has deep
worries that this is being eaten away by consumerism, and even
representative government can be an invitation to people to leave
their politics to others, or to see politics as simply a matter of voting
in elections. Like Jefferson she worried that the formal constitution,
even of the United States, left too little space for political
participation. She viewed referenda, for instance, as inherently
manipulative, not especially democratic, ways of containing,
managing and narrowing debate rather than encouraging and
broadening it. Ernest Gellner once expressed this more simply and
scathingly as 'the binary view of politics'. He proclaimed himself 'at
least a trinitarian, or else there is always some excluded middle';
well, say 'other', not necessarily 'middle'. Therefore, a rash appendix
was added to an edition of *The Origins* just after the Hungarian
Revolution, which saw hope in what was the old utopia of Proudhon
socialism, workers' councils rather than representative democracy.
And some topical essays showed interest and some sympathy with
the student radicalism of the 1960s, but only because they were
challenging 'thoughtless' institutions, that is institutions simply
carrying on without thought as to what was their real purpose, or
what they could do better. She quickly saw that most of the students
knew no better.

So the Left could not claim her. But conservatives could not
either. If she showed a deep understanding of the strength of
tradition, it was often in a pessimistic mode – how difficult it was
by thought and reason to invent new institutions. And to her the
American Revolution was a revolution, not just a rhetorical term for
a war of colonial independence: it had been the 'world's best hope'
indeed for civic republicanism, perhaps the 'last hope'. If she could
sound like Oakeshott for a moment when she argued that the idea of
starting with a blueprint and putting it into pratice was
preposterous, it was not because tradition determines or is always
the major factor conditioning human conduct and, therefore,
political invention, let alone revolution, is impossible; but precisely
because the invention of new political institutions is needed.
However, for them to last they must arise from a plurality of

political actors debating among themselves publicly until they can reach a consensus to act together.

She can give some comfort to contemporary communitarians or radical pluralists, so long as the community works with a political tradition, both internally and externally, and so long as the individual has the conscious courage to act alone should the community seek, except in times of dire and immediate emergency, to stifle public debate. In *The Human Condition* she remarks that no thing in nature is more unlike another thing and more unique than one man is unlike another, but that nothing is more like another either. But what most generally can resolve this metaphysical paradox is not, say, a belief that we are all children of one father, but that we can all act like, indeed be, citizens.

Always in the life of the citizen and the life of the mind, the greatest fault is quite simply not to think what we are doing and to think that we cannot think otherwise and then act otherwise. Her own position is never quite clear. Certainly anti-Platonist, there are no final solutions or single rational imperatives of any kind. But there are some moral limits and imperatives on *how* we should act in politics as well as acting politically – these she seems to draw from Kant and Jaspers, a refined modern humanism. Canovan well says that 'it is not so much a position as an internal dialogue, continually going back and forth between alternative standpoints'. In a literal sense this is free thinking. Perhaps this makes her rather careless of her philosophic presuppositions in essays on current problems, although in other essays she can parade them somewhat pretentiously. In more than one place, however, she expresses her preference for the 'political writer', who has had some experience of the political world, rather than 'the political philosopher'. She herself took on the role of a 'public intellectual' that got her into many scrapes when activists, unfamiliar with her writings, could not understand her special use of terms (she could not always start each time again as if from the beginning). But what was always important to her was the thinking mind offering reasoned justifications for actions based on reflection. And 'justifications' could never be (to get close to the present) mere soundbites or appeals to self-interest or a politics dominated by unwillingness to pay for any public improvements. Thinking to her is, quite simply, the antithesis of thoughtlessness, accepting things as they are, speaking, acting or voting as we are expected to, by order, by custom or appeals to personal loyalty. Yet freedom is not breaking from tradition as such, whether in a society or a party, but is understanding a tradition before attempting any new action. If radical breaks are needed, they are then more likely to be successful. We do not reach final conclusions, but by public debate, citizen's activity and the dispersal of power (she sees the very concept of 'sovereignty' as inimical to freedom) a plurality of voices can achieve not The Good, but always some betterment – not necessarily continual betterment, mind; our 'dark times' have seen quite as many downs as ups. Colonial liberation, indeed, but then new tyrannies. Mass enfranchisement and much economic progress, but still dehumanizing poverty and dehumanizing indifference to it, growing consumerism and neglect of the opportunities of citizenship. Is it her possibly too idealistic and demanding concept of citizenship and human nature that makes me stress her pessimism? I think not. There are many reasons for pessimism if we think about what is happening to trivialize the tradition and to corrupt the institutions of free politics. It is clear how worried she would be when, as I write, the leaders of both main parties in two great countries have been bending much of their energies in election campaigns into persuading their colleagues not to debate matters of public interest except by rote. Political parties and pressure groups have now too often developed as devices for limiting debate rather than encouraging it. Arendt might see great dangers in this. But she certainly can help us to put contingent events (not to use words like 'trivial' or 'thoughtless' again) in a broader context of the nature of our civilization – to see, in William Morris's homely words, 'what it is around us'. At least she helps us to struggle when we sometimes wonder what good it does to look the facts squarely in the face. We should read or reread her, both for memory of what is lost and some hope for what still could be, as we suffer the grotesque, distractive and trivializing plans to celebrate the millennium.

Notes

1. Elizabeth Young-Bruel's biography *Hannah Arendt: For Love of the World*, London, Yale University Press, 1982, is excellent both on thought and life. Arendt would, of course, have denied the disjunction, up to a point.
2. The commentator at an Arendt symposium at the American Political

Science Association's 1996 annual conference, George Kateb, who himself has written well and not uncritically about her (*Hannah Arendt: Politics, Conscience and Evil*, Oxford, Martin Robertson, 1984) demanded a five-year moratorium and complained that all kinds of people and causes, for which she had little sympathy or to which she gave little attention, such as environmentalists and feminists, anarchists and New Right conservatives, were now trying to claim her by arcane deconstruction of obscure or peripheral texts. Canovan (see below) cites 74 articles in her bibliography of 1991, and there are now eleven books in English alone.

3. Margaret Canovan, *Hannah Arendt: A Reinterpretation of Her Political Thought*, Cambridge, Cambridge University Press, 1992. Differing viewpoints can be found in M. A. Hill (ed.), *Hannah Arendt: The Recovery of the Public World*, New York, St Martin's Press, 1979; Bhikhu Parekh, *Hannah Arendt and the Search for a New Political Philosophy*, London, Macmillan, 1991; Gisela T. Kaplan and Clive E. Kessler (eds.), *Hannah Arendt: Thinking, Judging, Freedom*, London, Allen & Unwin, 1989; Phillip Hansen, *Hannah Arendt: Politics, History and Citizenship*, Oxford, Polity, 1993; Lewis P. Hinchman and Sandra K. Hinchman, *Hannah Arendt: Critical Essays*, Albany, State University of New York Press, 1994; and to mention only one article, Judith Sklar, 'Hannah Arendt as Pariah', *Partisan Review* 50 (1983), pp. 64–7.

4. Elsewhere I have argued that while the concept does not work descriptively – no 'totalitarian' system has ever exercised total control over society – yet the ideological attempt to do so was real and accounts for most of the ruthlessness, and lack of normal political and human restraints of Nazism and Bolshevism, not to mention Maoism and Pol Pot's Khmer Rouge. See my 'On Rereading *The Origins of Totalitarianism*' in Hill, *op. cit.*, pp. 27–47.

5. *Origins*, first edn, New York, Harcourt Brace, 1951, pp. 431–2.

6. Canovan, *op. cit.*, pp. 6–7 and 17–23.

7. As notably Ronald Beiner has pointed out, she sees political judgement, even action, as much closer to Kant's aesthetics than to his concept of practical reason; see Beiner's *Political Judgement*, London, Methuen, 1983, which arose out of his Oxford D.Phil., 'Hannah Arendt and Political Judgement'.

CHAPTER 18

On Isaiah Berlin

Isaiah Berlin, most famous English academic intellectual of the post-war era, outstanding lecturer, peerless conversationalist and superlative essayist, has died at the age of 88. His career began in pure philosophy but he became interested in the history of ideas, especially those claiming to offer a comprehensive view of human purposes. He had a genius in dazzling lectures and essays for expounding empathetically the plausibility of such ideas and evoking the character of their principal exponents, but always with determination to expose the danger to freedom and human diversity of all such ideologies that claim to have, or be leading us towards, a single goal or truth. To Berlin the plurality of human beliefs has to be accepted. Philosophy no more than brute force can resolve conflicts of values. His pluralism was not an uncritical exaltation of variety, still less the postmodern cynicism of 'anything goes', rather he recognized the recurrent pain, at times tragedy, of knowing that whatever values we pursue always have some cost to other values and often to other people. To be humane and tolerant and to act honourably we must both know our own limitations and appreciate the almost boundless oddity of others. Greater equality, he would say, may well be worth having, but it will be at the price – 'pray do not deceive yourselves' – of liberties significant to others, perhaps

An obituary in the *Guardian*, 7 November 1997, with some minor cuts restored.

even to ourselves if we stop to think.

He was born in Riga, Latvia, on 6 June 1909, the only child of Marie Berlin and Mendel Berlin, a prosperous timber merchant. His parents were secular Jews but his grandparents were pious Chabad Hasidim, the sect now known as the Lubavich. He grew up speaking Russian and German. The family moved in 1915 from Riga to Andreapol, and on to Petrograd in 1917, so he had vivid memories of the streets, the chaos, the elation and the fear of both the February revolution and the Bolshevik coup d'état of November. In 1921 his parents, finding conditions intolerable for them, left for England. The young Isaiah was put to school at St Paul's. He perfected his school English, he studied classics and picked up French as well, achieving a linguistic ease and proficiency that was to mark him out from most of his Oxford contemporaries when he read philosophy at Corpus Christi College. In 1932 he won a prize fellowship to All Souls, where he remained until he became a fellow of New College in 1938.

He quickly became renowned as a great talker in that famously self-important small world. His conversation bubbled and fizzed at astonishing speed with literary and philosophical speculation and anecdotes illustrative of this and that, but never plain anecdotes, always anecdotes deftly embroidered on some theme and festooned with references to Russian, German and French authors of years gone by, often quite unfamiliar to his listeners. His promise as a philosopher was clear in that he became one of a small circle, usually no more than four or five, convened by the formidable A. L. Austin and including A. J. Ayer, who met to discuss the purest problems of the new philosophy at the highest possible level. Are there *a priori* truths? What is the logic of counter-factual statements? What is personal identity? What is perception? Can we have knowledge of other minds?

'Discuss' is too weak a term for the intellectual violence when one of the group would assert a proposition, and the others would test it by trying to tear it to pieces by all means – a kind of group therapy in reverse. A. J. Ayer still used the same technique in his seminar at University College London after the Second World War, which by accident I attended. For how could Pamela possibly have a lover if her lover was not a philosopher too? Austin's seminar must also have been more like a sect than a seminar. When some bold idiot asked Ayer 'what is philosophy?', he replied, as Austin would have done, 'why, what we are doing, of course – philosophizing'. It was an activity, a *Ding an sich* – publication was almost irrelevant, a vulgarization of the need for instant rebuttal and reformulation. Berlin stayed with the circle until 1939, but after the war he decided that he had had enough. In his essay on 'Austin and the Early Beginnings of Oxford Philosophy' he recounts with good humour how it began to dawn on him that this esoteric activity, while exciting and pleasant, had its drawbacks: if knowledge could not be published and last a while, was it knowledge at all?

So very, very English he sounded, as was Oxford philosophy itself (Wittgenstein notwithstanding, and he always referred to Hume as English), yet he never forgot, or let it be forgotten, that he was deeply conscious of Russian and Jewish roots and concerns. Even during the time of apparent total immersion in that circle where logical positivism or linguistic analysis were the only alternatives and the history of ideas a total irrelevance, he wrote for the Home University Library a marvellously lucid and judicious *Karl Marx: His Life and Environment* (1939), almost the first remotely objective account of what Marx had said back then, who he was, why he said it, his Hegelian roots and Jewish background. This short book was, austerely and provocatively, about Marx and ignored Marxism and the international Communist movement. The critique of determinism was clear and bold but not laboured. He always had the good manners to enjoy unlikely company and, as it were, to bring out, not to put down or caricature, interesting people (living or dead) whose ideas he thought quite wrong-headed.

With unusual imagination the Ministry of Information sent him to New York in 1941 to show hesitant American intellectuals the honest face of an intellectual who was a belligerent English patriot, fiercely anti-Nazi but never anti-German, indeed even more than a little Zionist, which presumably helped. The Foreign Office soon brought him to the embassy in Washington where he wrote weekly despatches on the state of American opinion in his vigorous, flowing, complex long sentences, as if dictated at great speed with perfect control (someone said 'like Gibbon on roller-skates'). Churchill said they were some of his favourite war-time reading. But, alas, the famous tale is *not* true that when Roosevelt asked Churchill whom he might like to meet in Washington to relax with after dinner, that Churchill said 'Berlin', meaning Irving, and was as astonished as Isaiah himself to have the false counter-factual Berlin produced. 'It was not quite like that', he would say. However, something like that had occurred in London. Stories travel. But he made many friends among the Ivy League liberals who at that time dominated the State Department.

Before returning to Oxford, he served for a few months at the end of 1945 in the embassy at Moscow. There he met semi-clandestinely Boris Pasternak and the great poet Anna Akhmatova, and later wrote a memorable and moving account of their conversations about Russian literature and the condition of writers under Stalinism, indeed under Stalin's own eye in both cases, Stalin torn between his Slavophilism and his paranoia. Akhmatova was to attach an extraordinary, in her isolation almost a crazed, importance to their meeting: thus art and intelligence could rise above political conflict and oppression universally. And it affected Berlin greatly. To his natural gaiety, literary facility and pyrotechnic intellectuality was added a great moral seriousness.

When he returned to Oxford he did publish a handful of articles and notes on technical philosophical subjects, but his interests quickly changed. He had reread Tolstoy's *War and Peace* and plunged deeply into the Russian novelists, poets and social thinkers of the mid-nineteenth century.

> Their approach seemed to me essentially moral: they were concerned most deeply with what was responsible for injustice, oppression, falsity in human relations, imprisonment whether by stone walls or conformism – unprotesting submission to man-made yokes – moral blindness, egoism, cruelty, humiliation, servility, poverty, helplessness, despair, on the part of so many. In short, they were concerned with the nature of these experiences and their roots in the human condition.

Thereafter he turned his back on analytical philosophy, but with a mind sharpened by those ultra-intelligent mental exercises, he evoked the dilemmas inherent in great or hitherto obscure but interesting figures in the history of ideas. He generally called this 'political philosophy, which is but ethics applied to society'.

When Anna Akhmatova had told him everything she could about herself personally as well as her views on all great questions, as people will when they fear they will not survive and will be obliterated in memory, she asked Berlin who he was. He tells us he replied in kind, but not, of course, what he replied. He is the least autobiographical of writers in any psychological sense. But by then he must surely have known or suspected that his grandfathers, an uncle, an aunt and three cousins had all perished in the holocaust in Riga. That may have helped make the old ways seem parochial, deeply though he loved Oxford, college life and Englishness. He married in 1956 a most beautiful and rich woman, of Russian and French parentage, Aline de Gunzbourg.

The following year he succeeded the socialist historian, G. D. H. Cole, as Chichele Professor of Social and Political Theory while remaining a fellow of All Souls, to where he had been elevated or translated from New College in 1950. His inaugural lecture, 'Two Concepts of Liberty', made him instantly famous and provoked lasting debate among intellectuals on both sides of the Atlantic. Many called it 'a classic restatement of English liberalism'. But that was a two-edged judgement for few of us then knew anything of the more pessimistic tones of Russian nineteenth-century liberalism, something quite different from J. S. Mill's optimistic rationalism. But three things about its manner became the hallmark of all his writing. He could be and was read by both academics and general intellectuals – he joked against himself that he was 'a general intellectual, by analogy to "general domestic"; will tackle anything', for he affably ignored disciplinary boundaries. He combined rhetoric with analytical rigour in an unusual but characteristic way. He was always excited by ideas but invariably attached them to persons, rarely if ever to periods, movements or general tendencies. He translated Turgenev's *First Love* and later *A Month in the Country*. The melancholy tone of old Russian liberalism appealed to him more than the English liberal tradition still wedded to a belief in inevitable progress.

Essays flowed out and honours flowed in thick and fast. He was a director of the Royal Opera House, Covent Garden, from 1951 to 1965, then from 1974 to 1987, tolerantly suppressing his dislike of Wagner but not his excessive enthusiasm for early rather than late Verdi, and was a trustee of the National Gallery from 1975 to 1985. Through his friendship with Sir Isaac Wolfson, he was virtually the founder as well as the first president of Wolfson College from 1966 to 1975. He was elected to the British Academy in 1957, the same year he was knighted, and was its president from 1974 to 1978. For all his fame and authority, he had a certain amiable naivety. The story is told that when he received his CBE in 1946, as his turn in the line came the King said, as was his custom, 'I think we have met before'; but when he took that as a conversational opener, he was abruptly cut short by an equerry, guiding him because he was almost blind as his thick glasses has been removed in case the ribbon pulled them off: 'Bend your neck and stop talking'. These were two things he never, to his honour, otherwise did.

In 1971 came the Order of Merit. He willingly served on numerous time-consuming scholarship, fellowship and award committees in Britain, the USA and Israel, enjoying meeting the rising stars of each generation, asking them searching, interesting questions – and often, if they hesitated for a second, generously answering himself. He held 23 honorary doctorates (including Harvard, Yale, Oxford, London, Jerusalem and Tel Aviv) and gained several great prizes including the Jerusalem Prize for services to freedom, the Erasmus Prize for the history of ideas, and was the first to gain the Agnelli Ethics Prize in 1987.

His bibliography is confused since he rewrote speeches and essays for different occasions, and published some in different collections with varying titles. But basically there are four books: *Karl Marx, Four Essays on Liberty, Vico and Herder* and *The Magus of the North*, and six volumes of essays edited by his friend Henry Hardy (trying heroically, like Zuleika Dobson's maid packing her trunk, 'to make chaos cosmic!'), and also in 1997 a fine anthology of 'the best of Berlin', *The Proper Study of Mankind*. Letters have been prepared for publication as well as an authorized biography by Michael Ignatieff, but are to appear only after his death (*Isaiah Berlin: A Life*, 1998).

He spoke with astounding rapidity and in that very low-pitched Oxford accent, swallowing many vowels, eliding like a Frenchman, not the high-pitched drawling Oxford. American audiences often found him difficult to follow because of both the rapidity and the number of different names and ideas compounded in complex and unscripted but syntactically perfect sentences, always exciting to follow – what would come next, could he possibly regain the main subject, spoken two minutes and twenty dependent clauses ago, with an object sufficient for climax not bathos? Yes, always; often to massed sighs of relief and admiration. He was the most exciting and famously extempore of lecturers. I could never hear anything but Oxford in his voice, but the mother of an American friend, an uneducated woman born in Belarus, took a phone call from him one day, and calling her son remarked that a man with a very English accent was on the phone, 'but he was born in Russia, Mel'. It was always there, fortunately.

He loved England as sometimes only émigrés can and he appeared so very English, and it was 'England' almost too specifically; he never spoke or wrote of Great Britain or the United Kingdom, and had no interest in Scottish, Welsh or Irish literature. Well, he was aware that the Scottish enlightenment of David Hume and Adam Smith was part of the history of British empiricism, but on neither did he write. There were glancing references to Oakeshott, but no essay on Burke. So very English, in this sense, but also so naturally cosmopolitan, always introducing forgotten or misunderstood continental figures, especially those who had thought on a continental scale. Only large themes interested him, even in obscure authors; but he was endlessly kind to individuals. A young man received a letter as short as this: 'I have not the pleasure of knowing you, but I have read and admired your book and I will shortly say so in the *Observer*'. The pride and delight that gave me was only mildly diminished by his not actually getting round to reviewing it for two years, and then in a series on 'Neglected Books' in a dying monthly. He always had so much on the go, including a vast correspondence. But to call him workaholic would be quite wrong. What to others was work was to him pleasure. Leisure to him was good argument in good company. But the speed and restlessness of his thought made the essay his métier, not the book, never the monograph. Only his short book on Marx was other than an extended essay.

Most of his essays read as if they were dictated. Conclusions were not always as clear as they might have been had he written more slowly and with difficulty, but then the energy, facility, enthusiasm and the startling bursts of free-association, bringing unlikely figures together, might have been lost. There is a recording in the US National Sound Archive of the Mellon Lectures he gave at the Kennedy Centre, Washington, in which such runs and bursts are punctuated by the kind of applause that striking a six, or a home run, evokes from an excited crowd. For instance in his 'Joseph de Maistre and the Origins of Fascism' he remarked on 'the peculiar characteristic of a time of transition between sharply divergent outlooks, of which such psychologically complex figures as Goethe and Herder, Schleiermacher and Friedrich Schlegel, Fichte and Schiller, Benjamin Constant and Chateaubriand, Saint-Simon and

Stendal, Tsar Alexander of Russia and indeed Napoleon himself are typical representatives'. Useless to cry in the voice of Oxford philosophy, 'wait a moment, let us unpack quite what you mean by "peculiar" and "time of transition"' or to ask 'are all these twinnings apt?', for he then gallops on to a brilliant evocation of the mysterious man of destiny myth, the *'l'homme fatal'* as 'conveyed by the celebrated painting by Baron Gros, now in the Louvre, of Napoleon at Eylau'. To him Carlyle's great man theory of history was tosh, indeed dangerous tosh; yet there was value in being reminded that some great figures had altered the course of history, even if not always for the better.

So brilliantly evocative, but often at the end of the day so much of his writing, like that 'celebrated painting', is dramatic characterization: a cascade of evocative proper names and adjectives, but not explanation. The twists and turns of 'the crooked timber of humanity' (a phrase of Kant's that he used as the title of a book of studies) are, he held, perhaps not capable of explanation, in any scientific or logical sense, only of understanding. He is called a historian of ideas, but he showed little interest in either the pre-history of the ideas he discussed nor the sociology of knowledge: the when and how ideas emerge from obscurity to centre stage. Weber and Mannheim interested him not at all. The history of ideas is now a very specialized and method-conscious scholarly discipline, and its adepts look at Berlin with a mixture of admiration and exasperation. He wrote for intellectuals more than disciplinary scholars. What he did do with such unique brilliance was to evoke the plausibility of ideas, especially those that threaten freedom, and relate them to the character of particular thinkers. He was humanist through and through, sometimes in the almost reductionist sense that individuals alone move or personify events, but also in the moral sense that it is the happiness or dignity of individuals that counts, not the pride and power of nations or ethnic groups.

He was a Zionist, indeed, but not because he was Jewish, rather because Jews were persecuted and thus needed, contingently not in principle, the protection of a national home. He had a darker view of human nature than liberals who thought that good intentions and international organizations could achieve a peaceful coexistence in the Middle East without a most unfortunate price to be paid. We cannot live without group identities, hence his interest in Herder and the German romantics, but individuals can and sometimes should take on other identities, or challenge the dominant beliefs of the group in the name of freedom.

All this made this larger-than-life man, or this mortal Isaiah, kindly and helpful to young scholars: there were many, many such letters as the one to me. Some colleagues shook their heads that all his geese were swans, but he knew when to encourage, when to cut down or when to turn his massive back. He exemplified Ernest Gellner's maxim 'Social tolerance always, intellectual tolerance never'.

He had some blind spots. 'We seem to agree on most things. But I cannot share your enthusiasm for Baron de Jouvenal and Miss Arendt. Tell me what she is saying. Put it in a simple proposition.' 'That's a tall order. She is a rather complex thinker.' 'Precisely. There is nothing there to put simply. Fairy gold, Crick, fairy gold. Metaphysical free-association.' Occasionally he spoke as if his name did for argument. The *Observer* once had a foolish Christmas feature to designate the most over-rated writer of the year. Other contributors gave a name with a sentence or two of explanatory denigration. But Berlin simply pronounced ex cathedra: 'Hannah Arendt'.

His famous essay 'The Hedgehog and the Fox' on Tolstoy's view of history quoted a fragment from the Greek that 'the fox knows many things, but the hedgehog knows one big thing'. Many critics and friends firmly see Berlin as foxy; but if his medium was the essay, recurring through them all were two really big hedgehoging themes: his defence of freedom and his account of pluralism. In 'Two Concepts of Liberty', he famously distinguished between negative and positive senses, and argued that to seek to go beyond negative liberty – that is freedom from restraint – into positive liberty – that is freedom to achieve some positive good – is politically dangerous, morally dubious and even logically self-contradictory. Positive liberty is when I feel more free when I know the truth ('the truth shall set you free'), or am serving a just cause ('Oh God . . . whose service is perfect freedom'), or am relieving others from suffering. He simply pointed out that all these 'freedoms' involve either restrictions on others, or a certainty that the values of others or their views of truth are false, as in Rousseau's 'forcing people to be free'. There may be good reasons for restricting the freedom of others, or putting ourselves under the constraint of others; but let us recognize, he said, that to do so is not to increase freedom, otherwise the concept becomes simply a synonym for justified restraint. Freedom is a fundamental human value, underlying choice, personality, civilization and the possibility of true know-ledge; but it is not the only value. It may be right and just that I should be taxed so that you do not starve; but do not say that either of us is then positively free, otherwise freedom to debate the justice, the degree and the results of such actions is denied.

If he was a libertarian, it was in the sense that the protection of negative freedom is a necessary condition of any just social order; but it is not a sufficient condition, as the school of Hayek and the market liberals tried to argue. Like Popper, his views on social policy were pragmatic, though both were misrepresented by socialist critics. It took a long time for British Marxists to realize that bourgeois liberties *are* liberties, and that social problems and conflicts of values have neither unique nor complete solutions. 'Where does he stand?', some of us asked impatiently, some contemptuously. But at the time he was writing any British variations on freedom and justice paled into minor questions compared with the reality of the denial of anything sensibly called freedom by Soviet power; and Nazi marchers in the 1930s as well as German Communists had cried '*Freiheit!*'. To Berlin it was not the business of political philosophers to endorse one party rather than another, but to defend a strong but minimal (or strong because minimal) conception of freedom. But perhaps this was a little austere and closer than was often noticed to analytical philosophy, in its weakness as well as its strength, than to history. He was interested in the nature of freedom, and passionate to defend it against persecution, obvious or covert; but had no interest in the social conditions of freedom or in the history of citizenship, as in the work of those such as John Pocock, Quentin Skinner and many others who in the last decades have revived the idea of civic republicanism and traced its history. He was a great and definitive critic of single-truth systems of thought, what he called systematic ideologies; but with their threat diminished, some of his finest writings may lose the bite of relevance that once they had.

More lasting will be his understanding of pluralism, but it is not a comfortable one. He was not a relativist. Some values are universal, like freedom and science; and some value systems threaten or distort both. Nonetheless we live in a world of diverse values, not all of them equally pleasing for good reason, but which we can, with knowledge and empathy, understand; and too often we have to choose or compromise between them. In 'The Pursuit of the Ideal' he said:

> The notion of the perfect whole, the ultimate solution, in which all good things coexist, seems to me to be not merely unattainable – that is a truism – but conceptually incoherent; I do not know what is meant by a harmony of this kind. Some among the Great Goods cannot live together. That is a conceptual truth. We are doomed to choose, and every choice may entail an inseparable loss. Happy are they who live under a discipline that they accept without question . . . ; or those who have arrived at clear and unshakeable convictions about what to do and what to be that brook no possible doubt. I can only say that those who rest on such comfortable beds of dogma are victims of forms of self-induced myopia, blinkers that may make for contentment, but not for understanding of what it is to be human.

John Gray has well named this 'agonistic liberalism': the *agon*, the conflicts of character seen in Greek tragic drama as inherent and perpetual. Noel Annan saw Berlin's work as exhibiting 'the truest and most moving interpretations of life that my generation made'. Berlin's memory of Pasternak quoting Heine could be turned to himself: 'I may not deserve to be remembered as a poet, but surely as a soldier in the battle for human freedom.'

CHAPTER 19

The Legacy of Laski

None of us who heard him lecture will ever forget the experience nor have thought to hear the like again. But did the printed page or his political influence ever live up to his power at the podium? Not only those who did not hear him have doubted that. Now at last we are able to see in perspective and context the true stature of Laski with, like the portrait Cromwell ordered from Lely, 'roughnesses, pimples, warts, and everything'. Both books quote Max Beloff, no friend of Laski at all, calling the period 1920 to 1950, 'The Age of Laski'. Both books are well written, a pleasure to read as biographies, scholarly and judicious – if in somewhat different ways. And amazingly, considering the contentiousness of the man and the period, there is no substantial disagreement between them either in their assessment or, as far as I can see, in their accounts of particular events. I hope they can respect each other's work; that is not always the case with biographers.

That two real biographies should appear at once is neither tragedy nor farce: Harold Laski was born in 1893. These books are the centennial celebration, forcing on the London School of Economics (LSE), where Laski taught from 1920 when he left

A review in *Political Quarterly*, October–December 1994, of Isaac Kramnick and Barry Sheerman, *Harold Laski: A Life on the Left* (Hamish Hamilton, 1993) and Michael Newman, *Harold Laski: A Political Biography* (Macmillan, 1993).

Harvard until his death in 1950, a reluctant and minimal notice of its most famous or notorious teacher: an evening organized by the Government Students' Society with a platform of three voluble old Laski students, and one public lecture by Isaac Kramnick with Professor Kenneth Minogue in the chair, not the Director. The memory of Laski must seem the same kind of incubus to Dr Ashworth as the living Laski had seemed to William Beveridge (and also to President Lowell of Harvard) in the main academic business of raising money from business. ('Seems, madam! nay, it is'.) The wheel has gone full circle. Who talks of progress now? In some ways we are back in the 1930s. So it was modestly brave or shrewdly politic for John Smith MP to give a reception for the book of his fellow MP, Barry Sheerman, and the Indian High Commissioner fielded on another night his Vice-President, a most thoughtful old Laski disciple. Bad luck for Professor Newman that Macmillan's publicity machine was, for a rare once, outplayed. And their price suggests a bad underestimating of both the book's merits and its potential readership.

Professor Kramnick of Cornell (who has written on Burke and on Paine) did the research on America, where Laski was almost as famous as in Britain. Barry Sheerman (whose idea it was) did the British digging, although he seems to have used a narrower range of contacts than Kramnick. Kramnick did the writing, and he contextualizes sadly but firmly like the good historian of ideas he is: 'Laski's life speaks to a lost world. If we are now living through what some see as the twilight of socialism, then Laski's life speaks to its morning.' But at times I think I hear the rumble of muffled drums, perhaps from Barry Sheerman (who just missed Laski at LSE), playing a cautious recall for intellectuals (those that are left) to come back to the Labour Party again, but after reading his book with its salutary secondary themes of the dangers of rocking the boat and the disappointments of hoping for direct, personal influence. Sometimes they beat the drum too hard. To get a small niggle off my chest, they exaggerate the role of Laski in the founding of this journal (true he had a finger in every pie) and they have the first two editors as Leonard Woolf and Kingsley Martin rather than William Robson and Martin). But the bigger niggle is that in their division of labour Laski's French connection, his intellectual affinity, visits, friends and fame are almost forgotten. Newman is far more aware of how deeply Laski was influenced by

French rationalism, enlightenment and *les philosophes*, even if he does not explore it biographically.

The one book is a full biography, and Laski's life is fascinating. The other is slightly mistitled: 'intellectual biography' might have better conveyed its strength and deliberate limit. Kramnick deals with Laski's ideas equally sensibly, but the very scale and chronology of full biography and political events makes it hard to grasp his ideas as a whole, scatters shrewd analysis throughout a wide wood. (And it is no help to have a nominalist indexer who knows names but not concepts.) In Newman the ideas, both academic and popular, come together in a thematic treatment that correlates well enough with understanding of the main events of Laski's life; so he never loses the wood for the trees and can make a clearer assessment of Laski as thinker. Those more interested in the history of ideas will turn to Newman and those more interested in the history of the Labour Party and the international socialist movement to Kramnick. But, of course, it was always Laski's claim that his politics derived from his ideas: that theory must relate to practice. This was always one respect in which his Marxism of the 1930s was only skin-deep, even if a thick and glowing skin. Ideas were not a product of material conditions: they are the principles that drive us on to try to reform those conditions. Oh, of course, as he was fond of saying, 'Men who live differently, think differently'; but his whole life testifies to his belief that some intellectuals can cut through the oppressive natural habitat of social conditioning, at least enough to see ahead or to create new relationships.

He was born, we all know, into a well-off and orthodox Manchester Jewish household. But few of us realized, until Kramnick and Sheerman's researches, just how wealthy and how orthodox. His father Nathan was a cotton king all right and a leader of the Manchester Jewish community with political influence. He found the dispossessed young Liberal Winston Churchill a Manchester seat to nurse in 1904 which he won in 1906. Churchill stayed at the house quite often, had met the precocious Harold who then *did* have access to Churchill in later times. Both biographers agree that in letters, conversation and lectures Laski often stretched the yarn wide, but never spun cloth from an empty spool. Lord Haldane, Mr Justice Holmes, Felix Frankfurter, Louis Brandeis, FDR himself, all enjoyed and sought Laski's company – even Baldwin and Attlee, for a time, found something in it. Canards at 'that liar Laski' (such as the late George Catlin launched) won't fly any more. (Alas that neither Roy Jenkins nor Roy Hattersley, reviewing Kramnick and Sheerman in the *Sunday Times* and the *Observer*, appeared to have reached or gone back to that part of the exposition.) The problem now appears to be more that of a story-teller's exuberance, or the highly embellished anecdote-from-life so typical of the pulpit or 'Thought for the Day'. Both biographers are understanding of Laski's half boastful, half didactic but always entertaining foibles, if, quite rightly, not wholly forgiving.

He broke from home spectacularly by eloping in 1911 at the age of eighteen with a gentile PT teacher called Frida who was eight years his senior. His parents saw him through Oxford on condition that they did not live together, something that they pragmatically accepted, mostly. From then on she was his constant support, it was a life-long love affair. Newman quotes him writing to Frida when she was over sixty (they wrote constantly whenever apart): 'I can't bear to think of what I might have been if I had not found you. As it is, after all these years, I feel with all more heart that I begin to love you afresh every day. And to have you believe in me is the rock on which I build my truth.' His dependence was deep, but also very practical, for in domestic matters, it emerges, he was always hopelessly impractical and unskilled, even by male standards of the day. The Wellsian 'new woman' had a lot to put up with when she fell in love, or took on a super-intelligent partner as a good cause.

But at first it was Frida who had an ideology, which he promptly adopted, whereas he had only had a voracious, eclectic intellec-tuality, based on the dangerous gift of being able to scan, comprehend and retain a page at a glance, as could Sidney Webb, Kingsley Martin and Denis Brogan. Frida's ideology was eugenics. Harold submitted a paper on 'The Scope of Eugenics' to *The Westminster Review* (once J. S. Mill's paper), which they published. Sir Francis Galton wrote to congratulate the unknown author, and was startled to find a seventeen-year-old Manchester Grammar School boy. 'My wonderful boy Jew, Laski by name, came here to tea', he wrote, 'the boy is simply beautiful . . . He is perfectly nice and quiet in his manners. Many prodigies fade, but this one seems to have stamina and purpose, and is not excitable, so he ought to make a mark.' He nearly made the wrong mark. Frida began to think that female emancipation could not wait on the long generational breeding processes of the Shavian intelligentsia at summer schools, so instead, following the celebrated breach between Sylvia Pankhurst and her mother, Emmeline, on direct action and socialism, Laski planted a bomb (if only a small one) for Frida and the militant suffragette cause in Oxted station.

At Oxford, proving incapable at laboratory work, he switched from biology to history, concentrating on the history of political ideas, and became a skilled scourge of the debating chambers in the feminist cause. In 1914 he tried to enlist, despite already having written anti-war editorials for George Lansbury in the *Daily Herald*, but flat feet and a weak heart rejected him, so he took the chance of a job at McGill University, Montreal, and he soon escaped to Harvard for four very fruitful years – fruitful in two important scholarly works, *Studies in the Problems of Sovereignty* and *Authority in the Modern State*. But McGill in 1915 had a reputation far higher than its ability to remunerate its staff (just as I found it forty years later); so with no help from his family and big medical bills to pay when their daughter was born, Laski plunged into serious and continual journalism. He was already gravely workaholic, thinking nothing of sixteen to eighteen hours of 'meaningful activity' a day. There is surely some problem for and with people who preach the cause of humanity but who have no small human pleasures. His only hobby was book collecting and his only idea of a holiday was much like that of Sidney Webb, 'some new and challenging task'. From then on fluent writing became a vice of writing too much, seldom corrected or edited, not even by Frida. Political writing, however, brought him many friends, some already famous, and gained him the fame and notoriety he plainly craved.

His first two books were widely praised both in academic reviews and in, back then, the many serious general weeklies and monthlies. They criticized the theory of sovereignty and maintained that the strength of society is found not in the state but in semi-autonomous social groups. (As was bluntly remarked, it was an odd spectacle: a rationalist Jewish intellectual applying the social theory of the Anglo-Catholic J. N. Figgis about churches and the medieval historiography of Gierke and Maitland to defend, indeed to make central to the social question, trade unions. The influence of Leon Deguit's pluralism and of French radicalism was less often noted, indeed missed by both biographies.) But the *North American Review* did complain of Laski's tendency to repeat 'essentially the same thought in only a slightly different form'. It became widely remarked that he spoke as he wrote and that this was impressive; but that he wrote as he spoke was more of a pity. Both authors miss this.

So his essential intellectual habits were set even before he got to LSE in 1920, and his taste for public controversy, sometimes thrust on him, sometimes sought after, was whetted. (His 'intervention' in the Boston Police strike, that soured his relationships with Harvard but not with America, was a bit of both.) So too was his love of being in the know and knowing top people. Kramnick produces 'impressive evidence of Laski's skills in who he knew'. Newman quotes from a letter to Holmes about his decision to return to Britain: 'It brings (I dare to hope) some very real political influence within my grasp.' But both authors suggest a vivid mixture of self-importance and a conscience driven to speak out for political reform. Kramnick puts this shrewdly:

> Respectable Laski was still rebellious Laski . . . His strategic efforts to acquire 'real political influence' in England in the 1920s solidified his ability, forged at Harvard, to deliver sustained and bitter criticism of the ruling class while seeking their embrace. It is, of course, not uncommon for the radical intellectual to take an outside and critical stance, often devastatingly so, like Wells or Shaw, while thriving on the company, support and applause of the very people one has mocked, satirized and sought to topple. Magnify the ambivalence and the marginality in the case of a radical Jewish intellectual in Britain, however, and one can see that while his life strategy was not perhaps unique, its intensity was.

Both books show how Laski's fame grew rapidly as he wrote obsessively at every level from learned journals to the *Daily Herald*. He never lost his pure academic interests, as shown by his lecturing on French political thought from the sixteenth to the eighteenth century and superbly empathetic articles on Rousseau, Machiavelli and Burke. I used to think that his first two books were his best because the most purely scholarly, but Michael Newman is persuasive that the first edition of *The Grammar of Politics* (1925), deliberately written to be accessible to the general, intelligent reader, is his magnum opus as well as his most widely read book. 'All power is federal', he declaimed, striking at both Hobbes and Lenin, even if he never fully resolved the difficulties of pluralism in accounting for political order at all. He did not throw the state away entirely, indeed in the thirties brought it back to create a new social order in the interests of the working class; nor did he abandon or repudiate this pluralism in the 1930s when Marxism infused his language (Marx's, of course, not Stalin's, nor even Lenin's – 'interpretations can differ', he would quip, 'they read Marx in their way and I in his'). Marxism seemed to furnish an explanation of Nazism as late capitalism while liberal thought could only denounce, not comprehend, such violent and malevolent irrationalism. This was a nearly fatal misreading then shared by almost all the Left. Indeed, some capitalists fell into thinking that Nazism was simply (well, essentially) the only firm defence against Bolshevism. But his liberalism remained. If in any sense he was a fellow traveller, it was only on his own terms for tightly defined, anti-Fascist international purposes. He wrote several celebrated attacks on the Communist Party for their intolerance, brutality and duplicity. Using our published index, I find a pungent review in this journal in 1938 of the Webbs' *Soviet Communism: A New Civilisation* in which he chides them for, in that second Left Book Club edition, dropping the famous question mark of the first edition, and accuses them of a blinkered naivety on questions of civil liberties and human rights.

Laski soon took on board anti-imperialism. The timing of this was spectacularly fortuitous. He wasn't even looking for trouble when summoned for jury service in 1924: the libel action that lasted for five weeks was brought by General O'Dyer against an eminent Indian jurist, Sir Sankaram Nair, for accusing him of responsibility for the terrible Amritsar massacre. Jurymen *can* ask questions, it was not in his nature to remain silent and (in trumps) he didn't. He was genuinely, deeply shocked at the blatant racial prejudice revealed, as well as at the verdict. His fame in India lasts to this day. Leonard Woolf moved in on him with his network of Fabian colonial and League of Nations support committees; lasting friendships with Nehru and Krishna Menon resulted, and LSE became the magnet for nationalist intellectuals from the Empire. Laski's interventions in British politics began in the early 1920s with Lord Haldane as an ally, the Liberal Lord Chancellor in MacDonald's first government, as attempts to forge a Liberal and Labour alliance. But the rise of the National Government and the coming of Hitler to power led Laski to think that only a revolutionary transformation of society, albeit by politics, persuasion and Parliament, could prevent a new dark age over the whole world. So he became the leading spokesman of the Labour Left and an advocate of the Popular Front, trembling with Cripps and Bevan on the edge of expulsion from the party he favoured; yet soon to be elected to the NEC by the constituency parties. Throughout the Second World War he topped the poll each year. The liberal dictum in the *Grammar of Politics* that 'liberty is the absence of those conditions that prevent me from becoming myself at my best' turned sharp left, without signalling, into 'liberty is the presence of those conditions that can alone make me myself at my best'. In his lectures he would mock Hobhouse's version of 'the general will' ('I have never seen it walking down Houghton Street'), but an equally metaphysical virus began to infect Laski's writings and lectures, the 'Felt Needs of Our Time' – which happily led to different conclusions at different times. (In my student lecture notes of 1949 I find 'FNOOT etc.' several times in the margin. Psychologically and politically I was under the master's spell – and these good books bring it all back to me – but philosophically I had learnt in Freddie Ayer's seminar at University College London that that sort of argument wasn't good enough.)

Le Monde said in its obituary for Laski that he had consummated 'a necessary marriage' in the inter-war generation of 'Marxism of the mind' and 'liberation of the heart'. It seems rather that this differing couple somehow stayed together in the Laski kitchen, always in tension, sometimes quarrelling, sometimes papering over the cracks for the sake of the neighbours, but never seriously intending to separate. Michael Newman is especially interesting on the question of 'Constructive Contradictions' (the title of his last chapter).

The quarrel with Beveridge and the University of London over public confusion between the role of a chair and the power of a socialist publicist, which led him voluntarily to give up his weekly column in the *Daily Herald*, diminished his care to share in the work of the LSE. Kramnick and Sheerman show that once he had made that one compromise, the balance of left-wing socialism and liberal pluralism in his books and articles changed even more leftwards. But an alienation with LSE never affected his exceptional closeness to his students, his time-consuming helpfulness to almost anyone who came to him for assistant or just to talk about the big questions. I enjoyed both privileges briefly. He made one feel good and big and determined to serve the general will, the public interest or the FNOOT. But sometimes he was generous to a fault, not all his geese were swans; letters recommending 'this most brilliant young man' to his famous friends often needed heavy salting, even brining; and he made too many academic appointments of surprising mediocrity, not even necessarily disciples (as became Oakeshott's habit). No nonsense then about advertising and appointment committees; sometimes it seemed (as was old H. L. Beales's view) as if he appointed the first person who came to see him when a job happened to have come up. I think Barry Sheerman must have interviewed too many discreet loyalists among the survivors of the 1930s and 1940s to give a wholly accurate picture of the intensity of fratricidal strife. William Robson (this journal's founder) disliked Laski for what he saw as his neglect of the department and incapacity for regular administration. And neither book brings out the full scandal of Beveridge's dictatorial running of the school when the LSE's secretary became his mistress, a tyranny and duopoly that even brought Lionel Robbins and Laski into temporary alliance to get him out.

Before the war, Laski tried actively to get Attlee out as Labour leader, albeit relations never broke down completely, even after Attlee's celebrated rebuke in 1945. Attlee thanked Laski warmly for a fierce and brilliant polemic he wrote against the Communist Party when, on the outbreak of war, they defended the Hitler–Stalin pact. And Kramnick shows Laski dutifully writing some briefs for Attlee even when he was trying to get the NEC to assert authority over the Labour members of Churchill's coalition cabinet, especially to come out with a statement of war aims that would involve radical social reconstruction. Laski took the same line as Orwell in his *Lion and the Unicorn* that the war could only be won if there was a social revolution. Rebecca West told him, among others, not to be silly. He caused the Labour leadership endless trouble, but that was what the constituency parties liked, part of why he headed the poll all during the war and so had, in turn and turn about, to be party chairman; most unhappily in 1945. Kramnick is right to air many opinions (though such prejudices feed off each other, of course, and are not always independent evidence) that there was something 'childish' and attention-seeking in his pulling out the rhetorical stops on everything. His views on the aims of politics and policy were serious and profound, but his political judgement was often poor.

Yet, having said that, and basically agreeing with Rebecca West, Newman reminds us how prescient were some of his apparent exaggerations. In 1941 in a pamphlet 'Great Britain, Russia and the Labour Party' Laski wrote that if the three great powers failed to agree on a post-war order:

> There is the danger, first, that the power of the United States and Britain to provide relief for the peoples of the occupied and defeated countries may be restricted by doctrinal considerations; and . . . the further danger that governments may be imposed on Europe less with a view to the natural evolution of social and political forces in each of the constituent countries than with a view to the receipt of Anglo-American aid . . . conditioned by a desire to make certain that the future of capitalism is not seriously jeopardised . . . Immediately the prospect of Nazi defeat becomes imminent, there will be competitive manoeuvering all over the territory in enemy occupation to secure . . . a group whose purposes may be patronised by London and Washington, on the one hand, or by Moscow on the other . . . It may mean a return to power politics in a grim form in which the main purpose of Britain and the United States will be to prevent . . . the spread of Bolshevik ideas, while it is the main purpose of the USSR to promote that spread.

During the Cold War he became depressed and dispirited. But even during the Second World War his health began to suffer from over-work. For a few weeks he had a nervous breakdown. But on more or less recovering he went back to his old routines in the most difficult and exhausting of conditions, and now separated from Frida most of the week, LSE being at Cambridge and she doing war work in London. (However, not only Laski's tales grew, so did tales about him. Our twin authors were told that Laski was so exhausted in Cambridge, that Lance Beales would wheel him home on his bike. But there are dangers in memory, even Lord MacGregor's: what Beales wrote (*LSE Magazine* May 1971) was that he would walk with Laski to the lecture rooms, putting 'his impedimenta in my cycle basket because I doubted if his strength was equal to carrying them'.)

Frida began to wish that she could restrain him as well as support him: he did too much in politics, to the cost of the quality of what he could do best – his writing; and he did not always pick remotely winnable or prudent fights. But she found she could not. He felt passionately that the Labour Party must have democratic control over its leadership; but he also felt passionately that it was his duty to lead that fight. His inflated view of the authority of the party chairman made him an obvious electoral target, despite Churchill's gross exaggeration. But 'the period of silence' that Attlee publicly requested proved impossible, especially when he took up the Zionist cause against Ernest Bevin and the Foreign Office and when his *ex cathedra* views on French and American lecture platforms about anything and everything got reported, not always maliciously, as expressions of Labour Party, indeed government, policy.

There was the libel action following the claim in a local newspaper, but promptly reported by the *Daily Express*, that he advocated violent revolution; rather than that he said there could be violence from the right if the Labour Party, as he thought it should, tried seriously to dismantle the capitalist system. Some have said that he was foolish to bring the action, arrogantly over-confident. But both authors point out that he had little choice if, with ten days of the election campaign still to go, he had let the libel be repeated. And he plainly thought it dishonourable to let the action drop after the gagging writ had done its work. There was no reproach at the time from the party. Attlee and Morrison instructed Morgan Phillips to organize an appeal to cover the large costs, and an amazing number of prominent Americans contributed. All that was covered. There was no bankruptcy. But he was utterly humiliated. Frida wrote to a friend: 'Harold bore up well till he got home and then wept as I have never seen a man weep, and it just made me feel useless.'

Those who knew him before said that he never fully recovered his zest. But that was a relative judgement. Those of us who heard him lecture in the last two years of his life have to believe that from older witnesses, but it was hard to believe amid the high rhetoric and cut and thrust of his lectures, in his enthusiasm for strange scholarly things – that the *Vindiciae Contra Tyrannos* of 1579 should be in the canon of great texts of political philosophy, in his naughtiness – 'at least it can be said of Mr Attlee that he is the only prime minister of this century who has not committed adultery when in office', and in his quips and sarcasms, doubtless repeated yearly: 'And finally Rousseau developed persecution mania, for the very good reason that he was persecuted.' 'The Wars of Religion came to an end when Henri of Navarre decided "that Paris is worth a mass", which let me assure you, from my own experience, it is.' Finally he simply brought on a collapse by over-exertion in the general election campaign of 1950. Organizing the overflow meeting in Red Lion Square, I last saw Laski being supported against falling by Norman Mackenzie and others as they helped him from the car to the platform of the Conway Hall. On the platform he rallied.

Among the tributes when he died, Newman relates, Leon Blum compared him to Montesquieu and Tocqueville, claiming that no one else in Europe or America had had such a profound and original knowledge of democratic thought in the period since the seventeenth century. And in Britain Beloff spoke about 'the age of Laski'. But so quickly after his death his reputation declined dramatically. I think of how Orwell's increased dramatically after his death. Had it all been just the hypnotic magic of his spoken words? Of course, it is not the business of biography to discuss what happens after death, nor to speculate on what might have happened. But the question is interesting and both books touch on it and give much the same answer: the Cold War. His attempt to synthesize Marxism and liberalism, never much more than a rhetorical and emotional synthesis, was pulled apart violently, and not much was left useful to either side. And Kramnick shows how in America J. Edgar Hoover's long-kept 'Laski file' (ever since the Boston police strike in 1919) began to surface into the hands of predatory senators. Almost anyone he had met regularly or who had contributed to the libel trial fund, from Eleanor Roosevelt down, became some sort of Communist or un-American leftie. When James Forrestal, the US Secretary of Defence, went mad, thinking that the Reds were coming through his windows, he mouthed Laski's name repeatedly in paranoid terror. All this is now set down.

But there are other reasons too. The writing that gave him such a public reputation was almost all instant, reactive polemic, even if learned polemic ('theoretical polemic'?); and the shelf-life of that can be as short as Burke's 'flies of the summer' if its literary merit is not high. His best academic thinking was in the first two books and the associated articles, and his later books were too often repetitive and even tired. *The Grammar of Politics* could still have reached the educated public, but somehow after 1950 there was steady decline (why is a large question) in political publishing and political writing. The exception to this was the rise of the New Left after 1956 and one might have thought that Laski's attempt to fuse Marxism and liberty would have interested them; but though they

talked 'praxis' they had no interest in political practice or in writing
that could actually reach working people. The school of Althusser
and his Paris rivals saw Marxism as an almost autonomous realm of
high theory, so as much as any high Tory they dismissed Laski's
writings, if they knew them at all, as mere journalism; and they
wrote off the entire history of democratic socialism as bourgeois
revisionism.

With university expansion there was a great increase in academic
political publishing, but Laski's books were no longer professional
enough and the discipline became internalized; almost no one
seemed to see the need (except this good old journal) of reaching out
to the public (something for extra-mural departments, if at all). And
political philosophy as a discipline became very much more rigorous
under the influence of both logical positivism and then the
linguistic school, but just as internalized. Laski was not a real
philosopher by those standards, and perhaps only now has enough
time gone by to see that he must be an important part of the history
of ideas in this vanishing century, if ideas are admitted sometimes to
reach, even to reflect, public opinion.

So is there a lasting legacy or was his just a very interesting life at
a very interesting time in a bygone past? Both books end by saying
something more than a justification for a biography. Both agree that
the kind of pluralism that Laski advocated is now becoming
dominant in reformist thought, whether some of its advocates
recognize the paternity or not. Paul Hirst, an ex-Althusserian turned
Fabian, has edited an anthology on pluralism which is half Laski.
Newman gives the clearest account of the validity of this. Kramnick
and Sheerman incline to think more of the role of the publicist:
'Laski was at bottom a mass preacher and public teacher', a 'public
intellectual' they well say. They are kind to quote in their
conclusion my opinion on this: 'Laski's greatness was as a teacher
and preacher, not as a political philosopher.' But perhaps to split a
hair, I think what I meant, or should have said if I had had their
book then, was that while he is not a political philosopher as
academics understand it, yet he was one as the public once
understood it and, in principle, could again. So I would have him
enduring as not only a 'public intellectual' but as a 'public
philosopher'.

Forgive self-quotation but reviewing these two fine biographies
has been difficult, a little painful, obviously raising matters close to

the bone, revealing my feelings towards Laski as very ambivalent, and revealing almost an anger that he wasted too much of his talents, did not concentrate on what he did best. However Newman does attach a greater importance to Laski's political thinking than do Kramnick and Sheerman, and he does this by what theatre folk call 'a framing device'. And to my pleasure but slight worry he uses a recollection of mine to furnish that device. He concludes his Introduction:

> According to Bernard Crick, Laski's advice to students when studying Rousseau was as follows: 'Do not falter at the formal contradictions of his arguments, which are legion, but endeavour to discover what is the animating inwardness of the man.' As Crick suggested, I have tried to apply the same principles to Laski in an attempt to discover and explain his 'animating inwardness'.

I certainly agree that this 'charitable' interpretative principle should be applied to understanding Rousseau and I was, indeed, implying that it helps with Laski too; but precisely because of his unresolved philosophical contradictions. And Newman sees this so clearly. But it explains Rousseau and Laski's behaviour biographically and their great appeal historically and psychologically; it does not warrant a suspension of philosophical standards of judgement. There are some. Logical contradictions are not good for any argument. When he calls his last chapter 'Creative Contradictions' I am worried that some sort of dialectic is implied: that from out of contradictions comes a higher synthesis. No, the dynamic born of contradictions can only construct a life, activities, not a philosophical justification. Biography and the critique of texts are, though they may concern the same person, different activities: 'the life of the mind' is only a metaphor.

These are excellent biographies, of a different kind. But perhaps Michael Newman should now compile, now that interest is aroused again, a big enough anthology of Laski's political thought to show his depth, range and diversity. This might meet some of 'the felt needs of our time' – an example for each one of us (and that includes the Labour Party) to start thinking again in terms of principles, never mind that we will never wholly agree; that's life, that's politics.

CHAPTER 20

Shaw as Political Thinker, or the Dogs That Did Not Bark

Why is Shaw so ignored by my colleagues? I ask myself this question as a political philosopher with an interest in the history of ideas. He is not ignored by some literary scholars, but he is by academic political philosophers and by most historians of modern British politics. This may seem in this volume an inept attempt at a weak Shavian paradox. Shaw ignored! Well, perhaps I should bluntly say, not taken seriously. Any political history or history of ideas that mentions the Fabians mentions Shaw, but usually only a mention it is. *The Labour Party's Political Thought: A History* by Geoffrey Foote (an otherwise excellent book) has only four minor references to Shaw.[1] He tells us in thirteen lines, not wholly accurately, that Shaw attempted to convert the early Fabian Society to Marx but was himself converted to Jevons's theory of economic value. Foote devotes a more substantial paragraph to Shaw's defence against the anarchists of the Fabian theory of the state. He notes that the Fabians 'dabbled in eugenics, with Shaw proposing in his play

From *Shaw and Politics*, ed. T. F. Evans, *The Annual of Bernard Shaw Studies*, vol. 11 (Pennsylvania State University Press, 1991). The year after this, as if to comfort or confound my lament that political theorists ignore Shaw, there appeared from an Australian scholar, Gareth Griffith, *Socialism and Superior Brains: The Political Thought of GBS* (Routledge, 1992); my essay would have been better had I been able to read his far fuller account, but I have left mine as it stands for our interpretations differ interestingly.

Man and Superman that national suicide could be averted only by scientific breeding' and that 'Shaw eventually became disillusioned with parliament, and was to praise the national efficiency inculcated by Stalin and Mussolini' (why does he spare the references to Hitler?).[2]

Political philosophers ignore him. I am not aware of a single article on Shaw by an academic political philosopher; the gap in Britain between the academic and the general intellectual (which I am sure is greater than in the United States and Canada) is shown at its widest. Shaw was, after all, the most famous and prolific political intellectual of his time. But the suspicion remains with many scholars that he was mainly famous for being famous, into which he put so much successful effort over such a long time. The influence of the Webbs on British politics and social policy is acknowledged, even by those who detest it. But if every schoolboy knows that Shaw often said that they were the brain and he their megaphone or mouthpiece, only a schoolboy would take that at face value. Did he not have a mind of his own! When years afterwards Shaw told Lady Londonderry, 'All I could do for Webb was to beat the drum in front of his booth, as he could not master that useful instrument himself', his tone was of comic mock-modesty, and no one should doubt that such a drummer with a tone-deaf master will beat out some dominant rhythms of his own. Yet the actual influence of Shaw himself is either doubted or thought to be so difficult to assess that scholars shy away from the problem, fearful of making fools of themselves by trying to sort out what he really meant amid all the comic welter of sometimes provocative, sometimes defensive, badinage. And there is the awkward problem of how much of Shaw's political beliefs we can read into his plays. Do we take even the major assertions of a play literally, or as pointing to a Ph.D. doctor's dilemma? I first read Geoffrey Foote's summary of *Man and Superman* above with some unease, now with some disagreement.

Even those who recognize Shaw's great influence as a propagandist and publicist seem wary of assessing his ideas. Robert Skidelsky in writing on Shaw and 'The Fabian Ethic' makes the important general point that 'the heart of the Fabian ethic was an overwhelming sense of public duty'.[3] This distinguished them both from the religious, with their duty to God, and from the 'new lifers', with their duty to, or obsession with, self. But having made this general point, Skidelsky remains, as far as ideas are concerned, on a level of generalities; and the rest of the essay returns to the historian's familiar task, albeit with skill and wit, of establishing 'connections', personal connections. (I am sometimes puzzled whether modern historians simply see this as their only proper task as historians, or whether they actually believe that all ideas are simply a product of personal loyalties and interests – a kind of disease of liberalism.)

Michael Holroyd, even, fights shy of assessing Shaw's political ideas, indeed of taking them seriously. His approach is fundamentally reductionist, not in an economic sense, of course, but in a psychological one. He had showed his hand early in the entry for Shaw in *Makers of Modern Culture*:

> The Fabian Society became Shaw's new family and his socialist reforms a means of changing society so that no child should have to go through the sort of upbringing that he had endured. Believing himself to be unloveable, he made out of Collectivism a weapon against individualist romantic propaganda. . .
>
> He believed that he had inherited from his parents incompatible qualities which he must reconcile within himself. From this process emerged his concept of the Life Force which is not a symbol of power but a unit of synthesis.[4]

Small wonder that Holroyd called the first volume of the biography *The Search for Love*.[5] The passage just quoted shows that Holroyd or his publishers did not adopt that question-begging title partly to promote the book, as some reviewers naughtily hinted. It had long been his theory. But the evidence he advances (leaving aside that none of it was new, something masked by the lack of footnotes and sources)[6] shows that he may not merely have been over-interpreting, but also making, on balance, the wrong interpretation: the book could be as plausibly called on the evidence he himself presents 'The Search for Ideas' or 'The Search for Identity (through ideas)'. As a young man Shaw tried out different ideas even more energetically than he did different women, and the advantage of ideas over women was that they could be synthesized, for nothing was entirely wasted: even synthesized into a theory of evolution and creativity by sexual selection.

Holroyd obviously has little sympathy with rationalist humanism: that one adopts ideas by a process of reasoning. Ideas are simply rationalizations of psychological drives or traumas (or of economic self-interest, say others). The true intellectual historian can only say 'sometimes', not 'always'; and *never* for a person's entire ideology – there are too many variant doctrines on offer at any given time, and too many broken homes that do not throw forth a genius. The historian of ideas has to look at the intellectual context, not merely the social context, much less only the family history of the person concerned. The trouble with purely psychological explanations in biography, as Richard Ellmann once argued, is that they are perfectly reversible: an individual was moulded by childhood experiences, or reacted violently against them (what Karl Popper called 'the fallacy of psychologism').[7] It makes a good story either way, but the relation to historical truth remains problematic.

This psychologism makes it easy for Holroyd to bypass any serious discussion of Shaw's political ideas. To explain how he held them is always more important than what they are. In the encyclopedia article he even said that 'Shaw's socialism . . . *invades* many of his plays' (my emphasis). There is a whiff in Holroyd of a would-be old-fashioned English man of letters who wants politics and literature kept firmly apart. Now to some extent this foreshortening or separation is necessary in any biography of comprehensible size. But Holroyd makes it worse by actually mocking serious political discussion, or rather by retelling Shaw's own later comic accounts of what it was like and misrepresenting how seriously he must have taken the issues at the time.

Annie Besant in 1886 forced a confrontation between Fabians of anarchist persuasion and the collectivists:

> At the end of some high-pitched speeches, a mixed Fabian and SDF team that included Annie Besant, Shaw and John Burns . . . routed by forty-seven votes to nineteen the anarchists, led by William Morris and Mrs Wilson, who had argued that the inevitable compromise and concession of parliamentary politics would poison the well, obscuring socialist principles and hindering socialist education throughout the country. An immediate outcome of this rowdy debate was a notice from the manager of the hotel informing the society that further meetings could not be accommodated there. After an interval in a church, Sydney Olivier arranged for later functions to be held at Willis's Rooms which, decked with silver candelabra and patrolled by

liveried footmen, were famous as the least expensive, most aristocratic-looking, meeting-place in London.[8]

That is very funny, and probably an excellent and concise summary of the minority argument; but what – may one ask? – did the majority argue? One suspects (and without the missing references few readers can tell) that Holroyd's narrative is very close to some account by Shaw himself – too close perhaps and too uncritical, in effect trapped in Shaw's 'sure, it was all a joke' badinage. Almost every autobiographical statement by Shaw is for some present effect or polemic at the time he wrote; therefore they all need dating and putting into context to judge their truth for the time relative to which they nominally refer (and again, without references, few readers can tell). And his adopted persona was not, after all, the clown, but the wise fool. However comically he might have delivered his speech against the anarchists at that meeting, wrapped up in it must have been a deadly serious argument if he thought that, had the vote gone the other way, the Fabian Society as he knew it would have been at an end.

To be fair to Michael Holroyd, he ends that same chapter with a comment on William Morris's review of the *Fabian Essays* that clearly identifies the tension between the personal and the political, neither subsumed in the other:

> Morris and Webb were more than friends to Shaw: they were his political mentors. Morris was a great man and Webb a great brain; Morris a hero for all time and Webb a man of the time. Shaw wanted to unite the applied arts with the social sciences and use Webb's logic to circumvent Morris's sense of history. But as Morris's review of Webb's essay makes clear, they were two heralds beckoning Shaw in different directions. So Shaw continued speaking of the Fabians with two voices. His most persistent voice aggrandized the Fabian achievement. The other voice sounded his despair that they had not achieved more . . . He turned to the one and then to the other: and eventually he turned to the Soviet Union.[9]

Leave aside for the moment the last sentence, which is glib and too simple – it needs the word 'too' added, for one of the problems with taking Shaw seriously as a thinker rather than as a popularizer of utter genius is that he never gave anything up; yet there is another way of looking at 'different directions' rather than as political and philosophical contradictions arising from personal loyalties. The historian of ideas is familiar with very similar problems, such as occur famously in Rousseau. Can, with 'contextual charity', the contradictions between his individualism and collectivism, between romantic and austere classical values, be explained away empathetically; or must these contradictions, with 'contextual clarity' (confound it, that's what the fellow actually said), be exposed rigorously? Well, people say what they say and write what they write, but at different times and in different circumstances and to be understood by different audiences. Statements can presume or imply different time-scales. This is particularly characteristic of progressive thought. If you believe that the future will not resemble the past and will, indeed, be better, then there need be no absolute contradiction between visionary and tactician. Both are needed. Could we imagine a good (or even a better) society without either Webbs or Morrises? There can be Machiavellian utopians, so long as time-scales are distinguished;[10] and there is no particular reason why philosophers should be impractical (as Michael Oakeshott and F. H. Bradley have reminded us, the mind ranges through many different levels of experience or modes of being).[11] The economist will distinguish between short-term, middle-term, and long-term factors, and the theologian between things of this world and of the next; but the essayist, the satirist, and the entertainer may deliberately juggle with and confuse them, partly for fun ('laughter,' said Hobbes, 'is a sudden glory') and partly to stimulate new thought by desanctifying conventions (Pickering: 'Have you no morals, man?' Doolittle: 'Can't afford them, Governor. Neither could you if you was as poor as me.') In this sense Shaw is a speculative thinker, more in the tradition of Socrates and Voltaire than of the great system builders like Hegel, Marx and Herbert Spencer. The process of thought is almost as important as the content.

And the content? Let me now look at what a few academic students of politics, who have been brave enough to try to include Shaw in their narratives, think important about his ideas. One of the most impressive achievements of British political scholarship in our time is W. H. Greenleaf's *British Political Tradition*, of which three volumes have so far appeared and a fourth is to follow. Greenleaf is a disciple of Oakeshott, about whom he has written; in a broad sense he is of conservative persuasion. He has done what the Master and other disciples have mainly talked about, written an actual account of a tradition of politics, not simply a philosophic justification of tradition. And in looking at the full complexity of the tradition, his objectivity as well as his width of reading is awesome. He quotes Shaw sixty years later telling Kingsley Martin how he helped Webb sweep the 'perfect lifers' and 'all the nonsense and Bohemian anarchism' out of the early Fabian Society. And he quotes Shaw as saying that he put thoughts of the New Jerusalem aside in favour of a thorough understanding of the theory of rent and the sanitary regulations of a London borough. Instead of the 'scramble for private gain', the Fabians sought 'the introduction of design, contrivance and coordination in the conscious pursuit of collective welfare'. But Greenleaf cautiously notes that 'if recent commentary has properly indicated the ethical basis or undercurrent of early Fabian thought', yet Webb at the time was saying that the main effort of the English socialist movement 'was to bring about a society infused with collectivist principles and techniques'.[12] Greenleaf is right at least to remind us of the ethical undercurrent, and perhaps he takes Shaw's renunciation of New Jerusalem for free public lavatories for women a little too literally. Several of the great plays tell a different story, not only *Man and Superman.* Anyway, saints need not be unsanitary. On different time-scales both preoccupations are compatible or, if that sounds too socialist a methodology or hermeneutic for Greenleaf, then like Oakeshott or F. H. Bradley he might better construe them as on different levels of experience. Shaw's renunciation of bohemianism should have sounded critical alarm bells. That's either the pot calling the kettle black or should remind the reader, as any good tailor or couturier knows, that there are many shades of black. He too gets sucked into Shaw's wholehearted heroic rhetorical exaggeration.

Greenleaf is on firmer ground when characterizing Shaw's elitism. He quotes from Shaw's Fabian tract *Socialism and Superior Brains: A Reply to Mr Mallock* that always and everywhere – in this he agreed with the Tory Mallock – 'the few will . . . organize the many'.[13] Shaw was an elitist. Of that there is no possible doubt, no possible doubt whatever – except about what kind of elitist he was. Greenleaf fails to note that unlike Mallock, and like Major Barbara's evolutionary mate, Adolphus Cusins, he does think it necessary to educate the masses. Perhaps one day in the Life-Forced future when there is equality of income, imposed by the public-spirited and dedicated elite, and when the palpably unfit Snobby Prices (the Snopeses of Cockneydom) have been bred out or contracepted into genetic sterility, there will be virtual equality of ability. And, unlike Mallock again, Shaw says this on Labour movement platforms even. Greenleaf notes that he assured the trade unionists on behalf of the Fabian Society that extreme devices of democracy were undesirable and reassured them that the 'organized, intelligent and class-conscious Socialist minority' must not be placed at the mercy of the unorganized and apathetic rabble of electors and routine toilers.[14] The word 'organized' may have convinced the brothers that they were of the Elect. (The socialist historian Eric Hobsbawm has said that one of the difficulties of socialism, even in its Communist form, was that it was always in practice a doctrine of the skilled worker.)

In the same passage, however, Greenleaf notes 'the extreme and provocative tone' of the Shavian formulation in 'Sixty Years of Fabian Socialism' when he says, first, that the elite should be selected by experts, not by popular vote, and, second, that 'under Socialism social misfits should be "painlessly liquidated" and that those who are not able "to prove their social solvency" should be made to do useful work or be put to death'. Greenleaf wisely ruminates that:

> one never really knows with Shaw whether he means exactly what he says or is simply trailing his coat. Certainly this particular expression of opinion is the *reductio ad absurdum* of that alliance between eugenic selection and benevolent despotism that Shaw always favoured.[15]

But I put it to my fellow political philosopher that '*reductio ad absurdum*' is subtly wrong. Mr Dooley once said that every time Andrew Carnegie gave away a library, he gave away himself in a speech. But Shaw was not giving himself away; he surely picked his words deliberately, even if, by the time he did, they were grossly insensitive. So something like 'clownish melodramatic exaggeration' might fit it better, or simply call it SDH, 'Shavian dramatic hyperbole'. And while 'benevolent despotism' is all right, 'enlightened autocracy' would be better (these two terms mean something different in the history of ideas). Certainly Shaw and Webb's elite was programmed to work *through* the existing system – permeation as the tactic and the 'inevitability of gradualism' as the theory. Again Greenleaf himself notes this when he quotes from Shaw's Preface to the 1908 reprint of *Fabian Essays*:

> In 1885 the Fabian Society, amid the jeers of the catastrophists, turned its back on the barricades and made up its mind to turn heroic defeat into prosaic success. We set ourselves two definite tasks: first, to provide a parliamentary programme for a Prime Minister converted to socialism as Peel was converted to Free Trade; and second, to make it as easy and matter-of-course for the ordinary respectable Englishman to be a Socialist as to be a Liberal or a Conservative.[16]

Yet Shaw himself can mislead the reader by such a hearty contrast, helpful though it was to the Fabians, between revolution and permeation. For to him, if hardly to Sidney Webb, even permeation was part, cosmically a small part, of the unfolding of evolutionary progress and the Life Force, moving toward an eventual perfected or fully realized human nature. Beatrice Webb was to confide to her diary that 'religious ends and scientific methods are indivisible if mankind is to rise above the brute battle for life'.[17] It could even be argued that if socialism has revolutionary ends, it had best adopt political and evolutionary means.

Stanley Pierson in his *British Socialists* is a rare historian to take seriously, but not uncritically, Shaw's philosophy of history.[18] There have been more studies of popular religious or quasi-religious movements from American than from British scholars (such a book as Ian MacKillop's *British Ethical Societies* (1986) is rare). Pierson quotes Shaw as saying that had it not been for Webb, he 'might have been a mere literary wisecracker like Carlyle and Ruskin', but more clearly than Greenleaf he demonstrates that Shaw never gave up, even when he was beating the Fabian drum, a belief in the special role of the imaginative artist. 'He began to construct a personal religion or mythology', convinced that the secularists and the scientists had failed to explain 'the mystery of consciousness'. And Shaw, says Pierson, looked not to Darwin but to Samuel Butler's argument that 'man's mind disclosed the presence of a cosmic force working through evolution'; and he says that Schopenhauer and Nietzsche also influenced Shaw in this – he could have mentioned Bergson too.[19] He is surely right. And the road to this conclusion is a bold but clearheaded use of Shaw's plays, as well as his strictly political and polemical writings. A play cannot demonstrate an author's conclusions with finality (unless it is a very bad play), but it can demonstrate his or her main concerns: what the author thinks is relevant. Certainly it cannot be said of Shaw that he raises more questions than he answers. He, or his characters, answer everything, but often with different answers. His seriousness and originality as a political thinker should be judged by the questions he asks rather than by the dramatically arresting but varying answers he gives.

Man and Superman is, of course, Shaw's great testament to his evolutionary ethic and contains one powerful speculation about the nature and role of elites. Pierson quotes Sidney Webb, writing to Pease: 'I have just read Shaw's Don Juan play and I do not admire it at all.'[20] Small wonder. But there is also the view of Cusins as he prepares to share the Undershaft money and power with the former Major Barbara: 'I want a democratic power strong enough to force the intellectual oligarchy to use its genius for the common good.' That sounds more like a power for democracy than a democratic power; but this speculation is back closer to Sidney and further from Beatrice. However, on balance, Pierson is right to say that 'Shaw's desire for a more radical transformation of society was evident in his treatment of two phenomena which the Fabians tended to ignore – power and religion.'[21]

Shaw treats power and religion as, respectively, the means and the ends of Creative Evolution: the Black Girl will find that her god is perfected man, or at least a very greatly improved model. And the powerful means to that end will be a new elite, whose members will be part artist and part engineer – part Octavius Robinson and part Henry Straker. But in forcing us to face, however much we talk about democracy, that there will always be elites of some kind, an author can get trapped in his own rhetoric. Strictly speaking, Shaw was presenting elites as a disciplined and dedicated 'order', and it should follow that the members of such elites, like aristocrats or army officers, exercise a broad equality among themselves; collectively they are a hierarchy when facing other ranks and orders, but internally they are a fraternity. Yet Shaw's fascination with, intellectual generosity toward, and misreading of Hitler, Stalin and Mussolini, together with his lack of interest in their parties, is undeniable, regrettable and foolish. In 1933 he addressed the Fabian Society off the cuff and out of the back of his bursting head:

Herr Hitler – a very remarkable, very able man . . . But I cannot agree with Hitler on every point . . . I think he is the victim of bad biology and of a bogus ethnology . . . Now let us look at Signor Mussolini. What has he built up? He is trying to build up in Italy what he calls a corporate state . . . I approve of that, because it is precisely what the Fabian Society wants . . . Now let us come to another interesting gentleman whose personal acquaintance I have had the pleasure of making – Stalin . . . Now Stalin is a nationalist exactly like Hitler. He does not fall back on the world revolution, but understands that he has to have Socialism in Russia, which is quite big enough for him to look after without troubling himself about Socialism in Edinburgh, or anywhere else.[22]

In some ways he lapsed back to thoughts and concepts stirred by Carlyle: great men, not even dedicated elites, are the real catalysts of history. It cannot have escaped Shaw's attention entirely that each of his three heroes, however temporary their stand on his empty pedestal, could have rather short ways with surviving fellow leaders of the elite from the early days of the struggle. Shavian dramatic hyperbole (hereinafter called SDH) seems an appropriate rhetorical device when talking about evolution and the Life Force but less so when talking about the great dictators: the trouble with them, which Shaw did not realize in time, was that they meant exactly what they said about the need to eliminate the unfit and the unsocial; they were not joking.

Let us see how well SDH worked in the advocacy of the third side of the triangle of GBS's political philosophy: equality. In the last 25 years academic philosophers have written many books and articles on the concept of equality, and broad positions are taken, more or less for and more or less against. But none of them makes any substantial reference to Shaw.[23] Now, of course, they write for a different audience using more rigorous academic conventions of argument. Shaw addressed intellectuals and the self-educated whose only university was the free public library (the audience that Dickens, Mark Twain, H. G. Wells and Orwell have written for). In Shaw's day few intellectuals were found in or dependent upon universities; and even in our happy times one could exaggerate the intellectualism of university teachers: many are more concerned to build and maintain disciplinary barriers than to communicate widely through the free play of ideas. Great issues are more often debated in novels, plays, or minority-time television 'talking heads' shows than in seminars. But the academic political philosophers regularly devour the views of other past figures who had little or no lasting connection with universities: say Hobbes, Locke, Rousseau, Mill, Tocqueville, Marx, and perhaps Simone Weil. But the historian of ideas must look at the general preconceptions or dominant concepts or paradigms of an era wherever they are best expressed.

When Shaw put the case for a literal equality of income and outcome, not of opportunity (a view put forward by no other known socialist thinker since Gracchus Babeuf), he forced his audiences into mental movement, challenging them to come back with criteria for differentiation or to define what they meant by such concepts as 'an equal society', 'a radically more equal society', and 'an egalitarian society'. He began an address to the National Liberal Club on 1 May 1913 (the May Day holiday for radical labour), 'When I speak of "The Case for Equality" I mean human equality; and that, of course, can only mean one thing: it means equality of income. It means that if one person is to have half-a-crown, the other is to have two and sixpence.'[24] And he rattles on with a spectacular defence of this impossible position (impossible if taken literally – what if I use a penny of the half-a-crown, as William Cobbett once advised poor immigrants, to sow mustard seed, but then begin to sell it at profit as superior to the chemically doctored manufactured stuff?). But he is plainly fishing for stock responses in discussion.

A Mr Richard Whiteing rose to the bait and evidently put the familiar case that cultured human beings need more. First, Shaw hits him on the head with an idealized distinction (appropriate to the audience) between the 'real gentleman' and the 'sham gentleman'. The real gent is dedicated to public service: 'my ideal . . . shall be to strive to give to my country in return more than it has given me; so that when I die my country shall be richer for my life.' But sham gent says, 'I want a handsome and dignified existence; but a less handsome and dignified existence is good enough for other people.' Shaw concludes, 'If any man wants a better life, he should not seek that life for himself alone, but should attain it by the raising of the general standard of life.'[25] That is an impressive moral argument and rings true, even if it is scarcely a justification for his opening claim for literal equality of income – unless that claim is seen not as a programme for the next government but as a Platonic ideal or standard or as the telos of Creative Evolution.

In *The Intelligent Woman's Guide* he repeats the literal argument. His summary of the contents of Chapter 26, 'The Diagnostic of Socialism', includes, 'Many professed Socialists are so because they believe in a delusion called Equality of Opportunity, and would recant if they discovered that Socialism means unconditional equality of income for everyone without regard to character, talent, age or sex.' And the text robustly asserts that it is 'quite possible and practicable, not only momentarily but permanently. It is also simple and intelligible. It gets rid of all squabbling as to how much each person should have.' But the main thrust of his argument is in fact aimed at achieving a classless society, and 'the best test of that', one which must be supported by 'every device of taxation of income, restriction of inheritance and the like', is simply 'intermarriage-ability': social policy has 'no other object than to keep the entire community intermarriageable'.[26] At the National Liberal Club he had wrapped this up with comic badinage, not needed for intelligent women: he was not saying that every National Liberal must marry everyone else, nor need find everyone else equally attractive, nor that men and women under socialism would not say 'no' far more often than 'yes', especially in relation to marriage. All he was saying, he protested, was that only in a fully egalitarian society would social objections never be put in the way of a couple who wanted to marry.[27] That must have been close to his auditors' experience.

Intermarriageability is in fact a very shrewdly chosen indicator of class prejudice or classlessness, revealing a masterly 'sociological imagination'. And it is a cogent way of showing, as in his old arguments with the suffragettes, that full female emancipation needs not merely the vote but, at least, a radically more economically equal and ethically egalitarian society. (I now realize that I was unconsciously taking a leaf from the Master's book in my book, *In Defence of Politics*, when I used 'death' as the same form of counterfactual argument: *if* the life chances [that is, expectation of life] of any social group were equal to any other, we would know that we were in a classless society, in which there would be an almost perfect correlation between mortality statistics and social class.)[28] Even gaining the vote was a delusion of progress when unenlightened women continued to vote for men: therefore Shaw advocated 'the coupled vote' to gain equal numbers in elected assemblies – an elector should only be able to vote on one ballot for a man and a woman combined.

However, *The Intelligent Woman's Guide* makes clear that equality will be reached by levelling up to the income that is needed to sustain the professional elite who will guide and inspire the transition; the project is not levelling down.[29] And this is spelled out in some detail in 1945 in one of his very last newspaper articles, 'How Much Do We Need?' An arithmetical division of the national income cannot be immediate. A basic income must be imposed that is large enough to produce the professionals needed to run a modern society, whom he estimates to be about 10 per cent of the population. What is left will be distributed: 'from this point progress towards equality of income must depend on increased production'. During the transition 'the thinkers and directors' will be 'sufficiently paid, and the rank and file underpaid'. All increases in national wealth must be used 'to raise the family incomes of the rank and file until they, too, can afford the privacy, the leisure, the culture, and all the other amenities and opportunities which the basic income commands'.[30] I make no comment on the validity of this: whether in socialist terms it would simply entrench a new technocratic elite, or whether it demands an amount of regulation and control that would, indeed, convince many of us that the market is a lesser evil ('market socialism'?). I simply wish to establish what his view really was, a kind of realism: Rome could not be built in a day, but nonetheless there is a vision of a New Jerusalem. I think this combination was early Fabianism, Sidney Webb notwithstanding. SDH masked an unusual synthesis of idealism and realism, and it was well designed to do just that.

My lament has been for the neglect of Shaw by my fellow academics in politics and modern history. But as early as 1925 there was a book, *Contemporary Political Thought in England*, by Lewis Rockow (an historian at the University of Oregon), which gave Shaw a significant role in a cast that already included Hobhouse, Graham Wallas, Laski, Russell, and Cole.[31] He did this by adding to ten chapters on clearly certifiably serious political thinkers one on Wells, 'The Governance of a Utopia', and two last chapters on 'The State in Literature' dealing with drama and the novel. Shaw dominates the drama. Rockow summarizes his main themes well: equality in distribution, the public-service elite guided by and guiding the Life Force of Creative Evolution, and eugenics.

We must always make a hard conceptual leap to the context of the time, before Hitler's racism and the Holocaust discredited the whole speculation. Rockow, before all this, sagely noted that 'the subject of eugenics includes two separate questions, one of ends and one of means'. As regards ends, Shaw did *not*, Rockow argues, advocate a uniform pattern of a perfected humanity – what will emerge in better conditions is uncertain, will not be uniform, and is a matter of trial and error. And the means are largely through economic equality, which will increase the chances of intermarriage among the most talented: sexual attraction was a better form of natural selection than social snobbery. 'Some undesirable types he would exclude entirely from parentage, and the more extreme cases he would send to the lethal chamber.' But Rockow concludes, perhaps surprisingly but I think justly, 'Shaw's discussion of eugenics, if we omit some Shavian exaggerations, is moderate and helpful.' Can we omit 'the lethal chamber'?[32] On my analysis of Shaw's use of dramatic hyperbole in political speculation, I think we can – with contextual charity. But after the Holocaust and the Killing Fields? At least such language should not be used again even in humour in discussion of public policy; it must be contextualized as 'in literature'. We see what he meant, but it would not be easy to read Swift's *Modest Proposal* with tolerance, let alone relish, if during the great famine the Irish poor had practised cannibalism on their own children.

Rockow was wise to adopt the method of approaching Shaw through his drama. For in the plays it is obvious that SDH is at work and, as a literary strategy, usually or often works well. And the plays are obviously 'Shavian'. The exaggerations can be more easily discounted than in books, tracts, and speeches, but the substance of his views on what is overwhelmingly important in personal life and social relations cannot get lost – as it can in the badinage of his nonfiction, all written with the free use of the first person, thus tempting (from Holroyd and others) endless reductionist commentary about 'connections' or the childhood psychological roots of political ideology. 'Shaw,' concluded Rockow, 'is doing valiant service in educating the public mind.'[33] That was indeed his intent. And his method was to encourage speculation: most of the dogmatism was provocation and deliberate exaggeration.

This is not to say there were not blind spots, or that his political doctrines constitute a complete philosophical system. The common man of Rousseau, Kant, Wells, Orwell and the American Jeffersonian tradition can hardly be expected to sit around waiting for the elite to become perfected and then to perfect him. He must be up and about as a democratic citizen. Ross Terrill sadly comments, in his sensitive study of perhaps the greatest of the English socialist thinkers, R. H. Tawney, that 'it is a commonplace that the democratic component of socialist theories which claimed to be democratic has had an uncertain career. Not only at the hand of Communists but also of Fabians like Shaw and Labour Party intellectuals like Laski.'[34]

Shaw through his strategy of SDH forced people to put counter-arguments against literal equality, so it was probably intended to benefit a more discriminatory, relative equality, certainly an egalitarian ethos and morality. The philosopher John Rawls has argued that while 'equality' is not a clear or definable moral standard for social policy, yet all inequalities of rewards, goods, and power must be capable of being justified as contributing to the greater benefit of the least advantaged and must be attached to positions or offices open to all under fair conditions of equality of opportunity.[35] But they must in fact be justified. The presumption is that all such inequalities have to be challenged publicly. The boot is on that foot. And Shaw did much of the kicking where it most hurts, outside the academy. And he might have have relished the Rawlsian paradox that 'toward equality!' may not be a categorical imperative but that 'no unjustifiable inequalities!' is. Sometimes double negatives or the negation of the negation are as helpful as satire.

Notes

1. Geoffrey Foote, *The Labour Party's Political Thought: A History,* 2nd edn, London, Croom Helm, 1986, pp. 25, 28, 30, 32.
2. *Ibid.,* p. 30.
3. Robert Skidelsky, 'The Fabian Ethic', in Michael Holroyd (ed.), *The Genius of Shaw,* London, Hodder and Stoughton, 1979, p. 113.
4. Michael Holroyd, 'Shaw', in Justin Wintle (ed.), *The Makers of Modern Culture: A Biographical Dictionary,* London, Routledge & Kegan Paul, 1981, p. 475.
5. Michael Holroyd, *Bernard Shaw: The Search for Love, 1856–1898,* London,

Chatto & Windus, 1988.

6. Holroyd (*ibid.*, p. 467) explained that he would print his sources separately for scholars after the publication of his third volume. In a correspondence in the *Times Literary Supplement* (28 October 1988 ff.), I objected strongly to this procedure, first, on general grounds that it inhibits scholarly criticism and, second, because Shaw wrote so much about himself and so jokily that the reader needs to be able (since Holroyd quotes and paraphrases Shaw so much) to judge why, on what occasion, and for what effect Shaw was recalling and retouching the past. Also, in preparing this article, I have realized how heavily Holroyd has relied on certain key sources – Stanley Weintraub's edition of the shorthand diaries, *Bernard Shaw: The Diaries*; Dan H. Laurence's four volumes of *Collected Letters*; Lloyd J. Hubenka's edition of Shaw's essays and platform lectures, *Bernard Show, Practical Politics*; Margot Peters's *Bernard Shaw and the Actresses* (which in fact deals with all Shaw's women friends); and B. C. Russet's *Shaw of Dublin*. Doubtless, conventional acknowledgements will be made in due course. Holroyd's lack of important new findings perhaps tempted him into over-interpreting his material, sparing readers Shaw's often conflicting accounts of his own past states of mind and motives, but giving intelligent readers (who else?) no opportunity to judge for themselves.

7. See 'On the Difficulties of Writing Biography and of Orwell's in Particular', in Bernard Crick, *Essays on Politics and Literature*, Edinburgh, Edinburgh University Press, 1989, pp. 117–32.

8. Holroyd, *op. cit.*, p. 182.

9. *Ibid.*, pp. 189–90.

10. See Bernard Crick, *Socialist Values and Time,* Fabian Tract no. 495, London, Fabian Society, 1984, pp. 35–8, and *In Defence of Politics,* 2nd edn, London, Penguin Books,1982, pp. 236–41.

11. See Michael Oakeshott, *Experience and Its Modes*, Cambridge, Cambridge University Press, 1933; and F. H. Bradley, *Appearance and Reality*, 2nd edn, Oxford, Oxford University Press, 1959.

12. W. H. Greenleaf, *The Ideological Heritage*, vol. 2 of *The British Political Tradition*, London, Methuen, 1983, pp. 366–7.

13. *Ibid.*, p. 360.

14. *Ibid.*, p. 369.

15. *Ibid.*

16. *Ibid.*, p. 378.

17. Norman and Jeanne MacKenzie, *The Diary of Beatrice Webb,* London, Virago, 1984, 3: 367, entry for 17 September 1920.

18. Stanley Pierson, *British Socialists: The Journey from Fantasy to Politics*, Cambridge, MA, Harvard University Press, 1979.

19. *Ibid.*, pp. 102–5.

20. *Ibid.*, p. 107.
21. *Ibid.*, pp. 109–10.
22. Bernard Shaw, *Practical Politics: Twentieth Century Views of Politics and Economics*, ed. Lloyd J. Hubenka, Lincoln, University of Nebraska Press, 1976, pp. 234–7. These quotations are from a verbatim report of the lecture 'The Politics of Unpolitical Animals' given to the Fabian Society in December 1933.
23. A good bibliography for the 'equality' debate and controversy is in Barry Hindess, *Freedom, Equality and the Market*, London, Tavistock, 1987, pp. 168–72.
24. Shaw, *Practical Politics*, p. 122.
25. *Ibid.*, pp. 137, 143–4.
26. Bernard Shaw, *The Intelligent Woman's Guide to Socialism, Capitalism, Sovietism and Fascism*, London, Pelican Books, 1937, pp. 16, 478–9.
27. Shaw, *Practical Politics*, pp. 134–5, 140.
28. Crick, *In Defence of Politics,* pp. 223–35.
29. Shaw, *Intelligent Women's Guide*, pp. 477–9, a substantial qualification of splendid bombast on pp. 99–102, where the case for equality is stated in absolute terms (always, in Shaw, if one is patient, and looks hard enough, both principle and practice appear).
30. Shaw, *Practical Politics*, pp. 242–3, from the *Observer*, 13 August 1944.
31. Lewis Rockow, *Contemporary Political Thought in England*, London, Allen & Unwin, 1925, pp. 266–75.
32. *Ibid.*, pp. 271, 273.
33. *Ibid.*, p. 274.
34. Ross Terrill, *R. H. Tawney and His Times: Socialism as Fellowship*, London, André Deutsch, 1974, pp. 270–1.
35. John Rawls, *A Theory of Justice*, Cambridge, MA, Harvard University Press, 1971, pp. 101–8.

CHAPTER 21

The Complete Orwell

Most reviewers so far have written about Orwell the man. I want to write about what is in front of me – the twenty beautifully printed and immaculately edited heavy volumes that I can only just lift. Davison began his troublesome long march in 1981 and now it is out: twenty volumes, 3755 items in the last eleven volumes of essays, journalism, letters, diaries, etc., 7460 pages in all, 30,000 entries in the cumulative index, and footnotes and annotations beyond measure. His feat is awesome, even if he was not wholly alone: his wife Sheila and Ian Angus padded alongside, helping in everything.

Even rival biographers must close ranks in praise of Davison. Michael Shelden put it so well, writing, of course, in the *Daily Telegraph* (23 June 1998):

> One can only marvel at the devoted service that one British scholar has given to that genius. His is a real labour of love in a selfish age dominated by the greed and corruption that Orwell so eloquently warned against. And the edition itself is a national treasure which somehow survived the burdens of indifference and neglect.

Review article in *New Statesman*, 17 July 1998, of Peter Davison (ed.), assisted by Ian Angus and Sheila Davison, *The Complete Works of George Orwell*, twenty volumes (Secker & Warburg), 1998.

My only cavil is that 'genius' is a bit OTT and needs some discrimination, as I will argue, within Orwell's varied *oeuvre*. But this is a scholarly edition of world class. We can now be as sure as an already great textual scholar can help us to be that we can read all that Orwell wrote much as he meant it to appear after the often dangerous journey between manuscript and printed page.

We can never be completely sure. Davison knows that. Judgement cannot be avoided if there are different versions of the same text in print. Even a surviving author's corrected proof is no final proof that he did not change his mind later. For instance, in the early editions of Orwell's works from 1951 (the year after his death), the shattered Winston Smith when released from the torture cells 'almost unconsciously . . . traced with his finger in the dust on the table: $2+2=$ '. The first edition had the famous '$2+2=5$' of the torture scene. Davison says the startling blank space is 'the result, I imagine, of a piece of type slipping out unnoticed'; for otherwise it would show that Winston has been able 'to preserve his independence, his integrity; such a conclusion is optimistic', thus contradicting the book's pessimism. But I would read that blank as showing not that he is totally brainwashed to a new belief, but is rendered totally cynical and totally without care for truth – two plus two can mean what the — they like for all he now cares. Winston's earlier, better self is destroyed; a regime can do that, but he is only a broken man, not a reborn man. Having no belief itself, the regime can do no more. All they believe in is 'power for the sake of power'. So is this pessimism, or a kind of Orwellian sardonic optimism? I read the Appendix on Newspeak not as pessimism but as a satiric thrust that language cannot be trammelled by state power: the great works of the English language were 'difficult' to translate into Newspeak – hence the final adoption of Newspeak had been put off until 'so late a date as 2050'. Orwell could have made a change beyond the first edition. It is almost equally implausible that this '$2+2=$ ' if a mistake would have been missed so often (centred on a line of its own). It depends how one reads the text. In my Clarendon Press annotated edition of *Nineteen Eighty-four* I left the blank as an existential abyss. Now I am being quite as obsessive as Peter. He knew I would come back on this old big small point.

Now you will doubtless say (as Orwell would buttonhole his readers in his war-time *Tribune* columns) that these twenty volumes are a sledgehammer to crack a nut. What an odd fate for someone who wrote not for his fellow intellectuals but, in the tradition of Dickens and Wells, for the common man, a dying class whose education was the free public library not the grimly professionalized and demarcation-ridden universities. Not so. Some of the texts were very corrupt. Publishing conditions were very different *entre deux guerres*. Fears of prosecution for obscenity were understandably great, respectable publishers had gone to prison in living memory; and fears of libel were at least as great as now. Some of his tongue-lashings of foul hotel kitchens in Paris, corrupt Burmese, racist imperial civil servants, pig-ignorant private school entrepreneurs and advertising slogans led to many changes of text (some now restored, some lost for ever). From the beginning his publishers were aware of how close his fictions were to fact, even if later critics have too readily accepted that essays or sketches in the first person could sometimes be a clever use of the 'fictive I' as in Daniel Defoe and Edgar Allan Poe. His desire to set down how people actually spoke in the world down-under of the tramps and the spikes also engendered fear because of the Obscene Publications Act and the conventions of the day. 'Bugger, fuck and cunt, now I've said it all!', says the small girl of the story. Orwell tried but could not say it all. Letters to and from editors and his agent show him trying it on but accepting defeat with sardonic realism.

Davison uses as the legend to his general introduction Winston Smith ruminating that 'Ampleforth . . . was engaged in producing garbled versions – definitive texts, they were called . . .' He is Orwell's great ungarbler, as he has been of Shakespearean texts and even music hall songs. But this quote may also remind himself and us that a 'definitive text' is always a relative term, a haunting chimera. However, even if, as Orwell the socialist said of social and moral progress, there is no hope of perfection, there is reasonable hope of betterment. And so much better texts we now have, as well as some interesting new discoveries. These will never be for Minitrue's shredder. All future popular editions will now have texts as close to Orwell's intentions as is humanly possible.

Davison's tale of why it all took seventeen years is out of a black comedy by Iris Murdoch, and at times almost a Tom Sharpe farce. The commission was originally for a de luxe [*sic*] edition of Orwell's nine main books so as to celebrate or cash-in on the non-event of 1984. He was to produce a corrected volume a month for £100 each. I can imagine the then director of Secker & Warburg, Tom

Rosenthal, explaining earnestly, man to man, how it would not make money, and Davison feeling happy to be asked to do such a labour of love and to be paid at all. Saints are not of becoming simplicity in all things, only in some – the best forgery wouldn't last under Davison's tired eyes for five minutes. The task turned out to be almost Sisyphean. He finished on time, but three and a half years later he was summoned to Rosenthal's office to be asked why he had not delivered the corrected proofs. He admits to replying 'crossly'. A search revealed the missing proofs under a stack of books, coffee-stained and on a galley a pencilled schedule for a skiing holiday. They had never been sent to the printer. In 1986 three volumes were launched, but had to be withdrawn, being riddled with errors. The printer said that radar from ships passing on the Tyne had affected their computers!

Then surprisingly the stakes were doubled: the publisher decided to go for the complete edition of all published and unpublished material. Davison agreed when Ian Angus, the joint editor with Sonia Orwell of the familiar four-volume *Collected* [selected] *Essays, Journalism and Letters* of 1968 agreed to help him. The tale continues and gets worse, but let me pause to speculate why Tom Rosenthal and the Orwell Estate went for a complete scholarly edition, an *editio princeps* with, as they knew Davison by now, double-plus maxi annotation and apparatus. This was plainly beyond the capacity and capability of a small literary publisher, well-run or not. Such editions for good reason are the preserve of great university presses, and usually with a foundation grant for a large editorial team with thick glasses and Ph.D.s. Under the law as then was, Orwell having died in 1950, his works would come into the public domain in 2000. So a new edition, the more it was worked upon, the more likely it would be to be accepted in law as constituting a new copyright – as the Cambridge University Press had successfully doubled the life of the dead D. H. Lawrence. If my wicked surmise is true, they must have felt right Charlies when the EC eighty-year copyright came into force. Perhaps that explains part of what happened next.

Tom Rosenthal moved on. (He did not come to the launch party last week; like John Major he was watching cricket.) For two years the firm dropped the project. During the whole period of the labours of Davison, Secker went through seven changes of ownership and takeovers! The American co-partner for the edition, Harcourt,

Brace, Jovanovich, dropped it, came back again, dropped it, came again, dropped it. But from 1995 Max Eilenberg, then Secker's publisher, got the show on the road with great vigour. Then he went, and Random House took Secker over, and in the move of premises lost much of Davison's work, some having to be redone. And there is nearly no happy ending to the story. In bad health for two years, at the end of 1985 Davison had a sextuple heart bypass. He was told that otherwise he only had a year to live, which he knew would not be enough to finish the Orwell. In France he would have been a civic hero.

However, I do have two somewhat ungrateful worries. Yes, all textual scholarship involves difficult decisions. Orwell grumbled about *Homage to Catalonia* afterwards (as he did about most of his books, always dissatisfied – 'I've made a balls-up of it', apropos *Nineteen Eighty-four*); and he left clear instructions during his last illness that Chapters V and XI, 'the political parts of the book', should be better put at the end as appendices. Each of these chapters had begun by saying that if the reader was not interested in 'horrors of party politics', then 'please skip'. So Davison has followed Orwell's 'instruction' and blames (I would praise) the editor for ignoring it (as everyone has properly ignored Orwell's gloomy requests in the same document not to reprint *A Clergyman's Daughter*, *Keep the Aspidistra Flying* and *The Lion and the Unicorn*).

There is, indeed, a hiatus between Orwell's first-person narrative of what he himself saw in Catalonia and these two chapters explaining what was going on. But a new reader may find it hard to make sense of Orwell's narrative unless given, precisely where it occurs in the book as published in 1938 as Orwell thought necessary at the time, his commentaries on the political situation. If ten years later Orwell wished to give the book a more literary appearance than the original mix of plain observation and political polemic, yet that was the book he wrote at the time. One school of editorship would give priority to an earlier text and simply note the later change of mind. Here Davison may have gone too far, almost as if, in his admiration, he takes Orwell too literally, forgetting his sardonic self-deprecations of nearly all his books – 'every book is a failure'. I hope popular editions will not follow suit. After all, Orwell said that his great ambition after Spain was to 'make political writing into an art'. Davison's decision depreciates this, if never elsewhere in the gross way that Sonia Orwell in the four-volume edition ignored several key, late political essays and reviews to create the wholly false impression that his eccentric socialist fires were burning low; that in marrying her he had declared for 'literature'. That impression cannot be sustained now that we see everything, but everything; including, this must be said, some very poor and hasty book reviews, some excruciating film and theatre hack-work and some routine letters making appointments of no interest to anyone except another biographer in the archive where they best belong. Davison would think it wrong to exercise judgement on what is important or not, and yet he can tear into the political heart of the book that really was the turning point of both Orwell's thinking and his style.

My second concern is the basic decision to put everything, as far as possible, in strict chronological order in the eleven volumes of essays, journalism and letters. The essays are hard to find, interspersed with everything else and with no running-heads, only dates. Even the two books of essays that he chose and published together in his lifetime, *Inside the Whale* and *Critical Essays*, are scattered. The cumulative effect of reading in date order is to make the essays appear to arise all too closely from immediate context, a kind of reductionism that underestimates Orwell's skill as a writer, his thoughtfulness as a speculative essayist and his imaginative humour. Orwell sets that trap for any commentator. His use of the first person as a literary device leads many to think that the character of the man is the great thing not his skill as a writer – that plain, blunt, simple man who had gone to Eton and had read most of the modernist literature of the day, even if politically he chose to write so as to reach the common reader.

Several reviewers of these volumes have done the usual – a summary of his life followed by a discussion of his character. And those who wish to discredit his writings, too painful still for some romantic lefties because of his exposure of the mendacity of the Popular Front, had a go at his character. That lay behind those two *Guardian* journalists who were shocked out of their cotton socks two years ago that he should in 1949 have sent names to a close friend in a Foreign Office counter-propaganda unit of people unreliable for such purposes, as indeed most of them were. Davison puts it all in context excellently. There was a cold war on and Communists would stop at nothing by way of penetration and subversion. Two weeks ago the *Daily Telegraph* reheated all that stale soup from what Davison had printed (ignoring his very full gloss) with a front-page headline, 'Socialist Icon Who Became an Informer'. The right wing make character the issue so that no one can believe that there ever was a socialist of such honesty, integrity and patriotism.

So the nine big books are printed first, and his separately published war-time *The Lion and the Unicorn: Socialism and the English Genius*, perhaps his most important political writing, gets swallowed up as if an essay amid this and that, good writing and tat. The great essays are obscured. For if Orwell has genius, it is as an essayist. There is an uneasiness among critics about his reputation. Those pre-war novels would have few readers if it was not for his last two books. But will *Nineteen Eighty-Four* and *Animal Farm* survive fading memories of the events that triggered their satiric rage? Yet if puzzled critics consider his essays, then there is no need to think that his character inflates the reputation of his writings. The essay is a great English genre, and he is among the greatest exponents of that seeming-easy, most difficult craft: the humanist, speculative writer, raising moral dilemmas in ordinary language, humorous and serious at once, attacking cant of all kinds, and himself all the time longing for a just, egalitarian society but sadly aware of how far away it was, and is.

Index

INDEX